English in Action

Second Edition

Barbara H. Foley

Elizabeth R. Neblett

HEINLE
CENGAGE Learning™

Australia • Brazil • Japan • Korea • Mexico • Singapore • Spain • United Kingdom • United States

English in Action 4, Second Edition
Barbara H. Foley and Elizabeth R. Neblett

Publisher: Sherrise Roehr

Acquisitions Editor: Tom Jefferies

Managing Development Editor:
  Jill Korey O'Sullivan

Assistant Editor: Lauren Stephenson

Associate Development Editor:
  Marissa Petrarca

Director of Content and Media Production:
  Michael Burggren

Director of Marketing, U.S.: Jim McDonough

Sr. Product Marketing Manager: Katie Kelley

Sr. Content Project Manager:
  Maryellen E. Killeen

Sr. Print Buyer: Susan Spencer

Cover / Text Designer: Muse Group, Inc.

Compositor: PreMediaGlobal

For product information and technology assistance, contact us at
Cengage Learning Customer & Sales Support, 1-800-354-9706
For permission to use material from this text or product, submit
all requests online at **cengage.com/permissions**
Further permissions requests can be emailed to
permissionrequest@cengage.com

Library of Congress Control Number: 2010934069

ISBN-13: 978-1-4240-4993-6

ISBN-10: 1-4240-4993-8

Heinle
20 Channel Center Street
Boston, MA 02210
USA

Cengage Learning is a leading provider of customized learning solutions with office locations around the globe, including Singapore, the United Kingdom, Australia, Mexico, Brazil, and Japan. Locate your local office at
www.cengage.com/global

Cengage Learning products are represented in Canada
by Nelson Education, Ltd.

Visit Heinle online at **elt.heinle.com**

Visit our corporate Web site at **cengage.com**

Printed in the United States of America
2 3 4 5 6 7 17 16 15 14

Acknowledgments

The authors and publisher would like to thank the following reviewers and consultants:

Karin Abell
Durham Technical Community College, Durham, NC

Sandra Anderson
El Monte-Rosemead Adult School, El Monte, CA

Sandra Andreessen
Merced Adult School, Merced, CA

Julie Barrett
Madison Area Technical College, Madison, WI

Bea Berretini
Fresno Adult School, Fresno, CA

Mark Brik
College of Mount Saint Vincent, The Institute for Immigrant Concerns, New York, NY

Debra Brooks
BEGIN Managed Programs, Brooklyn, NY

Rocio Castiblanco
Seminole Community College / Orange County Public Schools, Sanford, FL

Sandy Cropper
Fresno Adult School, Fresno, CA

Carol Culver
Central New Mexico Community College, Albuquerque, NM

Shanta David
Union County College – IIE, Elizabeth, NJ

Luciana Diniz
Portland Community College, Portland, OR

Gail Ellsworth
Milwaukee Area Technical College, Oak Creek, WI

Sally Gearhart
Santa Rosa Junior College, Santa Rosa, CA

Jeane Hetland
Merced Adult School, Merced, CA

Laura Horani
Portland Community College, Portland, OR

Bill Hrycyna
Franklin Community Adult School, Los Angeles, CA

Callie Hutchinson
Sunrise Tech Center, Citrus Heights, CA

Mary Jenison
Merced Adult School, Merced, CA

Mark Labinski
Fox Valley Technical College, Appleton, WI

Rhonda Labor
Northside Learning Center, San Antonio, TX

Lisa Lor
Merced Adult School, Merced, CA

Eileen McKee
Westchester Community College, Valhalla, NY

Lynn Meng
Union County College – IIE, Elizabeth, NJ

Jennifer Newman-Cornell
College of Southern Nevada, Las Vegas, NV

Sonja Pantry
Robert Morgan Educational Center, Miami, FL

Eric Rosenbaum
BEGIN Managed Programs, Brooklyn, NY

Jodi Ruback
College of Southern Nevada, Las Vegas, NV

Linda Salem
Northside Learning Center, San Antonio, TX

Evelyn Trottier
Seattle Central Community College, Lynnwood, WA

Maliheh Vafai
Overfelt Adult Center, San Jose, CA

Nancy Williams
Bakersfield Adult School, Bakersfield, CA

Contents

Contents · **V**

Contents

Contents · **vii**

Contents

Contents · **ix**

To the Teacher

In our many years of teaching, we have found that most textbooks progress too quickly. There is a presentation of a new structure and a few exercises to practice it, and then another grammar point is introduced. We discovered that our students needed more time with the grammar—time to practice it, see it in context, use it to talk about a theme, and apply it to themselves. We could not find a series that provided sufficient practice and recycling, so we decided to write our own series—and *English in Action* was born.

English in Action is a four-level core language series for English language learners. Each level provides extensive practice and review with basic structures, as it gradually adds more advanced structures to challenge students. It teaches language through thematic units that are clear, engaging, and interactive.

English in Action, 2nd edition is a comprehensive revision and expansion of the first edition. Content has been added, deleted, and changed based on our experiences teaching with the text and feedback from our students and colleagues. In addition, one of the major goals of the revision was to provide a more explicit focus on language competencies.

Book 4 is designed for students who are familiar with the basic tenses and can apply them in everyday situations. Now they are ready for more difficult structures such as the present perfect tense. The text presents structures in more challenging contexts and encourages students to expand their use of English while discussing topics such as education, driving, travel, job performance, and citizenship. By the end of Book 4, students will feel comfortable talking, reading, and writing about their lives and the world around them.

Each unit will take between five and seven hours of classroom time. In classes with less time, the teacher may need to choose the exercises that are most appropriate for the students. Some of the activities can be assigned for homework. For example, after previewing Writing Our Stories, students can write their own stories at home instead of in class.

Features

- **Unit Opener:** Each unit opens with an illustration or photo and discussion questions to introduce the topic and draw the students into the unit.
- **Active Grammar:** The first half of the unit integrates the context and the new grammar. Users of the first edition will notice that there is enhanced grammar support, with full-color grammar charts and sample sentences. There are many whole-class, teacher-directed activities.
- **Pronunciation:** The pronunciation points, such as verb endings, contractions, question intonation, and syllable stress, complement the grammar or vocabulary of the lesson.
- **The Big Picture:** This is our favorite section. It integrates listening, vocabulary, and structure. A large, engaging picture shows a familiar setting, such as a restaurant, a doctor's office, or an office supply store. Students listen to a short story or conversation and then answer questions, fill in information, review structures, or write conversations.
- **Reading:** A short reading expands the context of the lesson. We did not manipulate reading selections so that every sentence fits into the grammatical structures presented in the unit. The readings include new vocabulary and structures. Teachers can help students learn that understanding the main idea is their primary goal. If students can find the information they need, it isn't necessary to understand every word.
- **Writing Our Stories:** In the writing section, students first read a paragraph written by an English language learner or teacher. Students then brainstorm and organize their ideas using graphic organizers. Next, students write about their experiences, ideas, or their research on a topic.

New to this Edition

The new features in the second edition include:

- The expanded and improved grammar feature presents easy-to-read charts and grammar notes throughout the units. In addition, grammar charts in the appendix provide a valuable student reference of all the grammar points covered in the book. A new exercise, Teacher Dictations, is located in the Active Grammar section.
- **Word Partnerships Boxes** This feature presents high-frequency word collocations that relate to the theme of the unit.
- **Working Together** These partner and group activities are spread throughout the units. They encourage students to work together in active ways. There are pictures to discuss, interview activities, conversations to develop, and discussion questions. Several units also include a **Student to Student** activity in which each student in a pair looks at a different page containing a different set of information. Students exchange information in order to answer questions about a picture, or to complete maps, charts, or menus with missing information.
- **Sharing Our Stories** These activities encourage students to read and talk about each other's writing.
- **Reading and Writing Notes** The notes give students additional support in developing reading and writing skills in English.
- **English in Action** This two-page section provides practice in the everyday skills students need to interact as community members, citizens, students, and workers. Activities such as role plays, presentations, and problem-solving exercises help students become more comfortable in real-life situations.

The second edition includes three new or adapted units. Unit 3 is now Changing Lifestyles. Unit 6, Travel, is a new unit that focuses on modals. Unit 13, Music, formerly Country Music, has been expanded to include more current musicians. All readings have been updated or replaced with a more current topic.

Ancillary Components

- **Student Book Audio CDs:** These include all of the audio in the Student Book: dialogs, descriptions, pronunciation exercises, and The Big Picture.
- **Workbook** and **Workbook Audio CD:** These components include vocabulary, grammar, reading, and writing activities related to key topics in the Student Book. Each unit also includes listening activities related to the audio on the Workbook Audio CD. The new edition of the Workbook includes new material to reflect content changes made to the new edition of *English in Action 4*.
- **Teacher's Guide:** The guide includes Student Book pages with embedded answer keys, audio scripts, and a grammar summary designed to give teachers more information about the grammatical structures and points taught in each Student Book unit. It includes new material to reflect content changes made to the new edition of *English in Action 4*. Each unit includes two new features, **More Action!** and **Teaching Tips.** These activities provide teachers with supplemental activities, explanations of difficult concepts, and a variety of classroom management topics.
- **Interactive CD-ROM:** This gives students the opportunity for practice and self-study at their own convenience. It provides interactive practice activities of the grammar, vocabulary, listening, and speaking skills taught in the Student Book.
- **Presentation Tool:** These pre-loaded interactive worksheets for every unit can be used on any IWB or data-projector. It also includes an asset bank with all Student Book 4 art files, grammar charts, audio files, and audio scripts.
- **Assessment CD-ROM with Exam*View*®: A bank of test items** allows teachers to create and customize tests and quizzes quickly and easily.
- **Website:** Teachers can access an *English in Action* website that provides additional practice activities, games, and the answer key to the Workbook.

The complete *English in Action* package includes everything necessary to facilitate learning. Visit **elt.heinle.com** to learn more about available resources.

Fun, engaging, and action-packed!

"**Active Grammar**" sections present clear, contextualized grammar explanations along with a rich variety of practice activities.

UPDATED FOR THIS EDITION!

"**Working Together**" activities build learner persistence through cooperative tasks, enhancing the classroom community.

"**Working Together**" activities build workplace skills with teamwork tasks such as labeling and presenting.

Fun, engaging, and action-packed!

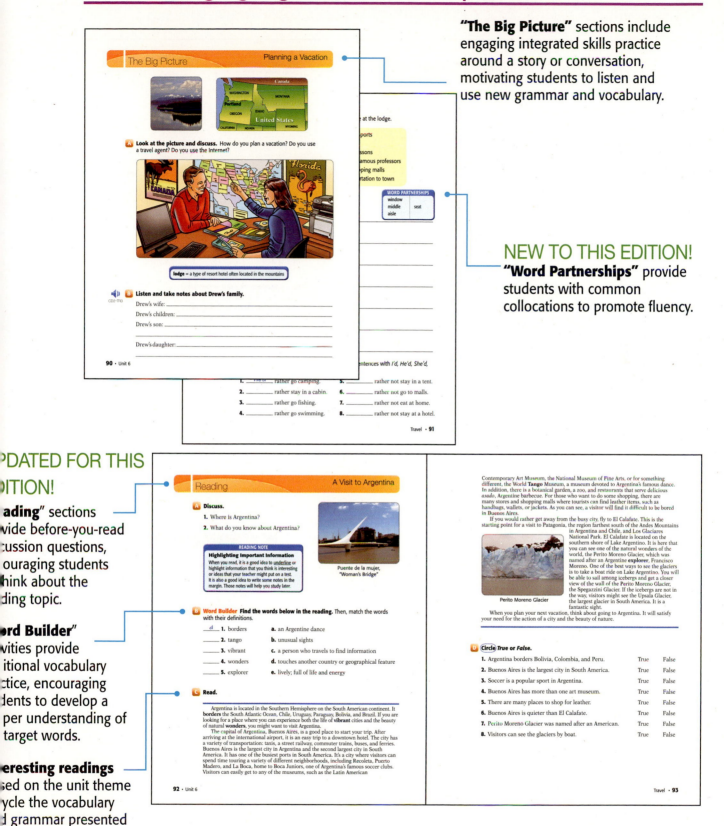

"The Big Picture" sections include engaging integrated skills practice around a story or conversation, motivating students to listen and use new grammar and vocabulary.

NEW TO THIS EDITION!
"Word Partnerships" provide students with common collocations to promote fluency.

UPDATED FOR THIS EDITION!

"Reading" sections provide before-you-read discussion questions, encouraging students to think about the reading topic.

"Word Builder" activities provide additional vocabulary practice, encouraging students to develop a deeper understanding of target words.

Interesting readings based on the unit theme recycle the vocabulary and grammar presented earlier in the unit.

The Big Picture — Planning a Vacation

A **Look at the picture and discuss.** How do you plan a vacation? Do you use a travel agent? Do you use the Internet?

lodge = a type of resort hotel often located in the mountains

B **Listen and take notes about Drew's family.**

Drew's wife: _____

Drew's children: _____

Drew's son: _____

Drew's daughter: _____

90 · Unit 6

WORD PARTNERSHIPS

window	
middle	seat
aisle	

... at the lodge.

...ports

...ssons

...amous professors

...ping malls

...rtation to town

...entences with *I'd, He'd, She'd,*

1. _____ rather go camping.
2. _____ rather stay in a cabin.
3. _____ rather go fishing.
4. _____ rather go swimming.
5. _____ rather not stay in a tent.
6. _____ rather not go to malls.
7. _____ rather not eat at home.
8. _____ rather not stay at a hotel.

Travel · 91

Reading — A Visit to Argentina

A **Discuss.**

1. Where is Argentina?
2. What do you know about Argentina?

READING NOTE

Highlighting Important Information
When you read, it is a good idea to underline or highlight information that you think is interesting or ideas that your teacher might put on a test. It is also a good idea to write some notes in the margin. Those notes will help you study later.

Puente de la mujer, "Woman's Bridge"

B **Word Builder** Find the words below in the reading. Then, match the words with their definitions.

_d_ 1. borders — a. an Argentine dance
___ 2. tango — b. unusual sights
___ 3. vibrant — c. a person who travels to find information
___ 4. wonders — d. touches another country or geographical feature
___ 5. explorer — e. lively; full of life and energy

C **Read.**

   Argentina is located in the Southern Hemisphere on the South American continent. It **borders** the South Atlantic Ocean, Chile, Uruguay, Paraguay, Bolivia, and Brazil. If you are looking for a place where you can experience both the life of **vibrant** cities and the beauty of natural **wonders**, you might want to visit Argentina.
   The capital of Argentina, Buenos Aires, is a good place to start your trip. After arriving at the international airport, it is an easy trip to a downtown hotel. The city has a variety of transportation: taxis, a street railway, commuter trains, buses, and ferries. Buenos Aires is the largest city in Argentina and the second largest city in South America. It has one of the busiest ports in South America. It's a city where visitors can spend time touring a variety of different neighborhoods, including Recoleta, Puerto Madero, and La Boca, home to Boca Juniors, one of Argentina's famous soccer clubs. Visitors can easily get to any of the museums, such as the Latin American

92 · Unit 6

Contemporary Art Museum, the National Museum of Fine Arts, or for something different, the World **Tango** Museum, a museum devoted to Argentina's famous dance. In addition, there is a botanical garden, a zoo, and restaurants that serve delicious *asado*, Argentine barbecue. For those who want to do some shopping, there are many stores and shopping malls where tourists can find leather items, such as handbags, wallets, or jackets. As you can see, a visitor will find it difficult to be bored in Buenos Aires.
   If you would rather get away from the busy city, fly to El Calafate. This is the starting point for a visit to Patagonia, the region farthest south of the Andes Mountains in Argentina and Chile, and Los Glaciares National Park. El Calafate is located on the southern shore of Lake Argentino. It is here that you can see one of the natural wonders of the world, the Perito Moreno Glacier, which was named after an Argentine **explorer**, Francisco Moreno. One of the best ways to see the glaciers is to take a boat ride on Lake Argentino. You will be able to sail among icebergs and get a closer view of the wall of the Perito Moreno Glacier, the Spegazzini Glacier. If the icebergs are not in the way, visitors might see the Upsala Glacier, the largest glacier in South America. It is a fantastic sight.
   When you plan your next vacation, think about going to Argentina. It will satisfy your need for the action of a city and the beauty of nature.

Perito Moreno Glacier

D **Circle** *True or False.*

1. Argentina borders Bolivia, Colombia, and Peru.	True	False
2. Buenos Aires is the largest city in South America.	True	False
3. Soccer is a popular sport in Argentina.	True	False
4. Buenos Aires has more than one art museum.	True	False
5. There are many places to shop for leather.	True	False
6. Buenos Aires is quieter than El Calafate.	True	False
7. Perito Moreno Glacier was named after an American.	True	False
8. Visitors can see the glaciers by boat.	True	False

Travel · 93

Fun, engaging, and action-packed!

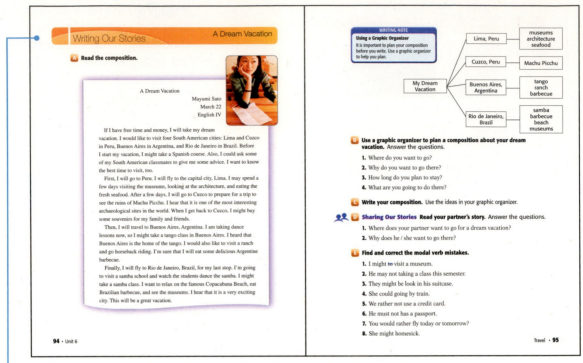

Writing Our Stories — A Dream Vacation

A Read the composition.

A Dream Vacation
Mayumi Sato
March 22
English IV

If I have free time and money, I will take my dream vacation. I would like to visit four South American cities: Lima and Cuzco in Peru, Buenos Aires in Argentina, and Rio de Janeiro in Brazil. Before I start my vacation, I might take a Spanish course. Also, I could ask some of my South American classmates to give me some advice. I want to know the best time to visit, too.

First, I will go to Peru. I will fly to the capital city, Lima. I may spend a few days visiting the museums, looking at the architecture, and eating the fresh seafood. After a few days, I will go to Cuzco to prepare for a trip to see the ruins of Machu Picchu. I hear that it is one of the most interesting archaeological sites in the world. When I get back to Cuzco, I might buy some souvenirs for my family and friends.

Then, I will travel to Buenos Aires, Argentina. I am taking dance lessons now, so I might take a tango class in Buenos Aires. I heard that Buenos Aires is the home of the tango. I would also like to visit a ranch and go horseback riding. I'm sure that I will eat some delicious Argentine barbecue.

Finally, I will fly to Rio de Janeiro, Brazil, for my last stop. I'm going to visit a samba school and watch the students dance the samba. I might take a samba class. I want to relax on the famous Copacabana Beach, eat Brazilian barbecue, and see the museums. I hear that it is a very exciting city. This will be a great vacation.

94 · Unit 6

WRITING NOTE

Using a Graphic Organizer
It is important to plan your composition before you write. Use a graphic organizer to help you plan.

My Dream Vacation
- Lima, Peru → museums / architecture / seafood
- Cuzco, Peru → Machu Picchu
- Buenos Aires, Argentina → tango / ranch / barbecue
- Rio de Janeiro, Brazil → samba / barbecue / beach / museums

B Use a graphic organizer to plan a composition about your dream vacation. Answer the questions.

1. Where do you want to go?
2. Why do you want to go there?
3. How long do you plan to stay?
4. What are you going to do there?

C Write your composition. Use the ideas in your graphic organizer.

D Sharing Our Stories Read your partner's story. Answer the questions.

1. Where does your partner want to go for a dream vacation?
2. Why does he / she want to go there?

E Find and correct the modal verb mistakes.

1. I might to visit a museum.
2. He may not taking a class this semester.
3. They might be look in his suitcase.
4. She could going by train.
5. We rather not use a credit card.
6. He must not has a passport.
7. You would rather fly today or tomorrow?
8. She might homesick.

Travel · 95

"Writing Our Stories" sections expand students' literacy by giving a closer look at real people in real communities and provide students with guided practice activities.

NEW TO THIS EDITION!

"English in Action" sections practice the everyday skills students need to interact and solve problems in the real world.

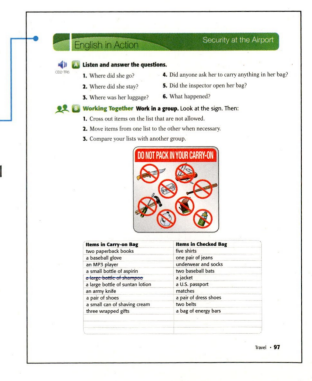

English in Action — Security at the Airport

A Listen and answer the questions.

CD2-TR8

1. Where did she go?
2. Where did she stay?
3. Where was her luggage?
4. Did anyone ask her to carry anything in her bag?
5. Did the inspector open her bag?
6. What happened?

B Working Together Work in a group. Look at the sign. Then:

1. Cross out items on the list that are not allowed.
2. Move items from one list to the other when necessary.
3. Compare your lists with another group.

DO NOT PACK IN YOUR CARRY-ON

Items in Carry-on Bag	Items in Checked Bag
two paperback books	five shirts
a baseball glove	one pair of jeans
an MP3 player	underwear and socks
a small bottle of aspirin	two baseball bats
a large bottle of shampoo	a jacket
a large bottle of suntan lotion	a U.S. passport
an army knife	matches
a pair of shoes	a pair of dress shoes
a small can of shaving cream	two belts
three wrapped gifts	a bag of energy bars

Travel · 97

About the Authors

Liz and I work at Union County College in Elizabeth, New Jersey. We teach at the Institute for Intensive English, a large English as a Second Language program. Students from over 80 different countries study in our classes. Between us, Liz and I have been teaching at the college for over 40 years! When Liz isn't writing, she spends her time traveling, taking pictures, and worrying about her favorite baseball team, the New York Mets. I love the outdoors. I can't start my day without a 15- or 20-mile bicycle ride. My idea of a good time always involves being active: hiking, swimming, or simply working in my garden. I also enjoy watching my favorite baseball team, the New York Yankees.

Barbara H. Foley
Elizabeth R. Neblett

Unit 1

Education

A **Discuss.** Look at the pictures and answer the questions.

1.

2.

3.

4.

1. Which classroom is most similar to a high school classroom in your native country?

2. Which classroom is similar to your English classroom?

3. Which classroom has the most students?

4. Which classroom has the fewest students?

5. Which classroom looks the most casual?

6. Which classroom looks the most formal?

7. Describe a typical classroom in your native country.

Learning About Your School

 A **Working Together** **Work with a small group of students.** Talk about your school and complete the chart. Then talk and write about two more places in your school.

> Does our school have a principal's office?

> Yes, it does.

> Where is it?

> It's on the first floor, near the entrance.

Place or Person	Does our school have _____?	Where?
1. A principal's or ESL director's office		
2. A teachers' room		
3. A bookstore		
4. A library		
5. A counselor		
6. A learning center or tutoring center		
7. A computer lab		
8. A cafeteria		
9. Restrooms		
10. A gym		
11. A student center		
12. A study room or a study hall		
13. A student activities office		
14. A copy machine for students		
15.		
16.		

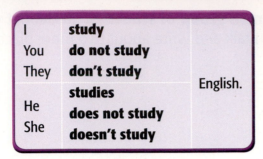

I	study	
You	do not study	
They	don't study	English.
He	studies	
She	does not study	
	doesn't study	

Use the present tense to describe everyday activities, habits, and repeated actions.

A **Circle** the correct verb to make true statements about high school in your native country.

1. The school year **begins / doesn't begin** in September.

2. The school day **starts / doesn't start** at 8:30 A.M.

3. School **meets / doesn't meet** on Saturdays.

4. High school students **choose / don't choose** some of their own courses.

5. Students **write / don't write** their papers on a computer.

6. Students **study / don't study** with students of the same ability.

7. Most students **work / don't work** after school.

8. Students **wear / don't wear** uniforms.

B **Complete the sentences about high school in your native country.** Use the correct form of the verb.

1. Teachers (move) _____ from classroom to classroom.

2. Students (call) _____ their teachers by their first names.

3. Teachers (wear) _____ jeans in class.

4. Teachers (sit) _____ on their desks during class.

5. There (be) _____ after-school programs for students.

6. Families (pay) _____ for textbooks.

7. The teacher (give) _____ many tests.

8. There (be) _____ homework every night.

C **Working Together** **Work with a small group of students.** Read the statements in Exercise B about your school. Discuss your answers.

Do	I you they	work?
Does	she he	study in the library? walk to school?

Yes, you **do**.
Yes, I **do**.
Yes, they **do**.
Yes, she **does**.
Yes, he **does**.

No, you **don't**.
No, I **don't**.
No, they **don't**.
No, she **doesn't**.
No, he **doesn't**.

CD1·TR1

A **Listen to the story about Sophie and Lizzy, two college roommates.** Complete the questions with *Do* or *Does*. Then, answer the questions.

1. _Does_ Sophie take all of her courses in the morning? Yes, she does.

2. _____ you take your English class in the morning? _____

3. _____ Sophie keep her side of the room neat? _____

4. _____ Sophie get up early? _____

5. _____ you get up early? _____

6. _____ Sophie study in the room? _____

7. _____ you study in your bedroom? _____

8. _____ Lizzy and Sophie have the same schedule? _____

9. _____ Lizzy keep her side of the room neat? _____

10. _____ you keep your home neat? _____

11. _____ Lizzy hand in her papers on time? _____

12. _____ you hand in your homework on time? _____

 B **Are you more like Sophie or Lizzy?** Explain.

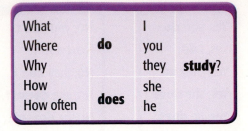

What Where Why	**do**	I you they	**study**?
How How often	**does**	she he	

	studies	English?
Who	**goes**	to work?
	lives	close to school?

 A **Working Together** **Work with a small group of students.** Interview each other about your daily schedules and habits.

Questions	You	Partner 1	Partner 2
1. What time do you get up?			
2. What time do you leave for school?			
3. How do you get to school?			
4. How long does it take?			
5. When do you study?			
6. How often do you study?			
Write one more question to ask your partners.			
7.			

 B **Pronunciation: Linking / *do you* /** **Listen and repeat.**

CD1·TR2

1. What do you do?

2. Where do you work?

3. How do you get home?

4. Where do you live?

5. Why do you study here?

6. What do you do on weekends?

C **Answer these questions about students in your class.**

1. Who always arrives on time?

2. Who wears a baseball cap to class?

3. Who often arrives late?

4. Who goes to work after class?

5. Who usually asks questions in class?

I do. You do. They do.	He does. She does.

 D **Write three more *Who* questions.** Then, ask a classmate your questions.

I	**am**		
He			us**ing** a computer.
She	**is**	(not)	study**ing** for a test.
We			sit**ting** at a desk.
You	**are**		
They			

 A **Working Together** **Work with a small group of students.** Write three sentences about each photo. Make one of the sentences negative.

1.

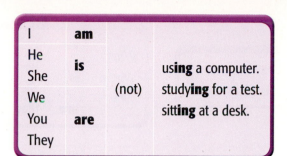

a. <u>The students are taking an important exam.</u>

b. _____

c. _____

2.

a. _____

b. _____

c. _____

3.

a. _____

b. _____

c. _____

4.

a. _____

b. _____

c. _____

Active Grammar

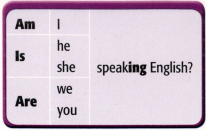

Am	I		
Is	he she	speaking English?	
Are	we you		

Who	**is**	speaking English?

Who takes a **singular** verb.

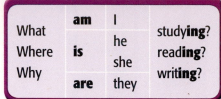

What Where Why	**am**	I	studying?
	is	he she	reading?
	are	they	writing?

A Work with a partner. Answer the questions about your class.

1. Are the students taking a test?
2. Are they working together?
3. Are they speaking English?
4. Is the teacher helping the students?

5. Is anyone using a dictionary?
6. Are any students writing?
7. Are any students drinking water?
8. Is the teacher writing on the board?

B Look around your classroom. Write your answers to these questions.

1. Who is sitting next to the door? _____
2. Who is talking to the teacher? _____
3. Who is speaking another language? _____
4. What is the teacher doing? _____
5. Where are you sitting? _____
6. What are you wearing? _____

C Dictation Your teacher will dictate the questions on page 263. Listen and write the questions you hear. Then, answer the questions.

1. _____
2. _____
3. _____
4. _____
5. _____
6. _____

appear	have	miss	smell
believe	hear	need	sound
belong	know	own	taste
feel	like	prefer	understand
hate	look	see	want

Use the *simple present tense* with non-action verbs.

> He **knows** my name.
> I **miss** my grandparents.

Exceptions:

> They **are having** a party.
> I**'m having** a cup of tea.

A In your notebook, write sentences about the students in the student center.

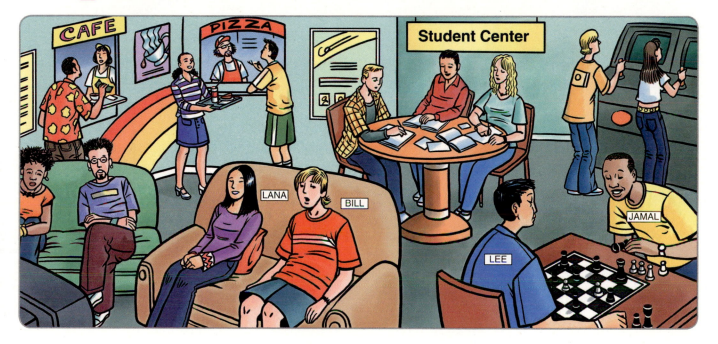

1. Students / like / to meet / student center
   Students like to meet at the student center.

2. They / need to relax / between classes

3. Two students / play / video games

4. Some students / study / together

5. Some music / play / in the background

6. Students / hope to pass / their exams

7. They / (not) hear / the noise

8. Lana and her boyfriend / watch / TV

9. Bill / look / bored

10. He / (not) like / daytime dramas

11. Two students / buy / pizza

12. The pizza / smell / good

T E X A S

★ San
Antonio

CD1·TR3

A **Listen to the description of the University of Texas at San Antonio.** (Circle) **or complete the information.**

1. Location: urban   suburban   rural

2. Degrees: two-year   four-year   four-year and graduate

3. Type of university: public   private

4. Number of undergraduate students: _____

5. Percentage of international students: _____

6. Number of graduate students: _____

7. Number of faculty: _____

8. Application Checklist

   a. Application fee: $ _____ Online application available: Yes   No

   b. _____ transcript

   c. Official ACT or _____ scores

9. Minimum SAT score for students in top 25 percent: _____

10. Two possible majors: _____

11. Services available for students:

   a. Academic _____

   b. A health clinic and _____ counseling

   c. Examples of student activities: _____

   d. Orientation for _____ and _____

WORD PARTNERSHIP	
undergraduate	stude
graduate	
associate's	
bachelor's	degr
master's	
doctoral	

B (Circle) *True* or *False*.

1. The University of Texas at San Antonio is a large university. (True) False

2. U.T.S.A. is a private university. True False

3. The main campus is in downtown San Antonio. True False

4. The university has two campuses. True False

5. U.T.S.A. has a graduate school. True False

6. U.T.S.A. employs about eight hundred faculty. True False

7. Students pay $35 for the application fee. True False

8. Transfer students can have an orientation. True False

C Listen and write short answers to the questions about the university.

CD1·TR4

1. No, it isn't. _____   5. _____

2. _____   6. _____

3. _____   7. _____

4. _____   8. _____

D Complete the sentences with the present tense form of the verb.

1. The University of Texas at San Antonio (have) _____ has _____ many campuses.

2. About 24,000 undergraduate students (study) _____ at U.T.S.A.

3. Future students (pay) _____ an application fee.

4. A student (take) _____ standardized tests before he or she goes to U.T.S.A.

5. U.T.S.A. (have) _____ a learning center with tutors and counselors for the students.

6. The university (give) _____ the students free career counseling.

7. Students (go) _____ to the employment service when they (need) _____ to find jobs.

A **Scan the reading to find the answers to the questions.**

1. Where is the school located?

2. Does N.J.I.T. have graduate programs?

3. How much is the application fee?

4. What is the suggested SAT score?

5. What is the minimum grade average that N.J.I.T. accepts?

6. Can students get degrees online?

New Jersey Institute of Technology, or N.J.I.T., is located in Newark, New Jersey,
ten miles from New York City. It is a four-year public university and technical college.
The college offers bachelor's degrees in engineering, computer science, management,
technology, and many other fields. N.J.I.T. also has graduate programs in many
subjects. <u>Ninety percent</u> of the students come from New Jersey and 70 percent
commute between home and school. The average age of entering students is eighteen.

In addition to an application, students who are interested in applying to N.J.I.T.
need to prepare the following materials for admission:

- the application fee; in 2010, the fee
  was $70
- an official high school transcript of
  grades
- official SAT I (Scholastic Aptitude Test)
  or ACT (American College Testing)
  scores; the recommended score is 1000
  total or above
- for non-U.S. citizens, students must
  send a photocopy of visas or permanent
  resident cards

The college requires interested students to have a strong math and science
background. Students must have a B average, four years of high school English, and
two years of science, including one of a laboratory science such as chemistry.

N.J.I.T. has a program available for students who prefer distance learning, or learning online. N.J.I.T. offers bachelor's and master's degree programs and graduate certificates online. Online courses are designed for students who need flexibility. Maybe they have demanding jobs that require overtime during the week, so they cannot take classes during the week. Maybe they have an odd work shift. Some students may have disabilities, which do not permit them to go to classes in person. Distance learning courses may be right for students who want to study from home.

In addition, N.J.I.T. offers many evening and early morning classes. It also has a summer session. Students who need extra preparation get special instruction, English as a second language classes, or tutoring. Like many other colleges today, N.J.I.T. requires that each student have a computer. The college offers good deals for students who need to buy computers and necessary software.

There are dormitories for students who prefer to live on campus or who live too far away to commute. Students can participate in many clubs, sports teams, and organizations. For example, there are organizations for groups such as the Korean Student Association and the Caribbean Student Organization. There are also many organizations for students in different majors.

If you think you might be interested in this college, look at its website for more information.

B **In the reading, number and <u>underline</u> the answers to the questions.**

1. What percentage of the students come from New Jersey?

2. What percentage of the students commute to the campus?

3. Does the college accept foreign students?

4. What is *distance learning*?

5. Who takes online courses?

6. Why do students like online courses?

7. What kinds of services are available for students who need more preparation?

8. What kinds of clubs and organizations can students join?

> **CULTURE NOTE**
>
> Most colleges and universities have websites that describe their programs, activities, and admission procedures. Their URLs (Internet addresses) end in **.edu**, which stands for *education.* Here are two examples: New York University's URL is www.nyu.edu. The University of Texas at San Antonio's URL is www.utsa.edu.

C **Go online.** Research a college or university that interests you.

> **Indent the first line of each paragraph. Use the tab key on your computer.**

> **Type your name, the date, and your course.**

Amelia Mendez
September 25
English IV

> **Write a title** —— My Schedule

    I am a student at Union County College. The school is in New Jersey. This is my first semester, and my major is education.

    I have a busy schedule. On Mondays and Wednesdays, I have an ESL grammar and listening class from 5:00 to 7:30. I have a reading and writing course on Tuesdays and Thursdays from 6:30 to 9:00. On Fridays, I have a math class from 6:00 to 8:30. I belong to a study group, and we study together for three hours on Saturday mornings. I do my homework at home after my classes. I spend about two hours a night on my homework. Math is my hardest subject.

    I like my classes and my school. I have a lot of friends. I like spending time at the student center.

A **Write a composition about your school schedule and your classes.** Answer these questions.

1. What school do you attend? Where is it located?

2. What is your weekly school schedule?

3. Are your classes difficult, easy, or just right?

4. How often do you have tests?

5. When and where do you study? How many hours do you study a week?

6. Do you like your school? Why or why not?

B **Complete each sentence with appropriate examples.**

1. My classmates come from different countries, such as _____ and _____.

2. In our English class, we are studying many things, such as _____ and _____.

3. Computers are useful for many things, such as _____ and _____.

4. A medical student has to study sciences, such as _____ and _____.

5. Languages, such as _____ and _____, are difficult to learn.

6. Sports, such as _____ and _____, are very popular in the United States.

C **There is one <u>underlined</u> verb mistake in each sentence.** Correct the mistakes.

1. The Division of Physical Education <u>offer</u> many recreational programs.

2. N.J.I.T. <u>is develop</u> many programs to attract women and minority students to engineering and the sciences.

3. U.T.S.A.'s campuses <u>provides</u> opportunities for many students.

4. Some students <u>are preferring</u> to study from their own homes, using computers.

5. What kind of exams <u>students usually take</u>?

6. The students <u>leave rarely</u> their classes without a homework assignment.

7. My roommate <u>is belonging</u> to the women's volleyball team.

8. This test <u>is looking</u> difficult.

A **Complete the story.** Use the simple present and the present continuous tense.

Joe is the manager of the student center, and this is his twentieth year working there. Joe (know) _____knows_____ the names of almost
1
all of the students who (visit) _____ the center every
2
day. He (like) _____ to talk to the students, and he
3
(miss) _____ them during vacations.
4

Today is the beginning of final exams, so the student center
(negative–be) _____ as busy as usual. A few
5
students (talk) _____ in a corner, soft music
6
(play) _____, and a group of students
7
(discuss) _____ a final project. Many students
8
(study) _____ in the library this week and
9
(write) _____ their papers in the computer center.
10

Today, Joe (prepare) _____ some special treats
11
for the students because he (understand) _____
12
that exam time is very stressful. The students (negative–have)

_____ a lot of free time during exam weeks, and
13
they (miss–often) _____ their meals at the dining
14
hall. It's 11:30 P.M., and Joe (make) _____ some
15
cookies, and pizzas (bake) _____ in the ovens.
16
The center (smell) _____ wonderful. Students
17
(look) _____ up from their books and (get)
18
_____ ready to take a study break.
19

B **In your notebook, write ten questions about the story.** Write five questions using the simple present and five questions using the present continuous.

A **Imagine that you are applying to college.** Complete the sample college application.

COLLEGE APPLICATION

ACADEMIC INFORMATION

Status: ☐ Full time ☐ Part time   **Term:** ☐ Fall ☐ Spring

Program / Major: [_____]   **Degree:** [_____]

Do you plan to take online courses? ☐ Yes ☐ No

Previous Education (Write all high schools and colleges attended.)

HIGH SCHOOL

Name of High School	Location	Graduation Date

COLLEGES / UNIVERSITIES

Name	Location	Dates Attended	Degree Received
Name	Location	Dates Attended	Degree Received

SAT / ACT   Date of exam: [/ /]

TOEFL   Date of exam: [/ /]

WORK EXPERIENCE

List current employer first.

Name of Employer	Location	Dates of Employment
Name of Employer	Location	Dates of Employment

I, [_____] , certify that the information on this application is true.
    Signature

[_____]
Date

Unit 2

Colonial Times

A **Look at the map of the original 13 colonies.** Discuss the questions that follow.

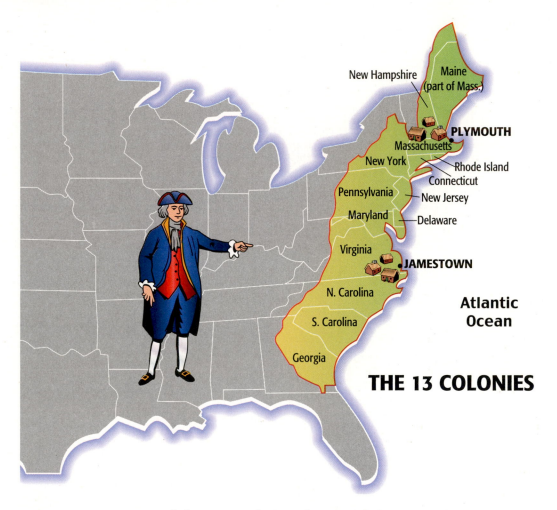

New Hampshire

Maine (part of Mass.)

PLYMOUTH

Massachusetts

New York

Rhode Island

Connecticut

Pennsylvania

New Jersey

Maryland

Delaware

Virginia

JAMESTOWN

N. Carolina

Atlantic Ocean

S. Carolina

Georgia

THE 13 COLONIES

1. Is your state one of the original 13 colonies of the United States?

2. Which colony was the farthest south?

3. Which state is Plymouth in?

4. Which state is Jamestown in?

5. From 1999–2001, the United States released new quarters representing the 13 colonies. Do you have any of them?

A **Write the past tense forms of the verbs.**

Regular verbs

1. call _called_
2. cook _____
3. milk _____
4. play _____

5. talk _____
6. use _____
7. travel _____
8. watch _____

I		
You	**moved**	
He	**didn't move**	to the United States.
They		

Irregular verbs*

1. buy _____
2. drive _____
3. go _____

4. grow _____
5. make _____
6. read _____

7. sleep _____
8. write _____

***Note:** See the chart of irregular verbs on page 116.

CD1·TR5

B **Look at the pictures and listen to the comparison between life in colonial times and life today.** Number the pictures in the order you hear them discussed.

C **Look at each picture.** Describe life in Colonial America.

A **Working Together** **Complete the sentences about life in Colonial America.** Write a verb from the box in the past tense. Some of the verbs are negative. You can use some words more than once. Look at page 19 for help.

buy	read
cook	sleep
go̶	talk
grow	travel
have	use
milk	watch
play	write

1. People ____didn't go____ to supermarkets.

2. They _____ their own food.

3. People _____ over open fires.

4. They _____ stoves.

5. People _____ their own cows.

6. They _____ milk at the supermarket.

7. Families _____ candles for light.

8. People _____ on mattresses.

9. At night, families _____ TV.

10. They _____ books and _____ games.

11. People _____ to one another on cell phones.

12. They _____ letters to one another.

13. People _____ by horse and wagon.

14. They _____ cars.

 B **Work with a partner.** Ask and answer the questions about your first year in this country.

1. When did you arrive in the United States?

2. How did you travel here?

3. Why did you come to this country?

4. What important things did you bring with you?

5. Who did you live with when you arrived?

6. Did you speak any English?

7. Was your first year in this country difficult?

A Complete the sentences with *was*, *wasn't*, *were*, or *weren't*.

1. Life _____wasn't_____ easy for the first settlers.

2. The first homes _____ small buildings made of wood and mud.

3. There _____ a kitchen in the house.

4. There _____ bathrooms, either. There _____ a small outhouse in the backyard.

5. Windows _____ small because no glass _____ available.

6. At first, there _____ only a few schools in the colonies.

7. There _____ a telephone to communicate.

8. By 1776, the population of the colonies _____ over three million.

I He She It	was was not wasn't	young.
You We They	were were not weren't	young.

	was	a garden.
	was not wasn't	a refrigerator.
There	were	few schools.
	were not weren't	large schools.

B **Working Together** Use the information below to talk about life today and life in 1790. Use the simple present or simple past tense.

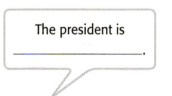

The president is _____.

George Washington was the president.

Today	**1790**
1. The president is _____.	1. George Washington
2. The president earns $400,000.	2. $25,000
3. The capital is Washington, D.C.	3. New York City
4. There are 50 states.	4. 13 states
5. The largest state is Alaska.	5. New York
6. The largest city is New York City.	6. New York City
7. The population is about 305 million.	7. four million

Active Grammar

Used to

| I You She They | **used to** | **live** in Peru. **use** candles for light. **grow** all of our vegetables. |

Use *used to* to talk about a habit or a routine that you did in the past but that you don't do now.
I **used to live** in New York. Now, I live in Sacramento.

A **Pronunciation:** *Used to* **Listen and repeat.**

CD1·TR6

1. In colonial times, people used to drive horses and wagons.
2. People used to cook over open fires.
3. People used to grow their own food.
4. They used to write letters.
5. They used to attend very small schools.

B **Work with a partner.** Read about life today. Talk about life in Colonial America. Use the words in the box and *used to.*

1. Today, girls wear jeans, dresses, or skirts.
2. Today, people drink from glasses.
3. Today, most children study in large public schools.
4. Today, most children wear sneakers.
5. Today, people read by electric lights.
6. Today, people eat with forks, knives, and spoons.

In colonial times, girls used to wear long dresses.

wooden mugs
long dresses
candlelight
spoons and their fingers
one-room schoolhouses
leather boots

C **Complete the sentences about life in your native country.** Then, read your sentences to a partner.

1. When I lived in _____, I used to _____.
2. My family and I used to _____ every summer.
3. My friends and I used to _____ on Saturday nights.
4. I used to eat typical foods like _____.
5. I never used to _____.

22 · Unit 2

D **Working Together** In a small group, try to find the 16 things wrong with this picture. Check your answers below.

Children **didn't play** with toy trucks.

Answers:
1. Children didn't play with toy trucks.
2. Houses didn't have air conditioners.
3. They didn't have electricity.
4. They didn't have helicopters.
5. Farmers didn't ride tractors.
6. They didn't have grills.
7. They didn't have traffic lights.
8. They didn't drive on paved roads.
9. Houses didn't have doorbells.
10. Carts didn't have rubber tires.
11. Teenagers didn't have music players.
12. Girls didn't wear short skirts.
13. Men didn't smoke cigarettes.
14. Teenagers didn't wear sneakers.
15. They didn't eat hamburgers.
16. They didn't have TVs.

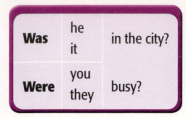

	he	in the city?
Was	it	
Were	you they	busy?

Where		you	**go** to school?
	did	she	
How		they	**get** to school?

Did you **have** any pets?
Did she **live** in the country?
Did they **play** sports?

CD1·TR7

A **Complete the questions.** Then, listen to Eric talk about his childhood. Take notes in your notebook. Answer the questions.

1. (be) _____ he born in the United States?

2. _____ he (live) _____ in a big city?

3. _____ he (have) _____ a big family?

4. (be) _____ he the oldest?

5. (be) _____ his relatives nearby?

6. _____ he (live) _____ in the city or in the country?

7. _____ he (walk) _____ to school?

8. (be) _____ his grandmother a good cook?

B **Complete the questions.** Use *did*, *was*, or *were*. Then, ask and answer the questions about your childhood with a partner.

1. Where __did__ you live?

2. _____ you have a big family?

3. _____ you spend time with your grandparents?

4. _____ your family close?

5. What sports _____ you play?

6. _____ you a good student?

7. How _____ your grades?

8. When _____ you begin to study English?

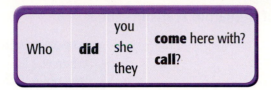

Who	did	you she they	**come** here with? **call**?

A **Answer the questions.**

1. **Who** did you come to this country with? _I came with my family._

2. Who did you stay with when you came? _____

3. Who did you ask for help to find a place to live? _____

4. Who did you talk to about this school? _____

5. Who did you talk to when you had a problem? _____

6. Who did you call after you arrived here? _____

B **Write two more questions.** Ask a partner your questions.

1. _____

2. _____

C **Work in a small group.** Ask and answer the questions. Write the name of the student or students on the line.

Who	**came** here alone? **brought** a pet here? **left** family behind?

1. Who came here alone? _____

2. Who brought a pet here? _____

3. Who left family behind? _____

4. Who found a job right away? _____

5. Who studied English before coming to the U.S.? _____

6. Who knew how to drive before coming to this country? _____

D **Write two more questions.** Ask your classmates your questions.

1. _____

2. _____

A **Listen.** Complete the outline about Benjamin Franklin's life.

CD1·TR8

A. Early life

1. Born in _____ on _____

2. Attended school for _____ years

3. Trained to become a _____

4. Moved to _____

5. Opened a _____

> When you listen to a lecture, take notes. Don't depend on your memory—depend on your notes.

B. Improvements to Philadelphia

1. Started the first _____

2. Helped to organize the first _____

3. Served as _____ and set up _____

4. Convinced city officials to pave the _____

C. Four inventions

1. _____ **2.** _____

3. _____ **4.** _____

bifocals
lightning rod
odometer
stove

D. Contributions as a leader

1. Signed the Declaration of _____

    a. It stated that the 13 colonies were a _____ and _____ nation.

2. Served as minister to _____

3. Signed the Constitution

    a. It established a new _____.

E. Death

    1. Died on _____

B **Look at your outline.** Ask and answer the questions.

  1. Where was Benjamin Franklin born?

  2. How long did he attend school?

  3. What trade did he learn?

  4. What city did he move to?

  5. What business did he open?

  6. What services did Franklin help to start?

  7. How else did he help the city of Philadelphia?

  8. What did he invent to measure distance?

  9. What important documents did he sign?

10. What was the Declaration of Independence?

C **Read the answers.** Then, complete the questions.

1. When _____?

He was born in 1706.

2. _____ from high school?

No, he didn't graduate from high school.

3. How many languages _____?

He spoke five languages.

4. What _____ when he was postmaster?

He invented an odometer.

5. What _____ with?

He experimented with electricity.

A reproduction of a Pilgrim house from 1627

A Discuss.

Name one historic place in your country. Why is it famous?

B Word Builder Scan the reading to find the words below. Then, match.

___f___ **1.** colony

_____ **2.** settlers

_____ **3.** archaeologist

_____ **4.** artifacts

_____ **5.** reconstruction

_____ **6.** reproductions

a. copies of original items

b. items or pieces of an item from the past

c. a person who studies artifacts to learn about the past

d. people who move to a place to start a new community

e. something that is put together again or rebuilt

f. a group of people who are living in a new place but who are still part of the original country

C Read.

Plymouth, Massachusetts is a popular tourist attraction. It was the second **colony** in America. On November 11, 1620, a small ship of people from England landed there and started a new colony. These **settlers** were looking for a better life and religious freedom.

One of the most popular attractions in Plymouth is Plimoth Plantation. Plimoth Plantation was the dream of Henry Hornblower II. When he was a boy, Hornblower read stories about the Pilgrims who lived in Plymouth. When he was older, he worked with **archaeologists** in Plymouth. The archaeologists found more than 350,000

artifacts from the original colony. At the same time, historians learned about the lives of the early colonists by reading their journals. In 1945, Henry Hornblower's father gave $20,000 to the Pilgrim Society to begin the **reconstruction** of Plimoth Plantation. The Society made **reproductions** of the clothes, tools, furniture, and houses of the 1620s. The museum opened in 1947, with just one reproduction of a colonial home.

Today, Plimoth Plantation looks like the original settlement of 1627. It is a living museum of more than 20 homes, shops, and gardens. Visitors can walk through the colonial town where each house looks exactly like a house of the 1620s. The museum staff are the "colonists." They wear the same kinds of clothes that the Plymouth colonists used to wear. The women cook on open fireplaces and make colonial recipes. The men grow the same vegetables and raise the same animals as people did in colonial times. Everyone uses the same kinds of tools that the colonists used. When visitors talk to the "colonists," the colonists answer with the same English language and accent that the original colonists had. A trip to Plimoth Plantation is a trip back in history.

D **Answer the questions.**

1. Why did the colonists leave England?

2. Was Plymouth, Massachusetts the first colony?

3. How did Henry Hornblower find out about the Pilgrims at Plymouth?

4. What did archaeologists find at the site?

5. How did historians reproduce the plantation?

6. Why is Plimoth Plantation "a living museum"?

7. What do "colonists" wear?

8. What kind of vegetables do they grow on Plimoth Plantation?

9. What language do the "colonists" speak?

E **Complete the sentences.** Use words from the box.

1. In the Caribbean, there are many former British _____colonies_____.

2. In my neighborhood, there is a _____ of a famous church. It looks almost like the original.

3. The first foreign _____ in New York were Dutch immigrants.

4. When I was a child, I wanted to become an _____.

5. After City Hall burned down, the city decided to do a _____.

6. Some workers found an _____ from a Native American tribe.

> archaeologist
> artifact
> ~~colonies~~
> reconstruction
> reproduction
> settlers

A **Read the composition.**

Laura Guigliano
October 18
English IV

The History of Pompeii

I am from Naples, in southern Italy. A popular historic city in southern Italy is Pompeii. Pompeii is an archaeological site by the Bay of Naples. It is at the bottom of Mount Vesuvius, an active volcano. In 79 A.D., the volcano erupted. The hot mud from the volcano poured down into the sea and towns and killed many people. The lava completely covered the city of Pompeii.

In 1738, workers accidentally discovered artifacts from Pompeii. They contacted authorities. Archaeologists and other experts went to the site. Over many years, these experts uncovered the ancient city of Pompeii.

Pompeii used to be an active vacation city for wealthy Romans. There were homes with beautiful gardens, shops, and places for entertainment. Residents used to spend time at the large outdoor theater. Today, visitors can walk around many parts of the city and look at the remains of the homes. Many of the streets are still in good condition. Visitors can see many of the artifacts in the Naples National Archaeological Museum.

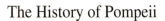

> ### WRITING NOTE
>
> **Brainstorming**
>
> Before writing, it is helpful to think about your topic. Many writers **brainstorm** for five or ten minutes. This means that they write down all their ideas. Then, they use the ideas that they like best for their compositions.

B **Read Laura's brainstorming notes.** (Circle) the ideas she used in her composition.

Historic Place	Location	What is it?
the Colosseum	Rome	old stadium; place for entertainment for Romans; original seating; lots of tourists; cats
Pompeii	near Naples and Mt. Vesuvius	old city buried by ash from volcano; ruins of homes, gardens; outdoor theater

C **Brainstorm about historic places in your native country.** Include the names and locations of a few places, what they are, what visitors do there, and other important information. If you need more information, search for it online. Take notes.

D **Write a composition about the historic place that you chose.** Use your own words to write your composition; do not copy.

E **Sharing Our Stories** **Read your partner's story.** What historic place did your partner write about? Where is it? What can tourists see there?

F **Find and correct the verb mistakes.**

1. Benjamin Franklin ~~help~~ *helped* to improve the city of Philadelphia.

2. Did Philadelphia a major city?

3. When Washington become the capital?

4. Boston use to be one of the major manufacturing centers.

5. Boston Latin School the first public school in America?

6. Who were the first vice president of the United States?

7. The original settlers didn't knew how to grow their own food.

8. People used to traveled by ship from country to country.

A Complete. Write the past tense form of the verbs in parentheses.

      In January 1607, three small ships (leave) _____*left*_____ England for America.
1

Four months later, they (arrive) _____ in America. Several of the men
2

(negative—survive) _____ the long, stormy journey. The men (choose)
3

_____ an area on the James River that is now in the state of Virginia.
4

They (begin) _____ to build a fort. The men (be) _____
5   6

"gentlemen" and (negative—work) _____ with their hands. Their purpose
7

in America (be) _____ to hunt for gold and to start a small colony for
8

England. Unfortunately, there (negative—be) _____ any gold. Winter
9

(come) _____ and there (negative—be) _____ enough food
10   11

for the colonists. Many men (get) _____ sick. By the end of the first
12

winter, only 40 men (be) _____ still alive.
13

      The first few years of the colony (be) _____ very difficult. Disease,
14

starvation, and Native Americans (kill) _____ most of the settlers.
15

Eventually, the colonists (learn) _____ more about farming and the
16

weather. They (make) _____ peace with the Native Americans. Tobacco
17

(be) _____ the business of the new colony. Gradually more and more
18

settlers (arrive) _____, and many small towns (grow) _____
19   20

along the river.

B Read the answers. Then, complete the questions.

1. When _____? In 1607.

2. How long _____? Four months.

3. _____? No, they didn't. They were gentlemen.

4. Where _____? On the James River.

5. What _____? Gold.

6. How many men _____? Only 40.

7. How _____? Very difficult.

8. Why _____? Because of disease, starvation, and attacks by the
Native Americans.

9. How _____? They grew and sold tobacco.

A **Read.** Then, write each sentence under the correct picture.

Making a class presentation takes a lot of practice. Here are some hints for making a good presentation.

- Use note cards or an outline. Don't read your presentation.
- Make eye contact with the audience.
- Smile and greet your audience.
- Practice your presentation.
- Thank your audience.
- Use visuals.

WORD PARTNERSHIPS	
give	
listen to	a presentation
practice	

1.

_____

2.

_____

3.

_____

4.

_____

5.

_____

6.

_____

B **Prepare a presentation for your class.** Use the information from your composition in Exercise D on page 31. Use visuals and notes or an outline.

Unit 3

Changing Lifestyles

  A **Listen.** Write the number of each statement under the correct picture.

CD1·TR9

1.

Kelly _____

2.

Sabrina _____

3.

Hugo ___1___

4.

James and Carla _____

5.

Laura _____

6.

Ahmed _____

7.

Dan _____

8.

Amy and Tom _____

9.

Sofia _____

I	am (not) 'm not		
You	are (not) 're not	going to	move. change jobs. get married.
He She	is (not) isn't		
We They	are (not) 're not		

Use *be going to* to talk about future plans.

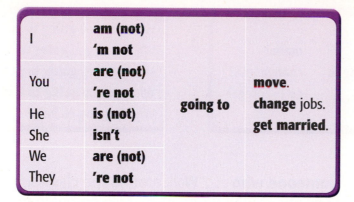

A **Listen.** Complete the sentences. Some of the sentences are negative.

CD1·TR10

1. Julie and Ellie __are not / aren't going to go__ away to college.

2. Julie and Ellie _____ to the community college.

3. Julie _____ education like her mother did.

4. She _____ engineering and architecture.

5. Ellie _____ a counselor on Monday.

6. Julie _____ full time.

7. She _____ at a department store, and

   she _____ classes at night.

8. They _____ the same schedules.

9. Ellie _____ classes at night because

   she _____ at her father's restaurant.

B **Look at the pictures on page 34.** With a partner, discuss how each person's life is going to change.

> Kelly is going to look for an apartment.

> Kelly is going to get a job.

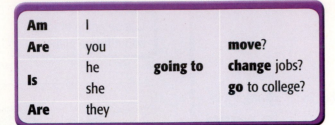

Am	I		
Are	you		**move**?
Is	he	**going to**	**change** jobs?
	she		**go** to college?
Are	they		

What **are** you **going to do**?
Where **are** you **going to move**?
How **are** they **going to get** there?
Who **are** you **going to visit**?
Who **is going to help**?

A **Working Together** **Find someone who . . .** Walk around the classroom and ask your classmates questions about their future plans. Use *be going to.* When someone answers "Yes, I am," write his / her name on the line. If someone answers "No, I'm not," ask another classmate.

1. get married? _____

2. move? _____

3. visit your native country? _____

4. buy a house? _____

5. attend a wedding? _____

6. have a party? _____

7. look for a new job? _____

8. eat out? _____

B **Talk about your weekend plans.** Use the words from the box or your own ideas. Your partner will ask you questions about your plans.

see a movie	visit a friend	clean
go to a party	work	go shopping
go dancing	play (a sport)	go to (a place)

My family and I are going to go to a wedding.

Who's going to get married?
Where's the wedding going to be?
What are you going to wear?

> If a specific time in the future is stated or clear, the present continuous can express future time.
>
> **I'm working** tomorrow.
> He **is leaving** at 4:00.

Tom and Amy are getting a divorce.

A **Write about Tom and Amy's plans.** Use the present continuous.

1. Tom / pack / tonight Tom is packing tonight.

2. He / hire / not / movers _____

3. Tom's friend / help / him / this weekend _____

4. Amy and the children / remain / in the house _____

5. Tom / buy / not / a new place _____

6. He / rent / a two-bedroom condo _____

7. Amy / meet with / a job counselor / Monday _____

8. They / meet with / their lawyers / next week _____

B **Listen and circle the meaning.**

CD1·TR11

1. (Now) Future   4. Now Future   7. Now Future

2. Now Future   5. Now Future   8. Now Future

3. Now Future   6. Now Future   9. Now Future

I			
You			
He	**will**	do it.	
She	**'ll**		
We			
They			

Use *will* to make an offer to help or a promise. It is common to use the contraction *'ll*.

I'll help you.

  A **Pronunciation: *'ll* Listen and repeat.**

CD1·TR12

1. I'll do it.
2. I'll get it.
3. I'll call you.

4. I'll help him.
5. I'll be there.
6. They'll paint it.

7. She'll do it.
8. He'll answer it.
9. We'll help you.

 B **Offer to help your classmate.** Use the expressions in the box.

I don't understand this homework.   I'll help you.

1. My car broke down and I don't have a ride to school.

2. I can't find my keys.

3. I don't know how to use my new DVD player.

4. I just moved in, and I don't know anyone around here.

5. I don't know how to get to the mall.

6. I wrote this report, but I need someone to read it over for me.

7. I received a letter in English, but I don't understand it.

8. My car has a flat tire.

9. My income taxes are due next week, but I don't know how to fill out the form.

explain it
introduce you
give you a ride
help you look
read it
show you how
give you directions
change it
translate it

> Use *will* to make a prediction about the future.
> The United States **will make** new immigration laws.
> There **will be** more electric cars.

A **Working Together** **Make predictions about the United States and your native country.** Use *will*. Then, read your predictions to the class.

1. The economy in the U.S. _____.

2. The economy in _____.
   native country

3. The population in the U.S. _____.

4. The population in _____.
   native country

5. There will be more _____ in ten years.

6. There will be less _____ in ten years.

7. _____.

B **Write three predictions about your future.**

1. I will _____.

2. I will _____.

3. I will not _____.

C **Dictation** **Your teacher will dictate the sentences on page 263.** Listen and write the sentences you hear.

1. _____

2. _____

3. _____

4. _____

5. _____

6. _____

7. _____

If I **study** hard, **I'll** graduate in two years.
(time clause)   (main clause)

When I **have** time, **I'm going to finish** my degree.
(time clause)   (main clause)

I'll graduate in two years if I **study** hard.
(main clause)   (time clause)

I'm going to finish my degree when I **have** time.
(main clause)   (time clause)

1. A time clause begins with time words such as *after, before, when,* and *if.*

2. Use a comma when the time clause is at the beginning of a sentence. Do **not** use a comma when the time clause is at the end of a sentence.

A Match the two parts of each sentence about a college student's plans.

_____b_____ **1.** If Sonia works hard,

_____ **2.** When Sonia takes a vacation,

_____ **3.** After Sonia saves some money,

_____ **4.** If Sonia meets the right person,

_____ **5.** After Sonia interviews for several jobs,

a. she'll buy a new car.

b. she'll get a promotion.

c. she'll accept the best offer.

d. she'll travel around Europe.

e. she'll get married.

B Complete the sentences about Sonia's future. Use your imagination.

1. Before Sonia gets married, _____.

2. _____ when she has children.

3. If she decides to become a stay-at-home mom, _____.

4. _____ after her children are grown.

5. If Sonia decides to change careers, _____.

6. When Sonia has enough money, _____.

7. _____ when she retires.

8. _____.

9. _____.

C **Ask and answer the questions.** Use a future time clause with *before, after, if,* or *when.*

> When are you going to get married?

> I'm going to get married after I graduate from college.

1. When are you going to travel out of the country?

2. When are you going to buy a new car?

3. When are you going to move into a bigger place?

4. When are you going to pay your utility bills?

5. When are you going to take a day off?

6. When are you going to become a U.S. citizen?

7. When are you going to leave this classroom?

 D **Working Together** **Number the events in George's life in order from 1 to 8.** Then, make sentences about his life. Use *before, after,* and *when.*

> Before George finds a job, he's going to graduate from college.

> He's going to get married when he meets the right woman.

find a job

buy a house

get married

graduate from college

have a daughter

have a son

meet a wonderful woman

save a lot of money

A **Discuss.** Laura and her husband are expecting their first child. How do you think their lives are going to change?

WORD PARTNERSHIPS	
maternity paternity family	leave
stay-at-home	dad mom

CD1·TR13

B **Listen.** Circle the changes that Laura and Brady are going to make.

buy a house	change a schedule	get a cat
find a bigger apartment	go out three nights a week	give away their cats
move	stay home	take some time off
change jobs	take a class	

🔊 **C** **Listen again and (circle) True or False.**

1. They're still looking for a house.   True   (False)

2. They like their building.   True   False

3. They're going to move soon.   True   False

4. All of the houses that they looked at needed work.   True   False

5. Their building is far from Laura's work.   True   False

6. She's going to take off two weeks from work. True   False

7. Laura and Brady are going to go out less often.   True   False

D **Match.**

_d_ 1. If they like the bigger apartment,

___ 2. When the baby arrives,

___ 3. They're going to do a lot of shopping

___ 4. When Laura's maternity leave begins,

___ 5. They're going to move

___ 6. Laura will call Melissa

a. before the baby comes.

b. Laura's mother is going to help.

c. if she needs help.

d. they'll move next week.

e. after they find a bigger apartment.

f. she'll stay at home.

E **Complete the sentences.** Use the future, simple past, simple present, or present continuous. Some of the verbs are negative.

1. Laura (tell) _____ told _____ her boss about her pregnancy.

2. Her company (give) _____ her two months off.

3. When Laura's mother (find) _____ out about the baby, she (decide) _____ to retire early.

4. Her mother (help) _____ for a while.

5. They (want / not) _____ to move out of their building.

6. They (get / not) _____ rid of their cats.

7. Laura and Brady (take) _____ a class.

8. Brady (take / not) _____ a lot of time off from work.

> **READING NOTE**
>
> **Finding Vocabulary Definitions**
> Sometimes you can find the definitions of new vocabulary words in the reading. Look for a comma after the word and a different word or short phrase that gives the definition. You can also read the sentence before or after the new vocabulary word(s) to find a clue to the meaning.
>
> This a big adjustment, or **change**, for the parents.

A **Discuss.**

1. Do you have any children? If so, how old are they?

2. At what age do you think children are ready to live on their own?

3. How do you think parents feel when their children move away from home?

B **Word Builder** **Find the words in the reading.** Then, write the definitions.

1. adjustment _____ *change* _____

2. syndrome _____

3. trigger _____

4. majority _____

5. cope _____

6. seek _____

C **Read.**

Parents whose children have recently left home are called "empty nesters." Their little birds, or children, have flown away to start independent lives. This is a big **adjustment**, or change, for the parents. The lonely, depressed feeling that parents have after a child becomes more independent is called "empty-nest **syndrome**."

Different sights and sounds can **trigger** the condition. A parent may suddenly start to feel sad. One empty-nester mother said, "I drove past my son's soccer field the other day, and suddenly I started crying. Another time, I heard my son's cell phone ring tone at the mall, and I became very emotional."

Although mothers still take care of the **majority** of childcare responsibilities, fathers also feel unexpected sadness. In general, fathers do not spend most of their time taking care of their children, so fathers do not expect to experience this feeling of loss. One father reported that he had to pull over to the side of the road after he heard his daughter's favorite song on the radio. "I never thought I would miss her so much," he said.

Children do not have to move out of the house for parents to experience empty-nest feelings. When children enter high school, they start going out on weekends, playing sports, and doing other activities with friends. Some parents report that they only see their children at breakfast or on their way out of the house. Parents miss the closeness that they used to have with their children when they were younger. They find it difficult to **cope** with the independence of their children. Parents must learn how to handle their feelings.

When parents do not recover from their sad feelings after a few months, they may want to **seek** professional help. In addition, they may look for assistance online, such as support groups, to help them through this difficult time.

There are many suggestions on how to recover from empty-nest syndrome. This is a good time for parents to remember the things that they wanted to do after the children grew up. Maybe they would like to travel or take some courses. Maybe they wanted to start a business; now they have the time. Cell phones and online chats also help parents to keep in touch with their children. Fortunately, empty-nest syndrome passes with time. Empty nesters should keep busy, renew old friendships, and take time for themselves.

D (Circle) *True* or *False*.

1.	Empty-nest syndrome is a problem for college students.	True	(False)
2.	Only sights can trigger a parent to feel sad.	True	False
3.	Both mothers and fathers can experience this syndrome.	True	False
4.	One parent became upset after she heard her son's voice.	True	False
5.	Parents with high school age children can also be empty nesters.	True	False
6.	High school children always spend a lot of time with their parents.	True	False
7.	There is professional help for empty nesters.	True	False
8.	One way to recover from empty-nest syndrome is to keep busy.	True	False

 E **In your own words, write a definition of empty-nest syndrome.**

_____

_____

_____

A Read.

Carlos Garcia

English IV

My Goals for English

I am an ESL student at Union County College. I came from Cuba three years ago. When I first came here, I did not speak any English, but now I can carry on a conversation in English and understand most people. I work at a warehouse, but only a few people speak English there. I am going to make some changes so that I will speak English much more fluently.

<u>First of all</u>, I'm going to continue my English classes. I think I will be able to speak English much better in about two years. After this semester ends, I am going to look for a job where I can use more English. When I find one, I am going to ask my co-workers to correct my English. Next, I think I will register for a pronunciation class because many people do not understand me the first time I say something. Then, I am going to try to find a study partner who speaks a different language. Finally, I am going to start shopping at stores where I will have to speak English. If I do these things, I think my English will improve.

WRITING NOTE

Transition Words

Use **transition** words to explain how to do something or to show what comes first, second, and so on. Use a comma after a transition when it begins a sentence. Here are some transition words and phrases:

First,   First of all,   Second,   Third,   Fourth,   Next,
Then,   After that,   After I . . . ,   Finally,   Last,

B Underline the transitions in the composition above.

C Number the sentences in the correct order.

    2   I'm going to look at the schedule of classes.

    1   I'm going to look for a good nursing program.

           I'm going to do the homework.

           I'm going to register for classes.

           I'm going to buy the books.

           I'm going to go to my first class.

D **In your notebook, write the sentences from Exercise C in order in a paragraph.** Use transitions.

E **Write a composition about your goals for improving your English.** Answer these questions in your composition. Use transitions.

1. Where do you study English?

2. What country are you from, and when did you come to the United States?

3. Which skills do you need to improve: reading, writing, grammar, listening, or speaking?

4. How are you going to improve your English?

F **Sharing Our Stories** **Read your partner's composition.** What are your partner's goals for learning English? Underline the transitions.

G **Find and correct the verb mistakes.**

1. In ten years, there ~~are~~ *will be* many more hybrid cars.

2. Before I quit this job, I going to find a new one.

3. He's going to stay home with his children if he will lose his job.

4. Is she going to go to college when she leave the military?

5. I take the citizenship test tomorrow at 4:00.

6. I pick it up for you.

7. Where they are going to live?

8. They need a bigger apartment if they have another child.

A **Complete the conversations with an offer to help or a promise.** Use *will*.

1. Child: Dad, I'm sorry. I broke the window when I was playing baseball.

Father: *Don't worry. I'll fix it.* _____

2. Wife: I'm tired tonight. I don't feel like making dinner.

Husband: _____

3. Father: You can use the car, but make sure you fill up the gas tank.

Son: _____

4. Daughter: I have to be at school tomorrow morning at 7:00.

Mother: _____

5. Son: Mom, my uniform is dirty, and we have a baseball game tomorrow.

Mother: _____

6. Son: Dad, my driving test is next week. Can you take me out to practice?

Father: _____

B **Combine the sentences.** Use the word in parentheses and a future time clause.

1. I'm going to get married. I'm going to meet the right person. (when)
I'm going to get married when I meet the right person.

2. They're going to get married. They are going to have separate bank accounts. (after)

3. The husband is going to cook dinner. His wife is going to feel tired. (when)

4. His wife is going to cut the lawn. He is going to be busy. (if)

5. They are going to have an argument. Their whole family isn't going to know about it. (when)

6. My mother will only stay for a week. My mother will come for a visit. (when)

7. She is still going to laugh. Her husband is going to tell the same joke twice. (if)

8. They are going to have a son. They are going to name him after his father. (if)

A **Match each person or couple with the home you think is best for them.**
More than one answer is possible. Compare your answers with a partner.

1.

We have a one-bedroom apartment. We are expecting another child soon, so we need a bigger place. We would like to buy a house with a yard and a garage.
Home _____

2.

Our children are grown, and our house is too big. We don't need four bedrooms, and we definitely don't need such a big yard. We want something smaller.
Home _____

3.

I have a full-time job, and I'm ready to buy a home. I'm excited about getting my own place, but I don't need a big place. I'd like a one-bedroom apartment with parking.
Home _____

a.

$239,000, 3 BDRM, 2½ baths; gas heat; frpl.; attached garage; built 1950s; nr parks, schools

b.

$249,000, 2 BDRM, 2 full baths, central A/C, gas heat, pool, prkg, tennis, nr schools/shops/trans

c.

$199,999, 1 BDRM, 1 bath, central A/C, gas heat, exercise room, pool, 24 hr doorman, nr shops/trans; built 70s

d.

$229,000, 2 BDRM, 2 baths, wall A/C; oil heat; nr shopping; built 80s

B **Go online.** Search for houses and apartments in your area. Multiple Listing Service (mls.com) lists many homes for sale and rent. Choose a home that you think would be good for you. Discuss your choice with your classmates.

Unit 4

Driving

A Match each traffic rule with the correct sign.

a. You must not ride bikes here.

b. Trucks must not use this road.

c. You must not turn left.

d. You must stop for pedestrians.

e. You must not park here or you will be towed.

f. You must stay to the right.

g. You must look out for deer.

h. You must slow down. This is a school zone.

i. You must not park here.

j. You must slow down. The road is slippery when wet.

k. You must slow down and be prepared to stop. Construction ahead.

l. You must turn right. One-way street.

1. ___f___

2. _____

3. _____

4. _____

5. _____

6. _____

7. _____

8. _____

9. _____

10. _____

11. _____

12. _____

Modals: *Must / Must not*

I You	**must**	**stop** at a red light.
He Drivers		**drive** at the speed limit.
	must not	**drive** without a license.

> *Must* shows rules, obligation, or necessity.
> You **must stop** at a stop sign.
> *Must not* shows that an action is not permitted.
> Drivers **must *not* drive** through a red light.

A **Use each sentence to state a traffic law.** Use *must* or *must not*.

1. Stop at a stop sign.
   You must stop at a stop sign.
2. Don't pass cars on the right.
   You must not pass cars on the right.
3. Pay traffic fines.

4. Don't drink alcohol and drive.

5. Register your car.

6. Don't drive over the speed limit.

7. Wear your seat belt.

8. Stop for a school bus with flashing lights.

9. Don't drive without a license.

You must stop at a stop sign.

You must not pass cars on the right.

B **Read each school rule.** Check (✓) *Yes* or *No* about your school.

School Rules	Yes	No
1. We must arrive on time.		
2. We must call or e-mail our teacher if we are absent.		
3. We must wear uniforms.		
4. We must speak English all the time.		
5. We must not copy from other students.		
6. We must not eat in class.		

C **In your notebook, write three more rules about your school or class.**

I You	**have to**	**stop** at a red light.
He She	**has to**	**drive** with a license.
They	**have to**	**wear** a seat belt.

> *Have to* shows necessity or obligation.
> I **have to get** car insurance.
> She **has to babysit** her niece.

A **Complete the sentences.** Use *have to* or *has to* and an appropriate verb.

1. She ___has to move___ her car.

2. She _____ for the ticket.

3. He _____ the tires.

4. He _____ new tires.

5. They _____ their sports car.

6. They _____ a car seat for their baby.

I You	**do not have to** **don't have to**	
She	**does not have to** **doesn't have to**	**buy** a new car. **work** today. **go** to school today.
They	**do not have to** **don't have to**	

> *Doesn't have to / Don't have to* show that something is not necessary.
> You **don't have to own** a car.

B **Restate each sentence.** Use *doesn't have to* or *don't have to*.

1. It's not necessary for a new driver to buy a new car.

2. It's not necessary for you to have a radio in your car.

3. It's not necessary for new drivers to have jobs.

4. It's not necessary for a learner to go to a driving school.

5. It's not necessary for drivers to have cell phones.

6. It's not necessary for you to wash your car every day.

> A new driver doesn't have to buy a new car.

C **Complete the sentences.** Use *must not* (prohibited) or *doesn't have to /
don't have to* (not necessary).

1. Students ___don't have to___ buy food in the cafeteria because there are
many restaurants nearby.

2. I ___must not___ copy from a classmate during a test.

3. I _____ wear a suit or a dress to English class.

4. The instructor _____ sell the books in class because there
is a bookstore at the school.

5. A teacher _____ wear a uniform at this school.

6. Students _____ buy new computers for classes.

7. We _____ use cell phones in the classroom.

8. Students _____ copy essays from the Internet.

9. We _____ bring drinks into the computer lab.

CD1·TR14

D **Listen.** Rebecca is talking about her schedule. Check (✓) the tasks that she has
completed.

Tasks	Completed
1. buy stamps	
2. mail her bills	
3. do the laundry	
4. go to the supermarket	
5. make a deposit at the bank	
6. confirm an appointment	
7. put gas in her car	

E **Ask and answer questions about Rebecca's to-do list.** Use the information
in Exercise D.

Do	I		
	you		**do** laundry?
Does	he	**have to**	**buy** stamps?
	she		**see** the dentist?
Do	they		

Does Rebecca have to
buy stamps?

No, she doesn't. She
bought some yesterday.

I		
You	**can**	
She		**drive**.
He		**park** in this area.
They	**can't**	

Can shows ability. *Can't* shows inability.

> I **can drive** a car.
> I **can't drive** a truck.

Can also shows that an action is permitted. *Can't / Cannot* shows that an action is *not* permitted.

> I **can drive** at night by myself.
> You **can't drive** through red lights.

CD1·TR15

A **Pronunciation: *Can* and *Can't*** **Listen.** Marcus is talking about his driving experience. Complete the sentences with *can* or *can't*.

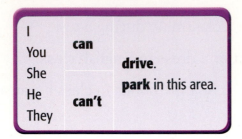

1. He _____can't_____ drive very well.

2. He _____ drive only with a licensed driver in the car.

3. He _____ back up.

4. He _____ parallel park.

5. He _____ drive on a busy highway.

6. He _____ drive at night alone.

7. He _____ drive with the radio playing.

B **Working Together** **Find someone who . . .** Walk around the room. Ask your classmates what they can do. If someone answers, "Yes, I can," write his / her name in the chart. If someone answers, "No, I can't," ask another person.

Question	Name
1. speak another language	
2. dance	
3. cook well	
4. bake a cake	
5. type fast	
6. swim	
7. play a musical instrument	

	I	
	you	**drive** a truck?
Can	she	**swim**?
	they	**speak** French?

I You	could	**speak** English.
He They	couldn't	**find** a job. **register** for classes.

Could shows past ability.
I **could drive** when I came to this country.
I **couldn't speak** English when I came here.

A **Complete the sentences.** Use *could* or *couldn't* and the verb.

1. When I came to this country, I (speak) _____ English.

2. When I came to this country, I (read) _____ a book without a dictionary.

3. When I came to this country, I (find) _____ a job.

4. When I came here, I (drive) _____ a car.

5. When I came here, I (use) _____ a computer.

B **Complete the sentences.**

1. When my family came here, _____.

2. When I came to this English program, _____.

3. When I started this class, I _____.

 C **Ask and answer questions about your first day in English class.**

Could you speak English?

Yes, I could speak a little English.

Could	you she he they	**speak** English? **find** a job? **register** for classes?

find the classroom

understand your teacher

read English

write in English

find a place to park

walk to school

do the first homework assignment

Should expresses an opinion or advice.

I **should buy** a smaller car. Small cars get good gas mileage.

Shouldn't / Should not shows that something is *not* a good idea.

You **shouldn't put** your packages in the back seat. Someone might see them.

You **should put** them in your trunk.

I You He They	**should** **shouldn't**	**drive** at night. **buy** that car.

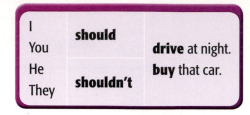

I agree that drivers should drive more carefully near elementary schools. Young children might run into the street.

 A **Working Together** **Read each statement.** Check (✓) your opinion. Then, discuss your reason with a small group of classmates.

Opinion	Agree	Disagree
1. Drivers should drive more carefully near elementary schools.		
2. Teenagers are too young to drive cars.		
3. Small children should always ride in the back seat of a car.		
4. People over 80 years old should not drive.		
5. Drivers should not eat and drive at the same time.		
6. The highway speed limit is too low.		
7. All drivers should have car insurance.		

  B **Give advice.** Use *should* or *shouldn't*. Discuss your answers with a partner.

1. A family with five children is shopping for a new car. What kind of car should the family buy?

2. Chen wants to learn how to drive. Who should teach him—his grandfather, his mother, or a private teacher?

3. Valeria is 16 years old. In her state, teenagers can drive at 16 years of age. Should she try to get her driver's license now, or should she wait until she graduates from high school?

4. Pierre is a new immigrant to the United States. Everyone at his job speaks his native language. He doesn't speak any English. What should he do?

I You She He They	had better 'd better	wear a seat belt. use a car seat.
	had better not 'd better not	drive without a license. forget to fill the gas tank.

Had better expresses a strong warning.
Had better is stronger than **should**.

You'd better check your tire.
(Or you'll get a flat tire.)

I'd **better not miss** another class.
(Or I'll fail the class.)

CD1·TR16

A **Pronunciation: *'d better / 'd better not*** **Listen and complete the sentences.** Then, listen again and repeat.

1. _I'd better stay_ home. I don't feel well.

2. _____ the baby in the car seat.

3. _____ the police and report the accident.

4. _____ the party inside. It's beginning to rain.

5. _____ another piece of cake. He'll get sick.

6. _____ a dog. Your landlord won't allow it.

7. _____ down. The roads are icy.

8. _____ that. I can't afford it.

B **Give warnings.** Use *'d better* or *'d better not.*

1.

2.

3.

4.

5.

6.

CD1·TR17

A **Jennifer is talking about how to get her driver's license.** Listen and complete the chart.

1

Complete D.A.T.A. (Drug, Alcohol, Traffic Awareness) course

2

Application with _____'s signature

+

Proof of _____

Original _____ Certificate

Permanent Residence Card

_____

Citizenship Papers

3

Written Test ____%

+

Vision Test
E
ONZ
KPMFS
UENWOASF

+

Hearing Test

Questions and Signs

_____

Languages

4

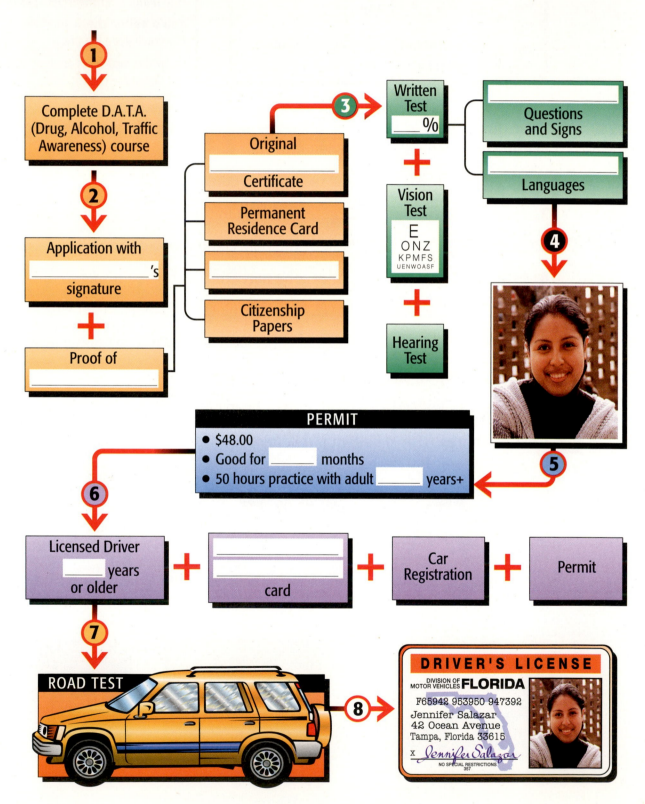

5

PERMIT
- $48.00
- Good for _____ months
- 50 hours practice with adult _____ years+

6

Licensed Driver _____ years or older

+

_____ card

+

Car Registration

+

Permit

7

ROAD TEST

8

DRIVER'S LICENSE
DIVISION OF MOTOR VEHICLES **FLORIDA**
F65942 953950 947392
Jennifer Salazar
42 Ocean Avenue
Tampa, Florida 33615
x *Jennifer Salazar*
NO SPECIAL RESTRICTIONS
357

B **Circle** *True* **or** *False.* If the answer is false, tell the correct information to a partner.

1. Jennifer must take two tests before she gets her permit. **True** False
2. Jennifer has to show her birth certificate for proof of age. True False
3. Jennifer can take the written test in her native language. True False
4. Jennifer has to get 90 percent correct to pass the written test. True False
5. She can practice six months with her permit. True False
6. Jennifer's sister can teach her how to drive. True False
7. Eighteen-year-olds must drive with someone 21 or older. True False
8. Jennifer has to show an auto insurance card to take the road test. True False
9. Jennifer must go to the road test with a licensed driver. True False

C **Discuss.**

1. What is the process for getting a driver's license in your state?
2. How is the process the same or different from Jennifer's state?
3. Has anyone in your class gotten a driver's license recently?

D **Ask and answer questions about getting a driver's license.**

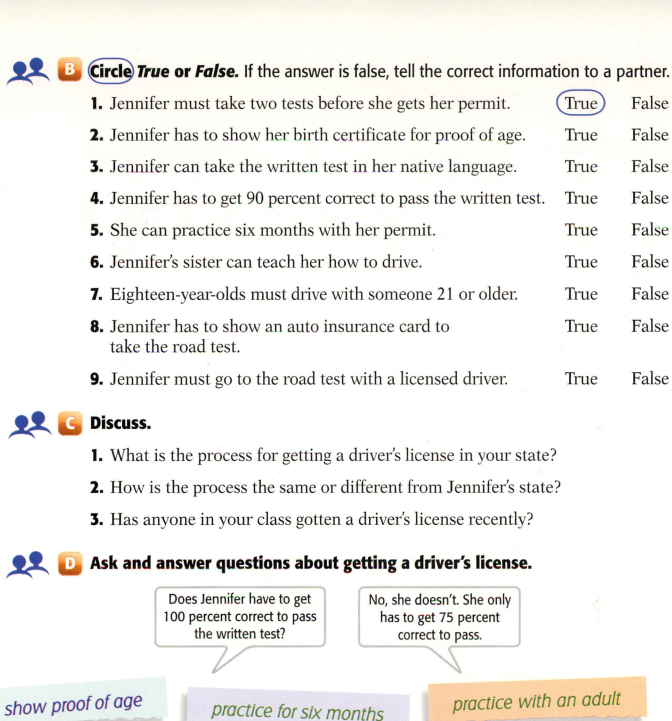

> Does Jennifer have to get 100 percent correct to pass the written test?

> No, she doesn't. She only has to get 75 percent correct to pass.

show proof of age

practice for six months

practice with an adult

take a vision test

have the registration for her car

buy a car

show citizenship papers

have auto insurance

have a parent's signature

A **Discuss.**

1. Do you have a driver's license?

2. If you have a driver's license, did you take the written test in English?

3. What was the minimum passing score on the written test?

B **Read the sample driving test questions.** Fill in the circle next to the correct answer.

● Yes   ⊗ No   ✓ No   ◑ No

> **READING NOTE**
>
> **Multiple-choice Questions**
> When you take a multiple-choice test, read each choice carefully. Then, try to eliminat one or two of the choices.

1. A driver approaching a flashing red traffic signal must . . .

   ○ **a.** drive carefully without stopping.

   ○ **b.** stop first, and then pass through the intersection.

   ○ **c.** go through the light slowly.

   ○ **d.** slow down at the intersection.

2. You must stop your vehicle . . .

   ○ **a.** at an intersection with a stop sign.

   ○ **b.** where there is a red light.

   ○ **c.** when a traffic officer orders you to stop.

   ○ **d.** All of the above.

3. You must turn on your headlights . . .

   ○ **a.** when you turn on your wipers.

   ○ **b.** in the evening.

   ○ **c.** one half hour before sunset.

   ○ **d.** All of the above.

4. If you are driving behind a school bus and it shows a flashing red light, you must . . .

   ○ **a.** slow down.

   ○ **b.** slow down and pass on the left.

   ○ **c.** stop at least 25 feet away.

   ○ **d.** All of the above.

5. You are driving on a highway with a 65 mph speed limit. Most of the other vehicles are driving 70 mph or faster. You may legally drive . . .

   ○ **a.** 70 mph or faster.

   ○ **b.** no faster than 65 mph.

   ○ **c.** between 65 and 70.

   ○ **d.** as fast as you'd like.

6. You have a green light, but the traffic is blocking the intersection. You must . . .

○ **a.** pass the traffic on the left. ○ **c.** wait until the traffic clears. Then, go.

○ **b.** honk your horn. ○ **d.** pass the traffic on the right.

7. You must obey instructions of school crossing guards . . .

○ **a.** at all times.

○ **b.** when school is closed.

○ **c.** in the morning.

○ **d.** when it is raining.

8. If you pass your exit on a highway, you should . . .

○ **a.** go to the next exit.

○ **b.** turn around on the highway and return to your exit.

○ **c.** cross to the other side of the highway and make a U-turn.

○ **d.** back up slowly to the exit that you want.

9. What does this sign mean?

○ **a.** Three-way intersection. ○ **c.** Railroad crossing ahead.

○ **b.** Stop. ○ **d.** No turns.

10. What does this sign mean?

○ **a.** One-way street ahead. ○ **c.** Left turn only.

○ **b.** Pass other cars on the right. ○ **d.** The road ahead is curvy.

Check your answers below.

1. b 2. d 3. d 4. c 5. b 6. c 7. a 8. a 9. c 10. d

| **8 or more correct** | *Congratulations!* You pass! Get your driver's license. |
| **Below 8** | *Sorry.* You're not ready to drive. Study for two more weeks. Then, come back and retake the test. |

A **Look at the street map.** Then, read the directions from the starting point.

Conversation 1

A: My sofa is getting old. I need to buy a new sofa. How do I get to Sofa World? I heard that there's a great selection of sofas there.

B: That's right. Sofa World has a large selection of sofas. You're on Sea Street. Go to the first traffic light and turn left. That's Paris Avenue. Traffic is usually light. Take Paris straight to Ocean Street. There's a gas station on your left and a soccer field on your right. Turn right. Go through one traffic light. Sofa World is the second building on the right. It's on the corner of Ocean Street and Athens Avenue.

Conversation 2

A: I have to pick up sandwiches for a meeting at my office. How do I get to Deb's Deli? I heard that I can get a great sandwich there.

B: That's right. The sandwiches are delicious. It's easy. This is Sea Street. Go to the second light, turn left. That's Rome Avenue. Go to the next corner. That's Lake Street. It's difficult to park around there, so you should park in the public parking lot on the corner. Deb's Deli is across the street from the parking lot.

B In your notebook, write directions from your school to your home or workplace. Include the names of important streets and places such as gas stations, banks, and stores.

 C **Sharing Our Stories** **Read your partner's directions.** Are the directions clear?

> **fender bender** = small accident

> **WRITING NOTE**
>
> **Unnecessary Information**
>
> When you write a story or composition, it is important to include details to help the reader understand what you wrote. It is also important to stay on topic. Do not include unnecessary information that may confuse the reader.
>
> *I was in a fender bender last week. There was a lot of heavy traffic because of a football game.* ~~*The Giants won 23 to 7.*~~ *The car that was behind me hit my rear bumper.*

D **Read the paragraph.** ~~Cross out~~ the unnecessary sentences.

> I think it should be legal to talk on a cell phone while driving. My parents gave me a cell phone when I got my driver's license. I have a part-time job, and I have to work in the evenings. It was very difficult for me to find a job, so I want to keep this job until I finish high school. I always call my mother from my car to tell her that I'm on my way home. My cell phone is very cute. It's red, and it plays my favorite song when it rings. A few months ago, I had a flat tire on the way home. I used my cell phone to call my father. He called our auto association to come and help me. Then, my father called me back and kept talking to me as he drove to my location to wait with me. I was very nervous and scared. I was very happy to have my cell phone.

E **Find and correct the mistakes.**

1. She must ~~puts~~ ^{put} money in the parking meter.

2. Can you driving a stick shift?

3. Drivers has to follow the traffic rules.

4. I didn't have to took the test in English.

5. He better not take another day off, or he'll lose his job.

6. We didn't have buy a new car.

Practicing on Your Own

A **Complete the sentences with the correct modal.** There is more than one correct answer for each sentence.

must must not	has to doesn't have to	have to don't have to	should shouldn't	had better had better not

1. You _____ take the written test in English.

2. You _____ drive over the speed limit.

3. You _____ drive immediately after you have an argument. Calm down first.

4. Children under seven _____ ride in car seats.

5. You _____ drive and talk on a cell phone.

6. Drivers _____ use a hands-free cell phone.

7. Drivers _____ drink and drive, or they will lose their licenses.

8. You _____ wash your car every day.

9. I _____ change the oil in my car a few times a year.

10. Bicycle riders _____ ride in the same direction as cars.

B **Compare the driving rules in your state to the driving rules in your native country.** Add an appropriate verb. Use negative forms when necessary.

1. In this state, I _____ a seat belt.

2. In my country, I _____ a seat belt.

3. In this state, children _____ in car seats.

4. In my country, children _____ in car seats.

5. In this state, drivers _____ auto insurance.

6. In my country, I _____ auto insurance.

7. In this state, you _____ a license when you are _____ years old.

can
could
must
have to
had to

64 · Unit 4

CD1·TR18

A **Listen and repeat.** Then, match. Write the letter(s) of the car part next to the word.

___ 1. accelerator   ___ 4. clutch   ___ 7. signal   ___ 9. gear shift   ___ 12. windshield

___ 2. brake   ___ 5. hood   ___ 8. steering   ___ 10. tires   ___ 13. windshield

___ 3. bumper   ___ 6. horn   wheel   ___ 11. trunk   wipers

WORD PARTNERSHIPS	
check	the oil
	the tire pressure
replace	the filters
	the wiper blades

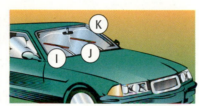

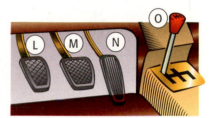

B **Word Builder** **Complete the sentences.** Use words from Exercise A.

1. _____ clean your windshield.

2. A _____ protects your car in minor accidents.

3. When you want to go forward or faster, press the _____.

4. Turn on the _____ before you make a turn.

5. Open the _____ to check the oil.

6. In the United States, many people prefer an automatic car to a car with a _____.

7. Put your packages in the _____ of your car.

8. Step on the _____ to stop your car.

9. Press the _____ to warn someone that you're coming.

10. In a manual car, the _____ pedal is to the left of the brake.

Unit 5

Leisure Activities

A Label the leisure activities.

cards	dancing	gardening	scrapbooking
cooking	~~dominoes~~	mah-jongg	sewing
cricket	fishing	photography	traveling

WORD PARTNERSHIPS

know how to	cook
	garden
	play cards

1. _dominoes_

2. _____

3. _____

4. _____

5. _____

6. _____

7. _____

8. _____

9. _____

10. _____

11. _____

12. _____

 B **Which activities in Exercise A do you like to do?** What other activities do you enjoy? Discuss your choices with a partner.

Present Tense		
Do	I	
	you	play
	they	soccer?
Does	she	
	he	

Past Tense		
	I	
	you	
Did	they	play
	she	soccer?
	he	

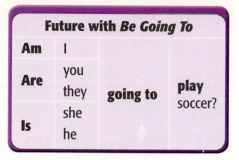

Future with *Be Going To*			
Am	I		
Are	you		
	they	going to	play
	she		soccer?
Is	he		

Present Continuous		
Am	I	
Are	you	
	they	playing
	she	soccer?
Is	he	

Past Tense of *Be*		
Was	she	
	he	athletic?
Were	you	
	they	

Can; Future with *Will*		
	I	
Can	you	
	they	play
Will	she	soccer?
	he	

A   **Complete the questions.** Use the activities from page 66.

1. Are you going to _____ *go fishing* _____ this weekend?

2. Are you going to _____ next month?

3. Were you _____ last weekend?

4. Were you _____ last month?

5. Do you like to _____?

6. Do you _____ every day?

7. Did you _____?

8. Did you _____ yesterday?

9. Are you _____ now?

10. Are you _____ right now?

 B   **Ask and answer the questions in Exercise A.**

| Yes, I am. | Yes, I was. | Yes, I do. | Yes, I did. |
| No, I'm not. | No, I wasn't. | No, I don't. | No, I didn't. |

Whose umbrella is that?	It's mine.
Who likes sports?	I do.
Who do you play cards with?	With my cousins.

Whose asks questions about possession.
Who asks questions about the subject or object.

CD1·TR19

A **People are talking about activities they enjoy.** (Circle) the question word. Then, listen and answer the questions.

Gina

Roberto

Yelena

1. **(Who)/ Whose** likes to go dancing? _____Gina_____ does.

2. **Who / Whose** father taught her chess? _____'s did.

3. **Who / Whose** has many books about his hobby? _____ does.

4. **Who / Whose** does Gina go dancing with? _____.

5. **Who / Whose** friends often meet at dance clubs? _____'s do.

6. **Who / Whose** does Roberto meet once a week? _____.

7. **Who / Whose** gets information online? _____ does.

8. **Who / Whose** has more free time now? _____ does.

B **Work in a small group.** Write the correct question word. Then, ask and answer the questions.

1. _____ has a hobby?

2. _____ family has a garden?

3. _____ family is planning a trip?

4. _____ plays a sport regularly?

5. _____ has a pet?

6. _____ mother or father likes to cook?

Active Grammar — *Who* Questions: Present and Past

Present	Subject	**Who** goes	to the gym every day?	<u>Beth</u> does.
	Object	**Who** does Beth go	to the gym with?	She goes <u>with her sister</u>.
Past	Subject	**Who** went	to the gym?	<u>Jim</u> did.
	Object	**Who** did Jim go	to the gym with?	He went <u>with his wife</u>.

A Complete the questions about the women's weekend activities.

Rosa   Melba   Paula

1. Who (take) _____took_____ a cooking class?   Rosa did.

2. Who (take) _did Rosa take_ a class with?   With a few other students.

3. Who (plant) _____ some flowers?   Paula did.

4. Who (play) _____ cards?   Melba did.

5. Who (Melba / play) _____ with?   With her friends.

6. Who (Rosa / give) _____ the food to?   To her grandson.

7. Who (help) _____ Paula with the flowers?   No one did.

8. Who (Paula / buy) _____ flower seeds from?   From an online store.

B Complete the questions about your classmates. Write the answers. Ask and answer the questions with a partner.

1. Who usually (arrive) _____ late to class?   _____

2. Who (sit) _____ next to you?   _____

3. Who (work) _____ full time?   _____

4. Who (your teacher / give) _____ tests to?   _____

5. Who (wear) _____ glasses?   _____

6. Who (you / come) _____ to school with?   _____

How do you get to work?	By bus.
How far do you live from school?	About three miles.
How long did you wait?	Thirty minutes.
How much money do you have?	$4.39.
How many tickets do you have?	Just two.
How often do you come to school?	Three days a week.

A **Complete the questions with the correct *How* expression.** Then, ask and answer the questions with a partner.

1. _____How often_____ do you visit your native country?

2. _____ siblings do you have?

3. _____ do you spend on transportation to school?

4. _____ are you going to live in this country?

5. _____ hours do you sleep a night?

6. _____ do you live from your job?

7. _____ did you find out about this school?

8. _____ do you go to the movies?

9. _____ did it take you to get to class today?

10. _____ is it from your home to school?

B **Take turns asking your teacher these questions.**

1. How did you find this teaching job?

2. How do you get to school?

3. How many students do you have?

4. How often do you give tests?

5. How difficult are your tests?

6. How far do you live from here?

C **Write three more questions to ask your teacher.**

1. _____

2. _____

3. _____

Present with *be*	You **are** from Thailand,	**aren't** you?
	It **isn't** cold today,	**is** it?
Present continuous	They **are having** a nice time,	**aren't** they?
	They **aren't having** a bad time,	**are** they?
Simple present	He **plays** soccer every day,	**doesn't** he?
	He **doesn't play** tennis,	**does** he?
Past with *be*	They **were** at the park,	**weren't** they?
	They **weren't** at home,	**were** they?
Simple past	You **took** some pictures,	**didn't** you?
	You **didn't take** these pictures,	**did** you?
Future with *will*	She **will plant** more roses,	**won't** she?
	She **won't plant** any vegetables,	**will** she?

CD1·TR20

A **Pronunciation: Tag Questions** **Listen and repeat.** Pay attention to the arrows.

1. They like to fish, don't they?

2. Fishing isn't expensive, is it?

3. They will cook their fish, won't they?

4. They don't fish every day, do they?

5. They're fishing in a lake, aren't they?

6. It isn't a hot day, is it?

7. Fishing isn't tiring, is it?

8. They hope to catch a lot, don't they?

B **Write the correct tag.**

1. You are studying English, __aren't you__?

2. You will be in class tomorrow, _____?

3. You were here yesterday, _____?

4. We won't have a test tomorrow, _____?

5. You have a car, _____?

6. It wasn't raining yesterday morning, _____?

7. You didn't come to class late today, _____?

A **Working Together** **Student to Student.**

Student 1: Turn to page 263. Read **Set A** questions to Student 2.

Student 2: Listen to Student 1 and write the questions.

1. _____?

My father did.

2. _____?

My father did, and I also taught myself from cookbooks.

3. _____?

Yes, I regularly watch cooking shows on television.

4. _____?

Not at first, but we remodeled it a few years ago.

5. _____?

I took Indian cooking, candy-making, and afternoon tea, to name a few.

Student 2: Turn to page 263. Read **Set B** questions to Student 1.

Student 1: Listen to Student 2 and write the questions.

6. _____?

Yes, sometimes. He took a couple of classes with me.

7. _____?

We took a Valentine's Day class and a Mexican cooking class.

8. _____?

I cooked oatmeal, but it was terrible!

9. _____?

He likes everything that I cook.

10. _____?

Because my job wasn't fun anymore, and I love to cook.

B **Read.** Then, complete the questions.

There are six people in the Yang family household. They live in San Francisco, but they are originally from Hong Kong. They moved to San Francisco three years ago and lived with relatives until they found jobs. The parents, William and Patricia, spoke English fluently when they arrived, so they found work quickly. William and Patricia work at the same hospital. William is an accountant in the billing department, and Patricia is a pediatric nurse. Their two oldest children, Charles and Margaret, are now college students. Charles is a medical student, and Margaret is studying architecture. Their youngest, Harry, is a high school student. The children are doing well in school. Grandmother Yang speaks English, too, and she volunteers in a library in Chinatown.

The Yangs love to travel. This summer they are going to Vancouver, Canada, to visit William's brother, Victor.

1. How many _____?

   Six.

2. When _____?

   Three years ago.

3. Who _____?

   With relatives.

4. Why _____?

   Because they spoke English.

5. How many _____?

   Three.

6. How _____?

   They're doing well.

7. Do _____?

   Yes, they do.

8. Whose _____?

   William's brother.

C **Write two *Who* questions about the Yang family.**

1. Who _____?

2. Who did _____?

A **Discuss.** Look at the pictures. What places do the Yangs plan to visit in Vancouver?

The Yang Family

Vancouver Harbor

Granville Island

Queen Elizabeth Park

Chinatown

CD1·TR21

B **Listen and take notes about the Yang family's trip.**

Victor	Lin	This morning	Later

C Listen again. Circle True or False.

1. The Yangs are staying in a hotel.   True   False

2. Victor and his family moved to Vancouver five years ago.   True   False

3. Lin likes Vancouver now.   True   False

4. Lin works part time.   True   False

5. Lin can speak both Cantonese and Mandarin.   True   False

6. They had tea at a hotel restaurant.   True   False

7. They are going to see some animals this afternoon. True   False

D Match.

_d_   1. What did Victor like about Vancouver?   a. No, she didn't.

____   2. Did Lin want to come to Vancouver at first?   b. In Queen Elizabeth Park.

____   3. How often does Lin work a week?   c. Next year.

____   4. Where did they go this morning?   d. The economic opportunities.

____   5. Where are they going to have dinner?   e. To Granville Island.

____   6. Where can they see a rose garden?   f. Three times.

____   7. When will Victor go to San Francisco?   g. In Chinatown.

E Go online. Search for information on another Canadian province or territory. Find three activities to do there. Report to your classmates.

Activities

1. _____

2. _____

3. _____

Leisure Activities · **75**

A **Discuss.**

1. Do you have a garden?

2. If you have a garden, what do you grow?

3. Did you have a garden in your native country?

B **Read.**

In January, the seed catalogs begin to arrive at homes all across the United States. Gardening has become one of the most popular hobbies in this country. For some people, it is not just a relaxing hobby, but it is also an economic bonus. For those who live in apartments and do not have yards where they can start gardens, there may be a community garden in the area.

In many cities throughout the United States, there are community garden programs. According to the American Community Gardening Association (www.communitygarden.org), a community garden is "any piece of land gardened by a group of people." Among the benefits of community gardening are the economic **benefits** for families, the **beautification** of neighborhoods, and the social **interaction** that people experience. You can find community gardens in every state, especially on the east and west coasts and in midwestern cities.

In cities around the country, **residents** grow gardens on **vacant** city lots, or empty spaces. The gardens are usually organized by community members, and they help other residents select tools, seeds, plants, and other materials. Sometimes there is a children's program, which teaches elementary children science and math using the gardens. The program can offer both online learning and class visits. Gardening can also teach residents about healthy, **nutritious** food.

Youth can participate in the gardens, too. Teenagers can do gardening, help people who visit the gardens, or do other activities in the gardens.

As you can see, the community garden does more than just grow fruit, flowers, and vegetables.

C (Circle) *True* or *False.*

1. Some people start gardens in order to save money.   True   False

2. According to the article, you need more than one person   True   False
   to make a community garden.

3. There are no community gardens in the Midwest.   True   False

4. All gardeners put their gardens on private property.   True   False

5. Members of the garden program always bring their   True   False
   own tools.

6. There are gardening programs for children online.   True   False

7. Gardening can help children learn science and math.   True   False

8. Community garden programs have many purposes.   True   False

D **Word Builder** **Complete the sentences with the correct word form.**

Noun	Verb	Adjective
benefit(s)	benefit	beneficial
beautification	beautify	beautiful
interaction(s)	interact	interactive
nutrition	_____	nutritious
resident(s)	reside	residential
vacancy(ies)	vacate	vacancy

> **READING NOTE**
>
> **Word Forms**
> It is important to learn how to use different forms of words. Most words have a verb form, an adjective form, and / or other forms. For example, *benefit* is the noun and verb form, and *beneficial* is the adjective form.

1. In my city, there is a _____ community garden on my block.

2. There was a _____ in my building, so I told one of my friends who was looking for an apartment.

3. The people who work in the garden enjoy the social _____.

4. Only people who _____ in my neighborhood can use our garden.

5. There are many _____ to gardening.

6. Many people garden because they want more _____ food.

A **Read.**

Linda Torres
October 25, 2010
English IV

How to Start a Garden

My husband and I enjoy gardening. We both had gardens in our old village, and now we have a garden in our new home. It is not difficult to start a garden, but it takes regular care and patience.

First, find a sunny spot in your yard. Try to find a place that gets sun all day long. Second, clear out the grass and large rocks in the space. Third, turn over the dirt, and add some compost to make the dirt better for growing vegetables. You can buy compost in a gardening store. After that, plan your garden. Decide what you want to grow. Next, buy the seeds and / or small plants. Plant your seeds and plants according to the instructions on the packets or boxes. Then, cover the ground with mulch to keep down the weeds. We use old newspaper and leaves, but some people use straw and bags of mulch from a store. Finally, water your seeds and plants regularly, and don't forget to weed your garden. After some time, you'll have delicious, healthy vegetables for your family.

> **WRITING NOTE**
>
> **Transition Words Review**
> In Unit 3, you learned how to use transition words to improve your English. You can use the same words to describe a process.

B **Underline** **the transition words in the reading in Exercise A.**

> First,   Second,   Third,   After that,   Next,   Then,   Finally,

C **Read about how to cut a pineapple.** Work with a partner. Number the sentences in the correct order. Then, rewrite the sentences in paragraph form in your notebook. Use the transition words from Exercise B.

_____ Cut the halves in half.

_____ Slice the pineapple off the tough outer skin, and slice the fruit into smaller pieces.

_____ With a sharp knife, cut the pineapple in half lengthwise.

___1___ Pineapple is a popular fruit in my country, but some people do not know how to cut one properly.

_____ Twist off the green top.

_____ It's ready to serve.

___5___ Take one quarter of the pineapple, and slice off the tough inner core.

_____ Don't throw away the core. Some people like this part.

D **In your notebook, write about how to do something related to one of your hobbies or interests.** Use transition words in your paragraph. Here are a few examples of topics: how to play dominoes, how to take care of a pet, or how to buy a bicycle.

E **Sharing Our Stories** **Read a classmate's composition.** How many steps are there? Underline each step.

F **Find and correct the mistakes.**

1. What _are_ you doing?

2. Why does she has so many pets?

3. Where did you found those stamps?

4. How long will they plays this game?

5. You going to work in your garden?

6. Who did play a sport last weekend?

7. Who you go dancing with?

A **Write questions and answers.**

1. who / your teacher?

_____?

_____.

2. who / immigrate / to this country with you?

_____?

_____.

3. when / you / come / to this country?

_____?

_____.

4. how / you / get / to school / every day?

_____?

_____.

5. who / write / on the board / right now?

_____?

_____.

6. what kind of leisure activities / you / like to do?

_____?

_____.

7. who / you / usually / speak English with?

_____?

_____.

8. who / tell / you / about this English program?

_____?

_____.

9. when / your class / have / a test?

_____?

_____.

 A **Look at the graph.** Work with a partner. (Circle) *True* or *False.*

ACTIVITY

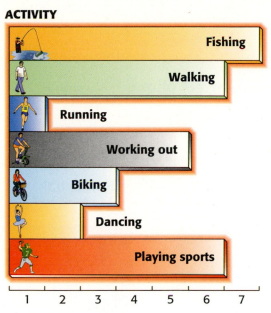

Fishing

Walking

Running

Working out

Biking

Dancing

Playing sports

1   2   3   4   5   6   7

1. Fishing is the most popular activity.　　(True) False

2. Biking is more popular than walking.　　True　False

3. Walking is as popular as playing sports.　　True　False

4. Working out at a gym is more popular than running.　　True　False

5. Running is the least popular activity.　　True　False

6. Dancing is more popular than biking.　　True　False

 B **Working Together** **Make a survey.**

1. One student asks the questions below to the whole class.

2. Two students count the responses from the class.

3. Complete the chart below.

Questions

1. Who plays a sport?

2. Who watches sports on TV?

3. Who socializes with friends and family?

4. Who rents movies?

5. Who goes to the movies?

6. Who uses the Internet?

Plays a sport																
Watches sports																
Socializes																
Rents movies																
Goes to movies																
Uses the Internet																

1　2　3　4　5　6　7　8　9　10　11　12　13　14　15　16

Travel

A Write the name of each place under the correct photo.

Boston, Massachusetts, U.S.A.   Shanghai, China   Paris, France
Cancun, Mexico   Los Angeles, California, U.S.A.   Rio de Janeiro, Brazil
Giza, Egypt   New York, New York, U.S.A.   Rome, Italy

1. Cancun, Mexico

2. _____

3. _____

4. _____

5. _____

6. _____

7. _____

8. _____

9. _____

 B **Discuss.** Which places would you like to visit? Why?

I	**may**	
You	**may not**	**go** on vacation.
They	**might**	**need** a visa.
He	**might not**	

Use *may* or *might* to express possibility.

I might go on vacation. = Maybe I will go on vacation.

He **may not need** a visa. = Maybe he will not need a visa.

A **Complete the conversation.** Use *may, might,* or *will*.

A: Where will you go for vacation?

B: We ___*might*___ go to San Diego.
1

A: Are you going to fly?

B: It's not too far. Maybe I _____ drive.
2

A: How long are you going to stay?

B: I don't have a lot of vacation time. I _____ only stay a few days.
3

A: Who is going to go with you?

B: Maybe my sister _____ go if she has time. Our cousin
4
_____ go, too.
5

A: That sounds like fun. Where will you stay?

B: We _____ stay with my brother. Or, we _____ stay
6   7
with my aunt.

A: Are you going to go to Mexico, too? It's a short trip.

B: That _____ be a good idea. We can go for the day.
8

A: Will you send me a postcard?

B: Sure. I _____ definitely send you a postcard.
9

 B **Practice the conversation in Exercise A with a partner.**

C **Answer each question with a possible answer.** Use *may* or *might*.

1. Why isn't Anna in school?
   She might be sick.

2. Why is the flight late?
   _____

3. Why does Pedro always go to the beach for vacation?
   _____

4. Why do they have to go to the consulate?
   _____

5. Why are you packing a bottle of aspirin in your suitcase?
   _____

6. Why is Beth packing heavy sweaters for her beach vacation?
   _____

7. Why are they driving to Florida instead of flying?
   _____

8. Why are so many people in the train station?
   _____

I			
You	**might**		**going** away.
They	**may**	**be**	**driving**.
She			

Use the continuous modal form to discuss possibilities about something that is happening now.

A: Where are they going?
B: They ***might be going*** to Europe.

D **Change each sentence.** Use the continuous modal form.

1. I might study tonight.

2. We might go to Beijing.

3. They may get a visa.

4. She might buy some new clothes.

5. The students might prepare for their trip.

6. He may buy a ticket.

7. She might call her mother.

8. They may take a tour.

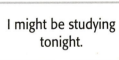
I might be studying tonight.

I			
You		**have** the flu.	
They	**must**	**speak** French.	
He			

Use *must* to make a deduction.

Situation: Ann is in Paris. She is talking to a store clerk in Paris and she is having no trouble communicating.

Ann **must speak** French.

 A **With a partner, answer the questions about the pictures.** Use *must.*

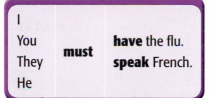
He must be in New York City.

1. Where is he?

2. Why are they sleeping?

3. What is he doing?

4. Why is she getting his autograph?

5. What is his occupation?

6. Where is she going?

7. Where is the traveler going?

8. Where are they?

9. Who are they?

Must for Empathy and *Could* for Suggestions

Use *must* to express empathy (show that you understand another person's feelings).

I spent ten hours on the plane.

You **must be** tired.

🔊 **A** **Listen.** Write the number next to the correct response.

CD1·TR22

_____ **a.** You must be tired.

_____ **b.** You must be excited.

_____ **c.** He must be homesick.

_____ **d.** She must be nervous.

___1___ **e.** You must be relieved.

_____ **f.** You must be bored.

_____ **g.** She must be cold.

_____ **h.** You must be worried.

👥 **B** **Work with a partner.** Talk about your life. Express empathy, using *must*.

I'm going to a party this weekend.

You must be excited.

Use *could* to make a suggestion.
A: How should I go to the airport?
B: You ***could take*** the shuttle.

🔊 **C** **Listen and complete each suggestion.**

CD1·TR23

1. A: My car broke down. I need to get to work.

B: You could *take the bus.* _____

2. A: We want to take a vacation, but we can't afford to spend a lot of money.

B: You _____

3. A: My sister's going to Rome, but the hotels are expensive.

B: _____

4. A: My family wants to stay at my house, but I don't have enough beds.

B: _____

5. A: My children are coming home from college, but flights are too expensive.

B: _____

6. A: My brother wants to study Spanish in another country.

B: _____

Would	you he she they	prefer to rather	drive or fly?

I You They He	would 'd	prefer to rather	fly. drive.

> To express a preference, use *would rather* and *would prefer to*. The contractions are *'d rather* and *'d prefer to*.
>
> I **would rather go** to New York than Miami.
> I **would prefer to go** to Chicago than Dallas.

 A **Ask and answer the questions with a partner.** Give reasons for your answers.

1. Would you rather fly or drive?

2. Would you rather travel by bus or by train?

3. Would you prefer to check a bag or take a carry-on?

4. Would you rather go to the beach or to the mountains?

5. Would you prefer to go to a large city or to a small town?

6. Would you rather visit an art museum or a historical site?

7. Would you prefer to visit Tokyo, Japan, or Barcelona, Spain?

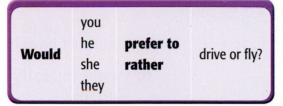

> Would you rather fly or drive?

> I'd rather fly. It's much faster.

 B **Working Together** In your notebook, write five questions about your classmates' preferences. Walk around the class and ask five students your questions. Then, report the results of one of your questions to the class.

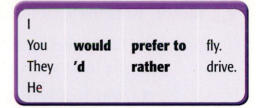

> Would you rather study in the morning or in the evening?

C **Write five sentences about your survey.**

Three students would rather study in the evening than in the morning.

1. _____

2. _____

3. _____

4. _____

5. _____

Active Grammar

Modals Review

A **Match.** Write the letter of the correct response.

_____d_____ **1.** I don't feel well, and I have a big test tomorrow.

_____ **2.** Why isn't Patrick here?

_____ **3.** The airline lost both of my suitcases!

_____ **4.** My son has just won a scholarship!

_____ **5.** It's boring to exercise at the gym.

_____ **6.** Who's that man with Ellen? Her husband's at work.

_____ **7.** Where's our teacher? She's never late.

_____ **8.** I babysat for twins last night.

a. You must be exhausted.

b. Would you rather go running with me?

c. He might be her brother.

d. You could call your professor.

e. He may not be coming.

f. You must be angry.

g. She might be stuck in traffic.

h. You must be so proud.

B **Write three sentences about each picture.** Use *may, might, must, would rather,* or *would prefer to.* Then, write one sentence from each picture on the board.

1. The mother _____.

2. The son _____.

3. _____.

4. He _____.

5. The shoes _____.

6. _____.

88 · Unit 6

Working Together Student to Student.

Student 1: Turn to page 264. Read **Set A** sentences to Student 2.

Student 2: Listen to Student 1 and write each sentence you hear next to the correct picture.

Then, change roles. Student 2, turn to page 264. Read **Set B** sentences to Student 1.

1. _____ .

2. _____ .

3. _____ .

4. _____ .

5. _____ .

6. _____ .

A **Look at the picture and discuss.** How do you plan a vacation? Do you use a travel agent? Do you use the Internet?

lodge = a type of resort hotel often located in the mountains

 B **Listen and take notes about Drew's family.**

CD1·TR24

Drew's wife: _____

Drew's children: _____

Drew's son: _____

_____

Drew's daughter: _____

_____

C **Listen again.** (Circle) the activities that are available at the lodge.

CD1·TR24

(sailing)   waterskiing   lessons for sports
camping   volleyball   movies
basketball   baseball   computer lessons
swimming   football   lectures by famous professors
snow skiing   tennis   trips to shopping malls
skateboarding   singing contests   free transportation to town

D **Answer the questions.**

WORD PARTNERSHIPS

window	
middle	seat
aisle	

1. What else can visitors do in the area?

_____

2. How far away is a major town?

_____

3. How often do shuttles leave the lodge?

_____

4. What can tourists do at the national park?

_____

5. What is Drew going to do now?

_____

6. Where would Drew prefer to sit on the plane?

_____

7. What is Gina going to do now?

_____

E **Pronunciation: 'd rather** **Listen.** Complete the sentences with *I'd, He'd, She'd, We'd,* or *They'd.*

CD1·TR25

1. ___We'd___ rather go camping.

2. _____ rather stay in a cabin.

3. _____ rather go fishing.

4. _____ rather go swimming.

5. _____ rather not stay in a tent.

6. _____ rather not go to malls.

7. _____ rather not eat at home.

8. _____ rather not stay at a hotel.

Travel · **91**

A **Discuss.**

1. Where is Argentina?

2. What do you know about Argentina?

Puente de la mujer,
"Woman's Bridge"

> **READING NOTE**
>
> **Highlighting Important Information**
>
> When you read, it is a good idea to underline or highlight information that you think is interesting or ideas that your teacher might put on a test. It is also a good idea to write some notes in the margin. Those notes will help you study later.

B **Word Builder** **Find the words below in the reading.** Then, match the words with their definitions.

_____d_____ **1.** borders   **a.** an Argentine dance

_____ **2.** tango   **b.** unusual sights

_____ **3.** vibrant   **c.** a person who travels to find information

_____ **4.** wonders   **d.** touches another country or geographical feature

_____ **5.** explorer   **e.** lively; full of life and energy

C **Read.**

Argentina is located in the Southern Hemisphere on the South American continent. It **borders** the South Atlantic Ocean, Chile, Uruguay, Paraguay, Bolivia, and Brazil. If you are looking for a place where you can experience both the life of **vibrant** cities and the beauty of natural **wonders**, you might want to visit Argentina.

The capital of Argentina, Buenos Aires, is a good place to start your trip. After arriving at the international airport, it is an easy trip to a downtown hotel. The city has a variety of transportation: taxis, a street railway, commuter trains, buses, and ferries. Buenos Aires is the largest city in Argentina and the second largest city in South America. It has one of the busiest ports in South America. It's a city where visitors can spend time touring a variety of different neighborhoods, including Recoleta, Puerto Madero, and La Boca, home to Boca Juniors, one of Argentina's famous soccer clubs. Visitors can easily get to any of the museums, such as the Latin American

Contemporary Art Museum, the National Museum of Fine Arts, or for something different, the World **Tango** Museum, a museum devoted to Argentina's famous dance. In addition, there is a botanical garden, a zoo, and restaurants that serve delicious *asado*, Argentine barbecue. For those who want to do some shopping, there are many stores and shopping malls where tourists can find leather items, such as handbags, wallets, or jackets. As you can see, a visitor will find it difficult to be bored in Buenos Aires.

If you would rather get away from the busy city, fly to El Calafate. This is the starting point for a visit to Patagonia, the region farthest south of the Andes Mountains in Argentina and Chile, and Los Glaciares National Park. El Calafate is located on the southern shore of Lake Argentino. It is here that you can see one of the natural wonders of the world, the Perito Moreno Glacier, which was named after an Argentine **explorer**, Francisco Moreno. One of the best ways to see the glaciers is to take a boat ride on Lake Argentino. You will be able to sail among icebergs and get a closer view of the wall of the Perito Moreno Glacier, the Spegazzini Glacier. If the icebergs are not in the way, visitors might see the Upsala Glacier, the largest glacier in South America. It is a fantastic sight.

Perito Moreno Glacier

When you plan your next vacation, think about going to Argentina. It will satisfy your need for the action of a city and the beauty of nature.

D (Circle) *True* or *False*.

1. Argentina borders Bolivia, Colombia, and Peru.   True   False

2. Buenos Aires is the largest city in South America.   True   False

3. Soccer is a popular sport in Argentina.   True   False

4. Buenos Aires has more than one art museum.   True   False

5. There are many places to shop for leather.   True   False

6. Buenos Aires is quieter than El Calafate.   True   False

7. Perito Moreno Glacier was named after an American.   True   False

8. Visitors can see the glaciers by boat.   True   False

Writing Our Stories

A Read the composition.

A Dream Vacation

Mayumi Sato
March 22
English IV

If I have free time and money, I will take my dream vacation. I would like to visit four South American cities: Lima and Cuzco in Peru, Buenos Aires in Argentina, and Rio de Janeiro in Brazil. Before I start my vacation, I might take a Spanish course. Also, I could ask some of my South American classmates to give me some advice. I want to know the best time to visit, too.

First, I will go to Peru. I will fly to the capital city, Lima. I may spend a few days visiting the museums, looking at the architecture, and eating the fresh seafood. After a few days, I will go to Cuzco to prepare for a trip to see the ruins of Machu Picchu. I hear that it is one of the most interesting archaeological sites in the world. When I get back to Cuzco, I might buy some souvenirs for my family and friends.

Then, I will travel to Buenos Aires, Argentina. I am taking dance lessons now, so I might take a tango class in Buenos Aires. I heard that Buenos Aires is the home of the tango. I would also like to visit a ranch and go horseback riding. I'm sure that I will eat some delicious Argentine barbecue.

Finally, I will fly to Rio de Janeiro, Brazil, for my last stop. I'm going to visit a samba school and watch the students dance the samba. I might take a samba class. I want to relax on the famous Copacabana Beach, eat Brazilian barbecue, and see the museums. I hear that it is a very exciting city. This will be a great vacation.

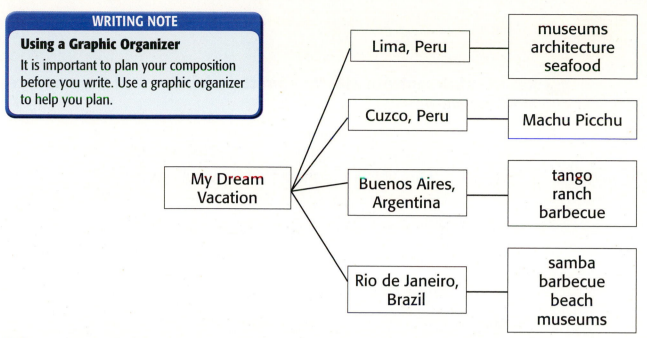
B **Use a graphic organizer to plan a composition about your dream vacation.** Answer the questions.

1. Where do you want to go?

2. Why do you want to go there?

3. How long do you plan to stay?

4. What are you going to do there?

C **Write your composition.** Use the ideas in your graphic organizer.

D **Sharing Our Stories** **Read your partner's story.** Answer the questions.

1. Where does your partner want to go for a dream vacation?

2. Why does he / she want to go there?

E **Find and correct the modal verb mistakes.**

1. I might ~~to~~ visit a museum.

2. He may not taking a class this semester.

3. They might be look in his suitcase.

4. She could going by train.

5. We rather not use a credit card.

6. He must not has a passport.

7. You would rather fly today or tomorrow?

8. She might homesick.

Travel · **95**

A **Rewrite each sentence with the correct modal.** Some of the sentences are negative.

could	may	must	would rather
have to	might	should	would prefer to

1. **I think it's a good idea for you** to apply for your passport early.

   You should apply for your passport early_____.

2. She **is required** to get a visa.

   She _____.

3. **Maybe** the flight is late because of the weather.

   The flight _____.

4. **Maybe** the students are not listening to the guide.

   The students _____.

5. We **would prefer to take** the shuttle to the airport.

   We _____.

6. My **suggestion** is for you to travel during spring break.

   You _____.

7. **It is necessary for him to pack** large bottles in his checked bag.

   He _____.

8. **Maybe** they are bringing your luggage right now.

   They _____.

9. They **would rather not** travel far from home.

   _____.

10. **He thinks that it isn't a good idea** for his sister to travel alone.

    _____.

CD1·TR26

A **Listen and answer the questions.**

1. Where did she go?

2. Where did she stay?

3. Where was her luggage?

4. Did anyone ask her to carry anything in her bag?

5. Did the inspector open her bag?

6. What happened?

B **Working Together** **Work in a group.** Look at the sign. Then:

1. Cross out items on the list that are not allowed.

2. Move items from one list to the other when necessary.

3. Compare your lists with another group.

Items in Carry-on Bag	Items in Checked Bag
two paperback books	five shirts
a baseball glove	one pair of jeans
an MP3 player	underwear and socks
a small bottle of aspirin	two baseball bats
~~a large bottle of shampoo~~	a jacket
a large bottle of suntan lotion	a U.S. passport
an army knife	matches
a pair of shoes	a pair of dress shoes
a small can of shaving cream	two belts
three wrapped gifts	a bag of energy bars

7

Sports

A **Write the letter of each sentence next to the correct name.**

a. She has been playing doubles for many years.

b. He has been trying to win the Super Bowl for a long time.

c. She has been racing cars since she was a teenager.

d. He has been talking to his fans for 20 minutes.

e. He has been playing soccer for a Brazilian team for two years.

f. She has been neglecting her schoolwork to play golf.

WORD PARTNERSHIPS	
female	
male	
high school	athlete
college	
amateur	
professional	

1.

_____ Angelica Jones

2.

_____ Marco Ronaldo

3.

_____ Dave Meese

4.

_____ Melinda Gomez

5.

_____ Kristine Park

6.

_____ Alfredo Perez

I	have		play**ing** tennis
You		**been**	for an hour.
He	**has**		
They	**have**		

Contractions

I have – I've

you have – you've

he has – he's

they have – they've

The *present continuous* describes an action that is happening now.

I **am playing** tennis.

The *present perfect continuous* describes an action that began in the past and is continuing now.

I **have been playing** tennis for an hour.

A **Complete the sentences.** Use the correct tense.

1. It's 5:00.

Carl ___is playing___ basketball.

Carl ___began___ to play basketball at 4:00.

He ___has been playing___ basketball for an hour.

He ___'s been playing___ basketball since 4:00.

2. It's 3:00.

The men _____ soccer.

They _____ to play soccer at 1:00.

They _____ soccer for two hours.

They _____ since 1:00.

3. It's 12:00.

The women _____ tennis.

They _____ to play tennis at 10:00.

They _____ tennis for two hours.

They _____ tennis since 10:00.

4. I _____ English.

I _____ to study English in _____.

I _____ English for _____.

I _____ English since _____.

CD2·TR1

B **Pronunciation: 've been / 's been** **Listen and repeat.**

1. **a.** She's taking dancing lessons.   **b.** She's been taking dancing lessons.

2. **a.** She's learning how to drive.   **b.** She's been learning how to drive.

3. **a.** He's playing baseball.   **b.** He's been playing baseball.

4. **a.** I'm looking for a new apartment.   **b.** I've been looking for a new apartment.

5. **a.** She's recovering from her accident.   **b.** She's been recovering from her accident.

6. **a.** He's studying Chinese.   **b.** He's been studying Chinese.

7. **a.** He's working hard.   **b.** He's been working hard.

8. **a.** I'm training for a new job.   **b.** I've been training for a new job.

CD2·TR2

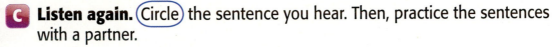

C **Listen again.** Circle the sentence you hear. Then, practice the sentences with a partner.

CD2·TR3

D **Listen to the conversation.**

A: Hi, Juan. What've you been up to?

B: I've been painting the house.

A: And how's your family?

B: We're all fine. Maribel is 16 now, so I've been teaching her how to drive.

A: Good luck with that! And your parents? How are they?

B: They've been enjoying their retirement. They've been visiting their grandchildren a lot.

A: Oh, that's nice. Tell them I asked about them.

B: I sure will.

E **Practice the conversation in Exercise D with a partner.** Then, write a new conversation in your notebook. Practice the conversation.

100 · Unit 7

> **For**
>
> *For* shows an amount of time.
> **for** a few minutes
> **for** three days

> **Since**
>
> *Since* shows when an action started.
> **since** 2009
> **since** Monday
> **since** she moved to the city

A **Write each word or phrase under *for* or *since*.**

several days	he joined the team	~~she began to play tennis~~
~~three hours~~	I was a child	a long time
about two weeks	a few minutes	many years
Saturday	he broke his arm	2:00

For	**Since**
three hours	she began to play tennis
_____	_____
_____	_____
_____	_____
_____	_____

B **Complete the sentences.** Use *for* or *since*.

1. She's been playing professionally ____for____ five years.

2. He's been working out _____ 8:00 this morning.

3. The team has been practicing _____ about three hours.

4. She's been riding her bicycle _____ two hours.

5. The girls have been practicing their routine _____ 3:00.

6. The players have been listening to the coach _____ 30 minutes.

7. He hasn't been running well _____ he hurt his leg.

8. The fans have been buying snacks _____ they arrived at the stadium.

Have	you		watch**ing** a game?
Has	she	been	play**ing** on a team?
Have	they		work**ing** hard?

Yes, I **have**.	No, I **haven't**.
Yes, she **has**.	No, she **hasn't**.
Yes, they **have**.	No, they **haven't**.

 A **Ask and answer questions.** Use the present perfect continuous.

> Have you been studying hard?

> Yes, I have.

1. you / study / hard

2. you / work / overtime

3. you / look for / a new job

4. you / get / enough sleep

5. you / exercise

6. your classmates / speak / English in class

7. the teacher / give / a lot of homework

8. the teacher / give / quizzes

9. you / listen to / music in English

10. you / watch / TV in English

B **Read the paragraph.** Then, complete the questions. Use the past tense or the present perfect continuous.

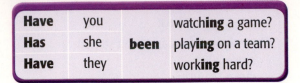

Daniel and Monica are skiers. Daniel has been skiing since he was a young child. Monica has been skiing since she was 14 years old. Now they're training for the Olympics. They have been training for a long time. Daniel won three competitions last year. Monica won the national competition and earned a second-place finish last month. They have been training together for only a short time. They both plan to become professionals after the Olympics.

1. <u>Has Daniel been skiing since he was a child </u>? Yes, he has.

2. _____ since she was a child? No, she hasn't.

3. _____? Yes, they have.

4. _____ last year? Yes, he did.

5. _____ last month? Yes, she did.

6. _____ for a long time? No, they haven't.

Working Together **Student to Student**

Student 1: Turn to page 264. Read **Set A** sentences to Student 2.

Student 2: Listen to Student 1 and write each sentence next to the correct picture.

Then, change roles. Student 2, turn to page 264. Read **Set B** sentences. Student 1, listen and write each sentence next to the correct picture.

"Roger is in the lead!"

"I'm not sure what's wrong."

"You haven't been finishing your work on time. Is anything wrong?"

"Could you take a look at it?"

1. _____

_____

2. _____

_____

3. _____

_____

4. _____

_____

5. _____

_____

6. _____

_____

7. _____

_____

8. _____

_____

Present Perfect Continuous:
How long Questions

How long	have	I	been	studying English? living here?
	has	you		
	have	he		
		they		

He**'s been studying** English for two months.
I've been living here for three years.

 A **Working Together** **Work in a group of four or five students.** Write each person's name in the chart. Ask the questions and write the answers in the chart.

1. How long have you been living in the United States?

2. How long have you been studying English?

3. How long have you been attending this school?

4. How long have you been working?

5. How long have you been working in the United States?

Names	Question 1	Question 2	Question 3	Question 4	Question 5
1.					
2.					
3.					
4.					
5.					

B **Complete the sentences.** Use the information from your chart.

1. _____ has been living in the United States the longest.

2. _____ has been studying English the shortest time.

3. _____ has been attending this school for _____.

4. _____ has been working the longest.

5. _____ doesn't work.

6. _____ has been working in the United States the longest.

CD2·TR4

C **Listen.** Then, complete the questions.

Does   How long   How often   How old   What   Who

1. _How old_ is Robert?

2. _____ did he win?

3. _____ has he been playing tennis?

4. _____ taught him how to play?

5. _____ he take private lessons?

6. _____ has he been taking private lessons?

7. _____ do his parents want him to practice?

8. _____ is his dream?

D **Ask and answer the questions in Exercise C.**

E **Read the timeline.** Complete the questions.

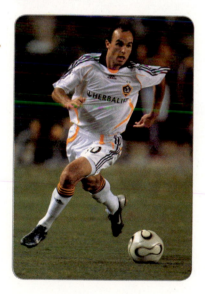

1. 1982	born March 4
2. 1990	started playing soccer
3. 1999	became a professional; signed with a German team
4. 2001	won MLS (Major League Soccer) championship with San José Earthquakes
5. 2003	won MLS championship with San José; named U.S. Soccer Athlete of the Year
6. 2005	won MLS championship with L.A. Galaxy
7. 2009	played in MLS finals; lost game; became captain of team; signed four-year contract extension

1. When _____?

2. How long _____?

3. Who _____?

4. What _____?

5. How many times _____?

6. How long _____?

7. How long _____?

A In each circle, write the number of the correct person from the box below.

 **B** **Listen to the story.** Then, answer the questions.

CD2·TR5

1. Is it the first half or the second half?

2. How many minutes are left in the game?

3. What's the score?

4. How many fans are at the game?

5. What have the concession workers been doing?

6. What have people been buying?

7. How long is the wait at the concession stand?

8. Has there been any fighting on the field?

9. Which players has the Stars' coach been putting in?

10. Which players has the Kings' coach been substituting?

1. players
2. fans
3. announcer
4. coach
5. official
6. concession workers

C **Complete the sentences.** Use the correct verb from the box in the present perfect continuous tense.

1. The fans ___have been making___ a lot of noise.

2. The fans _____ a lot of soda and water.

3. People _____ in line to buy food.

4. An announcer _____ the game.

5. The players _____ up and down the field.

6. A few of the players _____ each other's shirts.

7. The coaches _____ players.

8. Everyone _____ player number 7.

9. The fans _____ their favorite players.

| buy |
| call |
| ~~make~~ |
| pull |
| run |
| substitute |
| support |
| wait |
| watch |

D **Match the questions with the answers.**

___d___ 1. Is the stadium full?

_____ 2. Did the game start at 2:00?

_____ 3. Are there more than 20,000 fans?

_____ 4. Have the fans been cheering for their favorites?

_____ 5. Are the fans hot?

_____ 6. Has the Stars' coach been giving instructions?

_____ 7. Do the Stars have four goals?

_____ 8. Does player number 7 have the ball?

_____ 9. Is the score 4–1?

_____ 10. Have the officials been giving any red cards?

a. Yes, there are.

b. Yes, he has.

c. Yes, he does.

d. Yes, it is.

e. Yes, it did.

f. Yes, they are.

g. No, it isn't.

h. No, they haven't.

i. Yes, they have.

j. No, they don't.

A **Discuss.**

1. Where is the next World Cup going to be?

2. Which countries do you think are the strongest competition?

B **Word Builder** **Match the words with the definitions.**

____d____ **1.** still   **a.** a person or organization that holds an event

_____ **2.** amateur   **b.** all over

_____ **3.** exhibition   **c.** not professional

_____ **4.** host   **d.** continues; remains

_____ **5.** sparked   **e.** show

_____ **6.** throughout **f.** created

> **CULTURE NOTE**
>
> The word "soccer" is an abbreviation of "association football." The word first appeared in 1889.

C **Read.**

By January 27, 2010, two-thirds of the available tickets for the 2010 World Cup had already been sold. Even though soccer is not the top sport in the United States, there is **still** interest in the World Cup. The United States was the leader in sales for the 2010 World Cup, with over 50,000 applications for tickets.

In the United States, people call the sport "soccer," but in all other countries, people call it "football." FIFA (Fédération Internationale de Football Association) was founded in Paris, France, in 1904. At that time, seven countries, including France, Spain, and Switzerland, were part of FIFA. At the 1908 Summer Olympics, soccer became an official Olympic sport, organized by FIFA. At that time, only **amateur** athletes were allowed to participate in the Olympics. Because the best soccer players couldn't participate, the Olympic soccer tournament was considered an **exhibition** rather than a real match.

In 1914, FIFA recognized the Olympic soccer tournament as an amateur event. Belgium won the 1920 Summer Olympics, and Uruguay won the next two Olympics.

Soccer wasn't included in the 1932 Olympics. There were two reasons for this. One reason was that the games were in Los Angeles, and soccer was not popular in the United States. Second, the International Olympic Committee and FIFA could not agree about what an "amateur" was.

Uruguay was the **host** of the first World Cup in 1930. Thirteen countries participated: seven from South America, four from Europe, and two from North America. Uruguay was the winner again.

When the World Cup came to the United States in 1994, it **sparked** interest in soccer. Today, in school yards and on fields **throughout** the United States, many young people play soccer. With both men's and women's professional leagues, FIFA can expect to continue to have more and more fans in the U.S.

World Cup Winners 1930–2010	
Country	**Number of wins**
Brazil	5
Italy	4
West Germany	3
Uruguay	2
Argentina	2
Spain	1

World Cup Attendance		
Year	**Location**	**Attendance**
1990	Italy	2,516,354
1994	U.S.A.	3,587,088
1998	France	2,775,400
2002	Korea / Japan	2,705,566
2006	Germany	3,367,000
2010	South Africa	3,180,000

D (Circle) **the sentence that has a similar meaning.**

> **READING NOTE**
>
> **Sentence Sense**
> It is possible to understand the meaning of a sentence even when you do not understand every word.

1. Even though soccer is not the top sport in the United States, there is interest in the World Cup.

   a. Americans are interested in the World Cup, but soccer is not a very popular sport.

   b. Americans are very interested in soccer, but not in the World Cup.

2. The game was considered an exhibition rather than a real match.

   a. The teams preferred to see an exhibit.

   b. No one thought the game was a serious competition.

3. When the World Cup came to the U.S. in 1994, it sparked interest in soccer.

   a. The 1994 World Cup caused more Americans to think about soccer.

   b. Many Americans attended the fireworks at the World Cup in 1994.

E (Circle) *True or False.*

1. Soccer is becoming more popular in the U.S.   True   False
2. Many people in the U.S. are interested in the World Cup.   True   False
3. The U.S. organized the first Olympic soccer game.   True   False
4. Uruguay had a good soccer team in 1924 and 1928.   True   False
5. In the thirties, soccer was not popular in the U.S.   True   False
6. The first World Cup was held in Europe.   True   False
7. Since 1990, Europe has hosted five World Cups.   True   False

A Discuss.

1. Who is Lance Armstrong?

2. Is he still riding professionally?

B Read.

Lance Armstrong

Lance Armstrong was born on September 18, 1971, in Plano, Texas. His mother raised him alone. He began riding a bike at an early age, and he started entering triathlons (running, swimming, and cycling competitions) before he was a teenager. By the age of 20, Armstrong was the U.S. National Amateur Cycling Champion.

From 1991 to 1996, Armstrong won important races. In 1993, he became the U.S. Pro Champion, and he won one million dollars in the Thrift Drug Triple Crown. In 1995, he was the first American to win the Classico San Sebastian in Italy. In 1996, he was the number one cyclist in the world.

However, in October of 1996, Armstrong began to feel sick. He found out that he had cancer in his lungs, brain, and abdomen. This was the most difficult time in his life. Armstrong had three major operations and months of chemotherapy. In 1997, the doctors declared him cancer free.

After his health returned, Armstrong was very grateful, so he founded the *Lance Armstrong Foundation* to raise money for cancer research, awareness, and early detection.

Armstrong continued to enter competitions, and in 1999, he won the Tour de France, a three-week racing event through the valleys and mountains of France. He won the event again every year from 2000 to 2005. After the 2005 race, Armstrong retired, but he returned to the Tour de France in 2009, earning third place, but in 2010, he was twenty-third.

Armstrong considered a future career in politics, but he decided to spend more time supporting cancer research instead.

WRITING NOTE

Combining Sentences with *and*, *but*, and *so*

Combine two short sentences with words like *and, but,* and *so.* Each part of the sentence has a subject and a verb.

He began riding a bike at an early age, **and** he started entering triathlons.

Armstrong was very grateful, **so** he founded the *Lance Armstrong Foundation.*

Newspapers have been writing about his possible future in politics, **but** Armstrong has been spending more time talking about cancer research.

C In your notebook, combine the sentences with *and*, *so*, or *but*.

1. My sisters are going to arrive tomorrow. They are going to stay for a week.
   My sisters are going to arrive tomorrow, and they are going to stay for a week.
2. I've been calling Jack for a week. He hasn't returned my calls.
3. Bill hasn't been attending soccer practice. The coach is going to suspend him from the team.
4. Julie hasn't been feeling well. She made a doctor's appointment.
5. Ben wanted to attend a private college. He couldn't afford the tuition.
6. Karin goes to a gym three times a week. She walks in the park every morning.

D In your notebook, write a composition about a famous athlete. Use information from the Internet or from library books. Do not copy sentences.

E Sharing Our Stories Read your partner's composition. Answer the questions.

1. Which athlete did your partner write about? _____
2. Why is the athlete famous? _____

F Find and correct the mistakes.

1. I been playing a lot of soccer this year.
2. He has been show me how to play tennis.
3. She hasn't been go to the gym recently.
4. We have been playing well for September.
5. They have been live in Tampa for six months.
6. She been training for the Olympics.
7. You have been working out every day?
8. How long you been watching the game?

A Circle the sentence that has the same meaning.

1. Tara began to play volleyball at 1:00. It's 3:00, and she is still playing.

   a. Tara has been playing volleyball for two hours.

   b. Tara played volleyball for two hours.

2. Tom played tennis in the park from 4:00 to 5:00. Then, he went home.

   a. Tom has been playing tennis for an hour.

   b. Tom played tennis for an hour.

3. Yesterday, Martin rode his bicycle from 8 A.M. to 1 P.M.

   a. Martin has been riding his bicycle for five hours.

   b. Martin rode his bicycle for five hours.

4. The soccer fans sat down an hour ago, and they are watching the game.

   a. The fans have been watching the game for an hour.

   b. The fans watched the game for an hour.

5. Juan lifts weights at the gym every day from 7:00 to 8:00. It's 7:30 now.

   a. Juan has been lifting weights for 30 minutes.

   b. Juan lifted weights for 30 minutes.

B Complete. Use the present perfect continuous or the simple past.

1. **A:** How long (you / play) _____have you been playing_____ baseball?

   B: I _____ since I was a child.

2. **A:** How long (you / live) _____ in Chicago?

   B: I _____ there from 2007 to 2009.

3. **A:** How long (she / exercise) _____ at the gym?

   B: She _____ since January.

4. **A:** How long (you / wait) _____ in line for tickets?

   B: We _____ since 4:00 this morning!

5. **A:** How long (you / study) _____ for the test?

   B: I _____ for three hours, and then I went to bed.

A **Listen and repeat.**

CD2·TR6

1. I have a bruise.

2. She has a sprained ankle.

3. She has tendonitis.

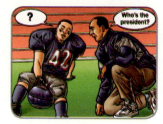

4. He has a concussion.

5. He has a pulled hamstring.

6. He has a torn rotator cuff.

  B **Listen.** Take notes about each injury and its treatment. Then, compare your answers with a partner.

CD2·TR7

Conversation 1: Injury: *torn rotator cuff* _____

Treatment: _____

Conversation 2: Injury: _____

Treatment: _____

Conversation 3: Injury: _____

Treatment: _____

Conversation 4: Injury: _____

Treatment: _____

Conversation 5: Injury: _____

Treatment: _____

Conversation 6: Injury: _____

Treatment: _____

Unit

8

Changes

A **Discuss.**

1. How many people are in your family?

2. How do you keep up-to-date on what is happening in your extended family?

3. What is a family reunion? Have you ever had a family reunion? If so, give some details.

WORD PARTNERSHIPS	
immediate	
extended	family
nuclear	

CD2·TR8

B **Listen.** Kathy and Gloria are talking about plans for a family reunion. Circle *True* or *False*.

1. Kathy and Gloria haven't spoken for a long time.	True	False
2. There's a date for the reunion.	True	False
3. The family has just had a reunion.	True	False
4. It's June now.	True	False
5. The reunion is going to be very expensive.	True	False
6. The invitations are in the mail.	True	False
7. Everyone's going to help with the food.	True	False
8. Michael has opened a small business.	True	False

I	have		for two years.
You	haven't		
He	has	taken a vacation	since January.
	hasn't	worked there	since the company opened.
They	have		
	haven't		

To form the present perfect, use *have / has* and the past participle.

Use the *present perfect tense*

- to describe an action that began in the past and is still <u>true in the present.</u>

    They **have been** in the city **for** many years.

    She **hasn't seen** him **since** they broke up.

- to describe changes.

    He **has lost** over 50 pounds **since** he started exercising.

    In the past year, Lily **has grown** three inches.

A <u>**Underline**</u> **the present perfect tense.** (Circle) *for* or *since*.

1. Kathy and Gloria <u>haven't spoken</u> (**for**) / **since** several months.

2. Tuan and Lana have been married **for** / **since** 1999.

3. Henry has belonged to the volunteer fire department **for** / **since** 2005.

4. Joanna has sold life insurance **for** / **since** six months.

5. Rita has been divorced **for** / **since** six months.

6. Richard has owned his own business **for** / **since** he moved to Ohio.

7. Tom has been in college **for** / **since** six years.

8. Anna has walked two miles a day **for** / **since** she had her heart attack.

9. Brian hasn't found a job **for** / **since** he graduated from college.

10. We haven't seen our cat **for** / **since** a few days.

B Make sentences with the information on the left and the *since* clauses on the right. Many combinations are possible.

1. I haven't had a good night's sleep.

2. I have had several complaints from my neighbors.

3. I have lost 10 pounds.

4. I've made several new friends.

5. I haven't been able to concentrate on my job.

since I fell in love
since I had the baby
since I joined a gym
since I bought a dog

 C Listen and repeat.

CD2·TR9

Base Form	Simple Past	Past Participle	Base Form	Simple Past	Past Participle
be	was / were	been	leave	left	left
bear	bore	born	lose	lost	lost
become	became	become	make	made	made
begin	began	begun	meet	met	met
break	broke	broken	pay	paid	paid
bring	brought	brought	put	put	put
buy	bought	bought	quit	quit	quit
catch	caught	caught	read	read	read
come	came	come	ride	rode	ridden
do	did	done	say	said	said
drink	drank	drunk	see	saw	seen
drive	drove	driven	sell	sold	sold
eat	ate	eaten	send	sent	sent
fall	fell	fallen	sit	sat	sat
feel	felt	felt	sleep	slept	slept
find	found	found	speak	spoke	spoken
forget	forgot	forgotten	spend	spent	spent
freeze	froze	frozen	steal	stole	stolen
get	got	got / gotten	take	took	taken
give	gave	given	teach	taught	taught
go	went	gone	tell	told	told
grow	grew	grown	think	thought	thought
have	had	had	throw	threw	thrown
hear	heard	heard	win	won	won
know	knew	known	write	wrote	written

Use the *present perfect* with words such as *just, lately,* and *recently* to describe
an action in the recent past.

Put *just* between *have / has* and the main verb.

   I **have just quit** my job.

Put *lately* at the end of a sentence.

   He **hasn't been** in class **lately**.

Put *recently* between *have / has* and the main verb or at the end of the sentence.

   They **have recently become** grandparents.
   They **have become** grandparents **recently**.

A **Complete the sentences.** Use the present perfect.

1. I (just / meet) _____ *have just met* _____ Juan.

2. She (recently / fall) _____ in love.

3. He (just / make) _____ the high school soccer team.

4. Stanley (recently / get) _____ his driver's license.

5. Silvia (see / not) _____ any new movies lately.

6. Ted and his family (just / move) _____ into a new home.

7. My sister (just / come) _____ from Japan.

8. I (recently / find) _____ a new job.

9. My uncle (visited / not) _____ us lately.

10. My aunt (bring / not) _____ us any cakes lately.

B **In your notebook, write two sentences about each picture.** Use *just* in one
sentence and *recently* in the other sentence.

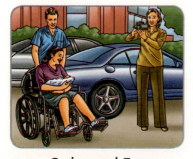

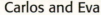

Carlos and Eva

A Pronunciation: Stress **Listen to the stress as each speaker clarifies the information. <u>Underline</u> the stressed word.**

CD2·TR10

1. A: I hear that David has recently bought a sailboat.

   B: Not exactly. He's bought a <u>motorboat</u>.

2. A: I hear that Amy has just moved to North Carolina.

   B: Close. She's moved to South Carolina.

3. A: I hear that Nora has just gotten her driver's license.

   B: No, just the opposite. She's lost her driver's license!

4. A: I hear that Joe and Tom have just opened an Italian restaurant.

   B: Not Italian. They've just opened a Mexican restaurant.

 B Practice the sentences above with a partner. Then, complete the conversations below and practice them with your partner.

1. A: I hear that Paul has just made the baseball team.

   B: No, he's made the _____ team.

2. A: I hear that Alex and Kathy have just gotten a cat.

   B: Not exactly. They've just gotten a _____.

 C Look at the pictures. Describe five changes in these people's lives.

1.

Allen ten years ago

Allen today

2.

Mary and Tom five years ago

Mary and Tom today

Already shows that an action is completed. Use *already* in affirmative sentences. You can use the present perfect tense or the past tense with *already*. *Already* with the past tense is more often used in spoken English.

> She **has already bought** the invitations.   She **already bought** the invitations.

Put *already* between *have / has* and the main verb or at the end of the sentence.

> She **has already bought** the invitations.   She **has bought** the invitations **already**.

Yet shows the action has *not* been completed. Use *yet* in questions and negative sentences. Use the present perfect tense or the past tense with *yet*. Put *yet* at the end of the sentence.

> **Has** she **sent** the invitations **yet**?   **Did** she **send** the invitations **yet**?
> She **hasn't sent** the invitations **yet**.

CD2·TR11

A   **Angela is planning a family reunion.** Listen and check (✓) the things that have already been completed.

Completed	Not completed	Things to do for the reunion
✓		form a committee to help plan the reunion
		set a date
		make the invitations on the computer
		send the invitations
		find the addresses of relatives who have moved
		plan the activities and games
		plan the menu
		order the cake
		buy the decorations
		hire staff to help cook, serve, and clean up
		gather photos for the party

   B   **Discuss each item on Angela's list.** Use *already* or *yet*.

> She has already formed a committee to help plan the reunion.

> They haven't sent the invitations yet.

C **George and Monica have just had a party.** With a partner, talk about what they have and haven't done. Use the cues in the box and *already* or *yet*.

put away the food	collect the cans and bottles
clear off the table	blow out the candles
take down the decorations	eat the last piece of cake
sweep the floor	close the windows
wash the dishes	get Monica's brother to leave
empty the garbage can	

> sweep – swept – swept
> blow – blew – blown

 D **Ask a partner about what she or he has done today.** Use *yet*.

> Have you gotten your mail yet?

> Yes, I have. I got it at 10:00.

go to work

buy anything

make a phone call

make your bed

do the dishes

speak in class

get your mail

do your homework

take a shower

watch TV

eat a piece of fruit

exercise

read the newspaper

120 · Unit 8

> Use the *present perfect tense* to describe actions that began in the past and are true in the present. The present perfect also describes events in the recent past.
>
> I **have been** in this country for three years.
> They **have just won** the lottery.
>
> Use the *present perfect continuous tense* to describe actions that began in the past and are continuing now.
>
> We **have been living** in this country for three years.
>
> Use the *past tense* to show an action <u>completed</u> in the past.
>
> She **graduated** from college in 2009.
> They **moved** to New Mexico two years ago.

A **Complete the sentences.** Use the correct form of the verb in parentheses.

1. Dave (move) _____ *moved* _____ into his apartment one year ago.
   He (live) _____ *has been living* _____ in his apartment for a year. The
   landlord (just / increase) _____ his rent by $200!

2. My mother and father (be married) _____ for a long
   time. They (get) _____ married in 1950.

3. I (begin) _____ working here in 2000. I (work)
   _____ here for more than ten years.

4. I (take) _____ my examination two weeks ago.
   I (just / receive) _____ my grade.

5. Rachel (look) _____ for a new job for several months.
   She (quit) _____ her job four months ago.

6. Nick (lose) _____ 15 pounds since he started
   his diet. He (start) _____ his diet two months ago.

7. George (buy) _____ his car in 1985. George (drive)
   _____ his convertible for over 25 years!

8. I (take) _____ my first art class five years ago.
   Since that time, I (paint) _____ over 100 pictures.

The Big Picture

A **Discuss these words.**

> gossip   grounded   face-lift
> clinic   broken off   date / go out with

B **Listen.** Write each person's name under the correct picture.

CD2·TR12

> Amy   Diana   Grandpa   Mary   Paul   Rosa

1. _____

2. _____

3. _____

4. _____

5. _____

6. _____

C **Answer the questions.**

1. Who has had a face-lift?
2. Who has just been promoted?
3. Who has recently begun to date a much older man?
4. Who has just broken off her engagement?
5. Who has bought a convertible?

6. Who has just been in an accident?

7. Who has just been at a clinic?

8. Who has been grounded?

9. Who has fallen in love with a neighbor?

10. Who has left to travel across the country?

11. Who has taken away their daughter's cell phone?

D (Circle) *True* or *False*.

1. Diana still has Chris's ring.	True	False
2. Rosa looks wonderful.	True	False
3. Rosa told all her friends that she had a face-lift.	True	False
4. Amy's parents have taken away her cell phone.	True	False
5. This is the first time that Amy has gotten in trouble.	True	False
6. Paul has been promoted.	True	False
7. Paul has the best sales record in the company.	True	False
8. Mary is dating a man who is much older than she is.	True	False
9. Grandpa has bought a new car.	True	False
10. Grandpa now has gray hair.	True	False

E **Pronunciation: Surprise Intonation** **Listen and repeat.**

CD2·TR13

1. A: He bought a new convertible. **B:** A new convertible?

2. A: He left yesterday. **B:** He left?

3. A: He's just been promoted. **B:** Promoted?

4. A: She's run off with a man twice her age. **B:** Twice her age?

F **Write three statements with surprising news.** Tell your partner the news. Your partner will show surprise.

1. _____.

2. _____.

3. _____.

A **Discuss.**

  1. Do you have a family newsletter?

  2. Why do some families have newsletters?

B **Read the first three sections of the newsletter on page 125.** What is each section about?

Section 1: _Plans for the family reunion_

Section 2: _____

Section 3: _____

C **Read the questions.** Then, skim the newsletter for the answers.

> **READING NOTE**
>
> **Skimming for the Main Idea**
> Each paragraph has a main idea or topic. Before reading, it is helpful to skim each paragraph to find out what the topic is.

  1. What are the dates of the family reunion?

  2. Where is the barbecue on Saturday?

  3. What was Alison's college major?

  4. What is Alison going to do next?

  5. How old is Grandma going to be on her next birthday?

  6. What does Fred do a few mornings a week?

  7. What does Fred do for volunteer work?

  8. What happened to Laura?

  9. Why does Karen need a new job?

D **Word Builder** **Match the words with their meanings.**

  __d__ **1.** adjust to   **a.** contribute money or time

  _____ **2.** hassle-free   **b.** became

  _____ **3.** elderly   **c.** job possibilities

  _____ **4.** turned   **d.** handle changes

  _____ **5.** chip in   **e.** in the future

  _____ **6.** ahead   **f.** easy

  _____ **7.** leads   **g.** people who are very old

The Nelsons in the News

June

Circle August 14th and 15th on your calendars! This year's reunion committee includes Doris, Frank, Lynn, and Gloria. For Saturday, we've already reserved a space at the Park Resort Hotel. The barbecue is going to be on the lawn by the pool. We'll all **chip in** for the food. We've also reserved a block of rooms for Friday and Saturday nights for anyone who wants to stay overnight. Contact Luisa at 888-555-2422 to reserve a room. People have requested a relaxing, **hassle-free** day on Sunday. We're talking to the resort caterer about a picnic lunch. Look at next month's issue for more details! Send your suggestions and comments to the committee members, or call Angela at 555-6739.

Congratulations to Alison Nelson. After eight years of college, sometimes full-time, sometimes part-time, Alison has just completed her course work in social work. She will graduate this month. Alison has accepted a position at Atlantic Community Services, where she will be working with troubled teens.

 Grandma Mayra Nelson **turned** 99 on May 2nd. She lives with her daughter, Eva, and son-in-law, Brad. Mayra enjoys TV, her flower garden, and visits from her four children, twelve grandchildren, and thirty great-grandchildren. She will become a great-great-grandmother in September! Mayra says that she is looking forward to her 100th birthday. She tells her children, "I expect you to give me a big party!"

Hi Everyone!

Our new home in Florida is only five blocks from the beach. Ann and I were wondering how we would **adjust to** retirement. It wasn't hard! Ann has joined a tennis club, and she plays three mornings a week. I've bought a fishing boat, and you'll see me on the water two or three mornings a week. I haven't caught "the big one" yet, but I'm trying! Ann and I also have been volunteering at the local community center. We deliver meals to the **elderly** one day a week. Two days a week, we read with children in an after-school program. Don't worry—we haven't forgotten about all of you. We'll see you at the reunion. If you are planning a trip to Florida, we'd love to see you. Call us at 813-555-3494, or e-mail us.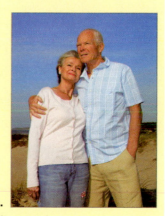

Fred

Send your get-well cards to Laura. Her knee replacement went well, but she has several weeks of physical therapy **ahead**. Her address is on page 3 of the newsletter.

Karen is looking for job **leads**. Her company closed, leaving 75 accountants looking for work. If you have any suggestions, please e-mail her.

Writing Our Stories

A **Has anyone in your extended family recently . . . ?**

☐ graduated   ☐ celebrated a birthday   ☐ lost a job

☐ gotten married   ☐ celebrated an anniversary   ☐ accepted a new job

☐ gotten engaged   ☐ taken a vacation   ☐ had an accident

☐ gotten divorced   ☐ moved   ☐ had an operation

☐ had a baby   ☐ retired   ☐ passed away (died)

☐ other _____

B **Read the paragraph from a family newsletter.**

> The Thompson Family Newsletter
>
> Lena Thompson
> June 4
> English IV
>
> Henry has just accepted a position as distribution manager at Davis and Bates. Davis and Bates is a growing furniture manufacturer in the West. Henry will coordinate all the company's deliveries. Currently, the company employs 25 people in its distribution center. They are planning to expand this to 50 employees. Henry is selling his house, and he will leave for California next month. His wife, Paula, and their two children will move to California after they sell their house.

C **Write details about each statement.** Use your imagination.

1. Thomas graduated from college.

   Thomas graduated from the University
   of Maryland in May with a degree in biology.

2. Randy and Lana had a baby.

   _____

   _____

> **WRITING NOTE**
>
> **Reporting the Facts**
> When reporting facts, it is important to include details. Specific facts provide interesting and clear information.

126 · Unit 8

3. Linda celebrated her birthday.

_____

_____

4. Tom was in a car accident.

_____

_____

5. Ken and Susan celebrated their wedding anniversary.

_____

_____

6. Karin and Juan have just returned from a wonderful vacation.

_____

_____

D **Write a factual article about an event in your family, your class, or your school.**

E **Sharing Our Stories** **Read your partner's article.** What did your partner write about?

F **Find and correct the mistakes.**

1. She have just found a new job.

2. They haven't gotten married already.

3. They have gotten married on October 10.

4. They has just celebrated their tenth wedding anniversary.

5. Jason has come already home from the hospital.

6. They have live in the same house since 1990.

7. Olga has graduated from Duke University last month.

8. Ron has take a job in Arizona.

9. Grandma Barnes pass away on June 15.

10. The whole family just has enjoyed a wonderful family reunion.

A **Complete the sentences about changes in one town.** Use the present perfect tense.

1. Ten years ago, there were two doctors. Now there is a small clinic with six doctors. The health-care system (improve) __has improved__.

2. The population (increase) _____ from 25,000 to 50,000.

3. Many new restaurants (open) _____.

4. The unemployment rate (decrease) _____ from 15 percent to 9 percent.

5. Tourism (become) _____ a major industry.

6. The city (hire) _____ 15 new police officers.

7. The crime rate (drop) _____ substantially.

8. Many new businesses (move) _____ into the area because of the strong economy.

9. The quiet village (change) _____ into a busy, noisy town.

B **In your notebook, write eight sentences about how your life has changed since you came to this country.**

C **Tim had a difficult first semester at college.** Now it is the second semester, and Tim has become a serious student. Compare his first and second semesters. Use the present perfect tense.

First semester: The "old" Tim

1. He missed ten days of school.

2. He was late for his classes.

3. He failed every test.

4. He didn't ask for extra help.

5. He didn't do his homework.

6. He failed two courses.

7. He didn't study for tests.

8. He didn't write any papers.

Second semester: The "new" Tim

1. He has missed only one day of school.

2. _____

3. _____

4. _____

5. _____

6. _____

7. _____

8. _____

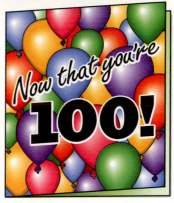

CULTURE NOTE

In the United States, groups of co-workers, friends, and family members often send a greeting card signed by the whole group. They send cards to a co-worker who is retiring or leaving, to someone who is getting married or having a baby, or to someone who is in the hospital or has lost a loved one. Each person writes a brief message and signs the card.

A Match each card message to the appropriate occasion.

_c_ **1.** A new baby

____ **2.** A retirement

____ **3.** A wedding

____ **4.** A gift

____ **5.** An illness

____ **6.** A death in the family

a. Get well soon! Hope you have a speedy recovery!

b. With appreciation for the beautiful gift.

c. Welcome to parenthood! Diapers, diapers, and more diapers!

d. We wish you joy in your new life together!

e. Good luck! We envy you!

f. We express our deepest sympathy in your time of loss.

B **Working Together** In a group of three or four students, create a greeting card for a classmate who is moving away. Then, everyone should sign the card.

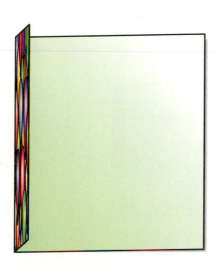

Unit 9

Job Performance

A **Under each picture, write the person's job.** Then, discuss the questions.

1. Does this person work in production or service?

2. What skills does this person need for the job?

3. Would you like this kind of work? Why or why not?

1. _____

2. _____

3. _____

4. _____

5. _____

6. _____

> *How long* asks about an amount of time. Use *how long* with the present perfect continuous.
>
> > **How long** has she **been repairing** TVs?
> > She **has been repairing** TVs <u>for two hours</u>.
>
> *How many* asks about a specific number. Use *how many* with the present perfect.
>
> > **How many** TVs has she **repaired**?
> > She **has repaired** <u>three TVs</u>.

 A **Read the conversation.** Then, practice it with a partner.

A: What <u>is Harry doing</u>?

B: He's registering students for classes.

A: **How long** <u>has he been sitting</u> at the registration counter?

B: He's been sitting there for two hours.

A: **How many** students <u>has he registered</u> **so far**?

B: He's registered 18 students so far today.

> **VOCABULARY NOTE**
> **so far** – until now

 B **Ask and answer questions about each picture.** Use your imagination. Use Exercise A as an example.

1.

2.

3.

4.

5.

6.

> Use the present perfect tense for repeated past actions. The following time expressions show a repeated action.
>
> *from time to time*   I have been late **from time to time**.
> *a few times*   She has worked overtime **a few times**.
>
> *Ever* and *never* are often used with the present perfect. *Ever* means "in your lifetime" or "in your experience."

 A **Ask and answer the questions about work.**

> A: Have you **ever** called in sick?

> B: No, I haven't. / I've **never** called in sick.

> C: Yes, I've called in sick **a few times**.

1. Have you ever called in sick?

2. Have you ever had an accident at work?

3. Have you ever quit a job?

4. Have you ever received a raise?

5. Have you ever gotten a promotion?

6. Have you ever received a performance evaluation?

7. Have you ever complained to your boss?

8. Have you ever complained about your boss?

9. Have you ever worked a double shift?

10. Have you ever had a problem with a co-worker?

B **Ask your partner two more questions about work.**

C **Ask your teacher about his or her job and interests.**

1. How long / you / teach / at this school?

2. you / ever / teach / another subject?

3. you / ever / study / another language?

4. you / ever / have / a different kind of job?

5. you / ever / visit _____?

6. you / ever / eat / _____ food?

7. you / ever / play on a sports team?

> How long have you been teaching at this school?

> Have you ever taught another subject?

D **Write two more questions to ask your teacher.**

1. Place definite and indefinite time expressions at the end of the sentence.

   I began to work here **in 2005**.
   I have changed jobs **twice**.

   I have been working here **for two years**.
   She's taken four breaks today **so far**!
   (Meaning: up until now)

2. Place adverbs of frequency before the main verb.

   Laura has **never** received a warning at work.

   She has **always** been an excellent employee.

3. Place *just* and *finally* before the main verb.

   Henry has **just** gotten a raise.

   Andrea has **finally** finished her project.

4. Place *already* before the main verb or at the end of the sentence.

   They have **already** repaired three computers.

   They have repaired three computers **already**.

5. Place *yet* and *recently* at the end of the sentence.

   I've spoken to him **recently**.

   Bill hasn't finished the project **yet**.

 A **Make three sentences about each picture.** Use the words in the boxes and the simple past or present perfect tense.

1. go on a job interview

twice   just   yesterday

2. take a vacation

last summer   recently   three times

3. get a promotion

yet   twice   in 2008

4. complete the order

finally   an hour ago   already

Some verbs can be used in either the present perfect tense or the present perfect continuous tense.

I **have lived** in this town for six years.
I **have been living** in this town for six years.

They **have worked** on this project since last month.
They **have been working** on this project since last month.

Other verbs, especially non-action verbs, can be used with the present perfect tense but not the present perfect continuous tense.

Non-action: hear   see   need   think (to express an opinion)

Maria **hasn't heard** about the promotion yet.

Refer to page 243 for a list of non-action verbs.

A **Complete the sentences.** Use the present perfect or the present perfect continuous tense. Some of the sentences can use either tense.

1. I (live) _____'ve been living_____ here for six months.

2. They (just / finish) _____ cleaning the trucks.

3. We (see / not) _____ the new schedules yet.

4. The manager (interview) _____ new job applicants this week.

5. My supervisor (ask) _____ for help with the new project every day this week.

6. I (know) _____ her since we first came to this company.

7. That company (have) _____ a lot of problems lately.

8. I (work) _____ on this program all day.

9. Adam (wear / not) _____ the same tie twice!

10. They (already / complete) _____ four repairs.

11. We (watch) _____ the new workers complete their tasks.

12. Henry (leave / not) _____ early since the new supervisor started working here.

13. Alexandra (work / not) _____ overtime since she got a promotion.

14. Our supervisor (hire) _____ any one new in over two months.

> Use the past tense to describe an action that happened at a <u>specific time</u> in the past.
>
> I **finished** my deliveries <u>an hour ago</u>.
> We **had to work** overtime <u>from 5:00 to 8:00</u>.
>
> Use the present perfect to describe an action that happened at an <u>unspecified time</u> in the past.
>
> They **'ve never used** this equipment.
> I **'ve applied** to that company twice.

A **Complete the sentences.** Use the correct form of the verbs in the past or the present perfect.

1. Bob (receive) _____*received*_____ a raise last year.

2. Orlando (receive) _____ two raises this year, and it's only July.

3. Laura (have) _____ six job interviews so far this year.

4. Samantha (have) _____ a job interview in Dallas yesterday.

5. We (hear / already) _____ that presentation many times.

6. I (see / never) _____ that presentation.

7. Sarah (take) _____ two sick days when she had the flu.

8. Ellen (take) _____ two sick days so far.

9. The company (hire) _____ three new workers, and we need one more.

10. My company (hire) _____ the four new workers that we needed.

B **Ask and answer these questions with a partner.**

1. Have you missed any days of school this year?

2. How many days have you been absent so far?

3. How many different jobs have you had in your life?

4. Where do you work now? How long have you been working there?

5. Where did you work before you started this job?

6. Why did you leave that job?

7. When did you come to this school?

8. How many classes have you taken at this school?

C **Listen. Circle the letter of the sentence with the correct meaning.**

CD2·TR14

1. **a.** The doctor is still seeing patients.

   b. The doctor is finished seeing patients for the day.

2. **a.** Jamie is still ironing shirts.

   b. Jamie is finished ironing shirts for the day.

3. **a.** The men are still planting trees.

   b. The men are finished planting the trees.

4. **a.** The teacher has more papers to correct.

   b. The teacher finished all the papers.

5. **a.** Carlos is finished for the day.

   b. Carlos is still in his truck, delivering packages.

6. **a.** Mary is not going to call any more people today.

   b. Mary will call 100 more people.

7. **a.** She retired from the hospital.

   b. She's still working at the hospital.

8. **a.** He will drive farther today.

   b. He's going to stop for the day.

D **Pronunciation: 've and 's Listen and repeat.**

CD2·TR15

1. **a.** I sold five cars.

   b. I've sold five cars.

2. **a.** She worked five hours.

   b. She's worked five hours.

3. **a.** They made 500 donuts.

   b. They've made 500 donuts.

4. **a.** She walked five miles.

   b. She's walked five miles.

5. **a.** I helped ten customers.

   b. I've helped ten customers.

6. **a.** He planted five trees.

   b. He's planted five trees.

7. **a.** She read 20 pages.

   b. She's read 20 pages.

8. **a.** I cleaned seven rooms.

   b. I've cleaned seven rooms.

E **Listen again. Circle the sentence you hear in Exercise D.**

CD2·TR16

F Working Together **Student to Student**

Student 1: Turn to page 265. Read **Set A** questions to Student 2.

Student 2: Look at the pictures and listen to Student 1. Write the answer under the correct picture. Use complete sentences.

Then, change roles. Student 2 will read **Set B** and Student 1 will write the answer under the correct picture.

1.

fired one   hired three

She has fired one employee this year. / She has hired three employees.

2.

ten patients   four doctors

_____

3.

five cars   eight years

_____

4.

one home   four years

_____

5.

at 5:00 A.M.   15

_____

6.

two systems   five years

_____

The Big Picture

CD2·TR17

A **Listen and complete the information about George's job.**

Job Description for Metro Transit Drivers

1. All applicants must have an in-person _____interview_____ and a _background_ check.

2. Employee pay starts at $ _____ an hour.

3. Report to work on time and in _____.

4. Drive _____ and obey all _____ and safety laws.

5. _____ and drop off passengers at designated bus stops.

6. _____ correct fares.

7. Greet and treat _____ with courtesy.

8. All employees with good evaluations receive a $ _____ pay increase.

9. If the employee has no accidents in five years, pay will increase to $_____ an hour.

CD2·TR17

B **Listen again and answer the questions.**

1. What year did George begin to work for Metro Transit? _____

2. How much was his starting salary? _____

3. Does he know the names of his passengers? _____

4. Has his salary increased each year? _____

5. How often does he receive an evaluation? _____

6. How long has George been working for Metro Transit? _____

CD2·TR18

C **Listen.** Write the questions to match the answers. Use the present or present perfect tense.

1. How much *overtime does George work* _____?

   About ten hours a week.

2. How much _____?

   Time and a half.

3. _____?

   Yes, he has.

4. How much _____?

   $300.

5. _____?

   Yes. George's friend got two.

6. _____?

   Yes, he does.

D **Complete the sentences.** Use the past or present perfect form of the verbs.

1. Before he started at Metro Transit, George (work) ___*worked*___ as a school bus driver.

2. He (negative-like) _____ the noise on the school bus.

3. When George began at Metro Transit, he (earn) _____ $14.80 an hour.

4. He (receive) _____ a pay raise every year since then.

5. His performance evaluations (be / always) _____ _____ _____ very good.

6. He (have / only) _____ _____ _____ two or three passenger complaints, which is less than the company average.

7. Two years ago, he (get) _____ a ticket for going through a red light.

8. He (pay) _____ a fine of $100 and the company (charge) _____ him another $200.

9. George (be / always) _____ _____ _____ polite and courteous to the passengers.

A Discuss.

1. What kinds of jobs do you think will be needed in the future?

2. Do you think your job will be needed in the year 2025? Why or why not?

B Word Builder Match.

___b___	**1.** to outnumber	**a.**	to grow larger
_____	**2.** to age	**b.**	to have a greater number than
_____	**3.** to increase	**c.**	to explain
_____	**4.** to be in demand	**d.**	to get older
_____	**5.** to account for	**e.**	to stay
_____	**6.** to remain	**f.**	to be needed or required

C Read.

The workforce of the United States includes everyone who is working now and everyone who is looking for a job. The Bureau of Labor Statistics evaluates the current workforce and employment opportunities. It makes predictions about the future workforce.

Between 2000 and 2010, approximately 17.1 million new workers entered the workforce, bringing the total number of workers in the United States to 149 million. What will the future workforce look like? The number of women **has increased** steadily. Sixty-two percent of all women will be in the workforce by 2016. The workforce is **aging**, too. Baby boomers—people born between 1946 and 1964—make up more than 13 percent of the workforce. Some people in this group are retiring, leaving job openings. However, because of the economy, others are **remaining** on the job longer than expected. One reason why baby boomers are staying in the workforce is because of education. They often have more education than younger workers. In addition, because of a slow economy, older workers continue working because they want to add to their retirement benefits. Health costs are rising, so baby boomers want to work as long as they can.

The workforce will become more ethnically diverse. In 2000, 73.1 percent of the workforce was classified as White, non-Hispanic. In 2010, this number was 69.2 percent, but soon the Hispanic workforce will **outnumber** all other ethnic groups, **accounting for** 16 percent of the total workers by 2016. African Americans will make up 12.3 percent and Asians will make up 5.3 percent.

The labor department divides jobs into two types: goods-producing jobs and service-providing jobs. Goods-producing jobs include manufacturing, agriculture, mining, farming, and fishing. There will be almost no growth in this type of job because most goods are produced in other countries and more machinery is used. For instance, the number of farmers and ranchers is expected to steadily decline. The government expects that service providers will **account for** 20.2 million new jobs for the years from now until 2018. Many of these jobs will require more than a high school degree. Registered nurses, home-care aides, nursing aides, and other health-care professionals will be **in demand**. Why? Because of technological advances in the medical field, preventive care, and the increasing number of older people, more health-care workers will be needed.

Every two years, the United States government publishes the *Occupational Outlook Handbook*, a document that presents specific information about the job market and the job outlook. Some of the information included is salary range, education required, and job responsibilities. This document can be found in the reference section of any local or school library, or online.

Source: Bureau of Labor Statistics; *Occupational Outlook Handbook*

READING NOTE

Interpreting Statistics

It is important to pay attention to and interpret the meaning of statistics in a reading passage. You might want to highlight or underline statistics.

WORD PARTNERSHIPS

manufacturing	
service-providing	jobs
goods-producing	
health-related	

D (Circle) *True* or *False*.

1. There are approximately 17.1 million workers in the U.S.   True   False

2. More than half of all U.S. women will be working in the future.   True   False

3. The workforce is getting younger.   True   False

4. Some baby boomers are retiring later than expected.   True   False

5. Baby boomers continue to work because of health-care costs.   True   False

6. By 2016, Hispanics will outnumber both African Americans and Asians in the workforce.   True   False

7. The jobs most in demand in the future will be in goods-producing.   True   False

8. The government expects to see more jobs in medical fields.   True   False

9. The government revises the *Occupational Outlook Handbook* every two years.   True   False

A Read.

My Future Career

Pamela Simmons

October 23

English IV

I am considering a career as a dental hygienist. A dental hygienist usually works in a dentist's office. A dental hygienist removes plaque and deposits from teeth, takes dental X-rays, and tells patients how to clean and floss their teeth. In some offices, dental hygienists administer anesthetics, fill cavities, and assist the dentist.

All dental hygienists receive a license from their state. It is necessary to attend an accredited dental hygiene program. Students must pass a written and clinical examination. Many community colleges offer dental hygienist programs and many dental hygienists who work in dental offices have an associate's degree. Others have bachelor's degrees or even a doctorate.

At school, students study in different settings. They study in classrooms, in laboratories, and in model dental offices. They may take many science courses, such as anatomy and pharmacology. There is a strong job outlook for dental hygienists. In this field, people can work flexible hours or part time. The average salary is $66,570 a year.

I'm interested in this career because I like working with people, and I like the medical field. The working conditions are good. I don't have time to attend a four-year program. A career that only requires a two-year degree and that has a good salary and job outlook appeals to me.

B Check (✓) your job skills. Then, discuss your skills with a partner.

☐ selling   ☐ drawing   ☐ typing

☐ managing money   ☐ designing   ☐ repairing

☐ writing   ☐ working with numbers   ☐ teaching

☐ organizing   ☐ supervising people   ☐ public speaking

☐ operating equipment   ☐ using a computer   ☐ helping people

C **Discuss the meaning of each job characteristic.** Then, check (✓) the characteristics that are the most important to you.

☐ salary ☐ benefits ☐ job training

☐ job status ☐ job security ☐ flexibility

☐ possibilities for promotion ☐ possibilities to travel

> ### WRITING NOTE
>
> **Taking Notes**
> College papers usually require you to do some research. It is important to take notes and to write your paper using your own words. Do not copy word for word. When you take notes, you do not need to write complete sentences.

D **Go online.** Find information about a job that interests you. Use the *Occupational Outlook Handbook*. You can also find the handbook at your local or school library. Complete the chart.

Career title	
Job description	
Working conditions	
Education or training	
Earnings	
Job outlook	

E **Write a paper about the job you chose.** Explain why this career is a good choice for you.

F **Find and correct the mistakes.**

1. I have never ~~take~~ *taken* a sick day.

2. She has gotten along with her co-workers always.

3. He has spoken to the boss a few minutes ago.

4. She has receive an award as the top salesperson twice.

5. Have you never attended a performance review?

6. They have never went on a job interview.

7. She has been writing two reports so far.

8. We have had to work on weekends last month.

Practicing on Your Own

A **Rewrite the sentences.** Put the adverb or time expression in the correct place in the sentence.

1. Susan has worked overtime. (several times this month)

   Susan has worked overtime several times this month.

2. She has followed company policies. (always)

   _____

3. She has spoken to the human resources department about a promotion. (already)

   _____

4. We have received a complaint about her work. (rarely)

   _____

5. She has taken an advanced software course. (recently)

   _____

6. She has been able to solve problems. (usually)

   _____

7. She has completed a sales management course. (just)

   _____

B **Look at the monthly evaluation reports for two employees at Excel Electronics.** Karl is going to receive a promotion. David is going to lose his job. Complete the evaluations. Use the present perfect.

Karl	David
1. He has always arrived on time.	**1.** David has been late ten times.
2. He has taken one sick day.	**2.** _____
3. He has sold 150 televisions.	**3.** _____
4. _____	**4.** He has made mistakes on seven bills of sale.
5. He has always written the correct address on delivery notices.	**5.** _____
6. He has often worked overtime.	**6.** _____

English in Action

A **Katie is a sales assistant.** Read her job description.

Davis Jewelry: Sales Assistant

Assist customers
Maintain and restock displays
Perform sales transactions
 accurately
Follow all store procedures and
 polices

 B **Listen to Katie's performance evaluation.** Check (✓) the correct boxes.

CD2·TR19

	Exceeds Expectations	Meets Expectations	Needs Improvement	Unsatisfactory
Reports to work as scheduled				
Appearance is neat				
Shows initiative				
Behaves professionally				
Uses effective sales techniques				
Performs sales accurately				

 C **With a partner, discuss and evaluate Katie's work performance.**

1. Has Katie always arrived on time? Has her on-time arrival improved?

2. How are Katie's sales? How are her sales techniques?

3. When does Katie make mistakes?

4. What has Mr. Davis decided to do?

Unit 10

Regrets and Possibilities

A **Read the thoughts and discuss each picture.**

1.

2.

3.

4.

5.

6.

7.

8.

9.

Use *should have* to discuss regret about a past action.

I **should have studied** more.
   Meaning: I didn't study enough.

We **should have brought** warm clothes.
   Meaning: We didn't bring warm clothes. Now we're cold.

They **shouldn't have left** their umbrellas at home.
   Meaning: It rained; they weren't prepared.

A **Write the past participle form of each verb.**

Base Form	Past Participle		Base Form	Past Participle
buy	bought		leave	
try			meet	
drive			see	
forget			lose	
fill			pay	
send			sleep	
eat			take	
break			tell	
feel			write	

CD2·TR20

B **Listen and complete.**

1. I _____ should have bought _____ a new one.

2. I _____ a used one.

3. She _____ harder.

4. I _____ so many courses.

5. I _____ earlier.

6. I _____ to bring it.

7. They _____ the tank.

8. He _____ without a license.

9. We _____ the check on time.

10. She _____ it.

C **Complete the sentences.** Use *should have* or *shouldn't have* and the correct form of the verb in parentheses.

1. I registered for too many courses, and now my grades are falling.

   I (take) _____ so many courses.

2. Akiko forgot to bring her book, and she needs it for the exam.

   She (forget) _____ her book.

3. Sandra's cell phone rang during the exam.

   She (turn off) _____ her phone before the exam.

4. Jim stayed up very late. The next morning, he overslept and was late.

   He (stay up) _____ so late.

5. Marie wanted to take a psychology course, but she registered too late.

   She (register) _____ earlier.

6. Paul didn't type his paper and received a low grade.

   He (type) _____ his paper.

D **Make a statement about each picture.** Use words from the box, *should have* or *shouldn't have*, and your imagination.

bring	put	remember	take	wear	eat

1.

2.

3.

4.

5.

6.

Should have for Expectation

> Use *should have* to show an expectation.
>
> The bus **should have arrived** by now.
> Meaning: The bus is late.
>
> I **should have done** better on this exam.
> Meaning: My grade is lower than expected.

CD2·TR21

A **Listen and write the number under the correct picture.**

a. _____

b. _____

c. <u>1</u>

d. _____

e. _____

f. _____

B **Complete the sentences.** Use *should have* or *shouldn't have* and the correct form of the verbs in parentheses.

1. Our professor isn't here. She (arrive) ___should have arrived___ at 9:00.

2. Why hasn't the movie started? It (begin) _____ at 8:20.

3. Paul hasn't gotten his degree yet, but he (graduate) _____ last semester.

4. The library (charge / not) _____ me a late fee. There was a snowstorm yesterday.

5. The contractors (replace / not) _____ the carpet. It was brand-new!

6. It's 4:00, and Lina (find) _____ out if she has been accepted in the special program.

7. The snow (stop) _____, according to the weather forecast.

8. She (gain / not) _____ weight if she followed the doctor's diet.

Regrets and Possibilities · **149**

> Use *may have, might have,* or *could have* to express past possibility.
>
> I **may (not) have gone** to the movies.
> You **might (not) have forgotten** to bring the tickets.
> She **could (not) have bought** a new car.
>
> Use *could not have / couldn't have* to express past impossibility.
>
> He **couldn't have been** at work that day. He was in the emergency room with his daughter.

A **Match each statement with the correct possibility.**

_____ *e* **1.** Frank didn't come to work yesterday.

_____ **2.** I wonder where the neighbors went.

_____ **3.** I saw Tariq with a strange woman. Who was she?

_____ **4.** Marco was wearing a suit yesterday. He usually wears jeans.

_____ **5.** Madeline was in a toy store yesterday. What did she buy for her niece?

_____ **6.** Anna isn't happy with her new job.

_____ **7.** I can't find my cell phone.

a. He might have had a job interview.

b. They may have gone to Florida

c. She might have bought her a teddy bear.

d. You could have left it in the restaurant.

e. He may have been sick.

f. She could have taken that other job.

g. That might have been his sister I hear that she's in town.

 B **Read each sentence.** With a partner, write two possibilities in your notebooks. Use *might have, may have,* or *could have* and a verb.

1. A classmate missed an important exam.

2. A classmate looked sick yesterday. Today, she was absent.

3. A friend was at a travel agency last Saturday.

4. A strange woman was talking to your friend's husband.

5. A friend called you to pick her up at a hospital emergency room.

6. A very large package was delivered to your neighbors' house.

> Use *must have* to express a deduction about a past action.
> I **must have left** my keys at home.
> You **must have left** your cell phone at home.
> They **must not have remembered** their notebooks.

CD2·TR22

A **Listen.** A man is calling 911 to report a problem in his apartment. Write the letter of the correct deduction under each picture.

1. _g_

2. _____

3. _____

4. _____

5. _____

6. _____

7. _____

8. _____

Deductions

a. The burglar must have used it to hide the other clothes.

b. The burglar must have taken it.

c. The burglar must have dropped the gloves when he left.

d. The burglar must have scared the cat.

e. The burglar must have gotten scared and left through the window.

f. The burglar must have been hungry.

g. Someone must have broken in.

h. The burglar must have put on one of your suits.

B **Pronunciation: Past Modals** **Listen and repeat.**

CD2·TR23

1. You must've left your book at home.

2. She might've studied French.

3. I should've made an appointment.

4. We could've gone on a vacation.

5. He must've had to work.

6. She couldn't have walked that far.

7. We shouldn't have spoken to her.

8. They shouldn't have arrived late.

9. He may not have had an opportunity.

10. I must not have heard you.

 C **Practice saying the sentences in Exercise B with a partner.**

 **D** **Pronunciation: Word Stress** **Listen to the conversation and underline the stressed words.**

CD2·TR24

A: Hi, Julia. Why didn't you come to my party? Everyone missed you.

B: What party?

A: I had a party last Saturday.

B: Really? You should've called me.

A: I did. I left a message on your voice mail.

B: I changed my number. You could've sent me an invitation.

A: I did. I e-mailed it two weeks ago.

B: You must've sent it to the wrong address. I've changed my e-mail.

A: You should've told me.

B: Sorry. Anyway, how was the party?

A: It was fun. You should've been there.

  E **Practice the conversation in Exercise D with a partner.** Use the correct stress. Use your partner's name.

Active Grammar

Must have for Empathy

Use *must have* to express empathy.

My daughter didn't make the soccer team.

She **must have been** disappointed.

 A **Take turns reading the statements.** Your partner will respond. Use the subject in parentheses, *must have been*, and an adjective from the box.

angry ~~bored~~ embarrassed excited disgusted proud

You must have been bored.

1. We spent ten very long hours at the museum. (You)

2. My family and I were on vacation when we saw one of our favorite singers. (You)

3. They ordered soup, and there was a cockroach in one of the bowls. (They)

4. I was talking about my boss when she walked in to the room. (You)

5. We were taking a test when my cell phone rang. (Your teacher)

6. My sister was the first person in our family to graduate from college. (Your family)

  B **Working Together** Student to Student.

Student 1: Turn to page 265.

Student 2: Use cues 1–5 to say what happened last weekend. Student 1 will respond.

Example: My homework / be / very difficult

My homework was very difficult.

You must have been frustrated.

1. I / have to work overtime / all weekend

2. I / can't find / keys / for two hours

3. I / not get / the new job

4. my son / win / football championship

5. my brother / get / promotion

Now change roles. Student 2, turn to page 265. Student 1, use cues 6–10 to tell Student 2 what happened last weekend. Student 2 will respond.

6. my daughter / get engaged

7. I / get lost in a strange neighborhood / for an hour

8. at the bank / I / can't express myself in English

9. I / receive a bonus / at work

10. my friends / have a birthday party / for me

A **A high school counselor is talking to Amber, a student.** Listen and take notes below.

Notes: Amber	Notes: Miguel

 CD2·TR26 **B** **The counselor is talking to Miguel, another student.** Listen and take notes above.

C **Match each student with the correct problems.**

Student	Problems
Amber _____	**a.** relationship
_____	**b.** problems with a class
_____	**c.** college plans
Miguel _____	**d.** poor grades
_____	**e.** lost a job
_____	**f.** needed a job

🔊 CD2·TR25 **D** **Listen again to Amber's conversation.** Then, answer the questions.

1. What job does Amber have at school?

2. What does the counselor think about Amber's work on the school newspaper?

3. Why is Amber upset?

4. Is Amber good at her job?

5. Why is the job important to her?

6. What did Amber do? Why?

7. Is she sorry?

8. What is the counselor going to do to help her?

E **Complete the sentences.** Use *should have* or *shouldn't have* and the verb to express the facts and your opinion in parentheses.

1. Amber (write) _____ false information.

2. Amber (speak) _____ to her boyfriend about her feelings.

3. Amber (think) _____ more carefully before she wrote the article.

4. In my opinion, the vice principal (take) _____ away her job.

🔊 CD2·TR26 **F** **Listen to Miguel's conversation again.** Then, answer the questions.

1. Is Miguel a good student? Has he improved?

2. Did Miguel do the things that the counselor suggested?

3. What could Miguel have done to improve his math grades?

4. Which is harder for Miguel—speaking English or writing English?

5. Why didn't Miguel get help from a tutor?

6. Where is Miguel working now?

7. What is Miguel's work schedule?

G **Complete the sentences.** Use *must have, could have,* or *couldn't have* and the correct form of the verb in parentheses.

1. Miguel (find) _____ a math tutor, but he didn't need to.

2. Miguel's math instructor (be) _____ pleased with his progress.

3. Miguel (make) _____ a good impression at his job interview.

4. Miguel (find) _____ a different writing tutor.

5. Miguel (get) _____ the job without his counselor's help.

A Discuss. Then, read.

1. Do you have children, grandchildren, or nieces and nephews?

2. Can the children speak, read, and write your native language?

3. Do you want the children to learn your native language and culture? Why or why not?

READING NOTE

Preparing to Read

Before you read a passage, look at the title. Then, read the first two sentences of each paragraph. Think about the topic. Then, continue to read the passage.

WORD PARTNERSHIPS

after-school	
cultural	program
intensive	
weekend	

Family 1

I'm from Argentina. My family and I are living in the United States. We've been living here for almost three years now. My children can speak English fluently, and they are in regular classes. I'm disappointed that they don't speak Spanish anymore. They've forgotten our language. I should have done something to help them maintain our language and learn about our Argentinean culture, but it's too late now.

Family 2

My daughter is very excited. This summer, we're going to visit my parents in Korea for the first time. I've been sending her to a Korean school every weekend for the past year. Some friends told me that I should have concentrated on her English, but my husband and I decided that we wanted her to learn Korean, too. She's been writing letters to her grandparents, and the grandparents are thrilled to receive a letter that they can read. We made the right decision.

What can immigrant parents do to help their children learn or **maintain** their native language and culture? Children who grow up speaking one language outside the home and a different language inside the home learn to speak two languages. However, it is hard for these children to learn to read and write their parents' native language at an advanced level. Therefore, many parents send their children to special programs for an average of three to five hours a week. The **mission** of most programs is to help children of immigrant parents and / or grandparents learn their native language and culture. There are Polish schools and Chinese schools, to name a few.

One Korean school in New York City offers six hours of instruction every Saturday. The school teaches reading and conversation, Korean history, and Korean **fine arts**, including art and music. Students include Korean children who were adopted by American couples, Korean-Americans, Koreans, and Americans.

A Greek school in Chicago teaches Greek language to children in their Greek Orthodox Church community. The school day lasts two and a half hours every Saturday. The students can learn to read, write, and speak Greek. One parent explained why she sent her child to the Greek school. She said, "I studied Greek in an after-school program when I was a child, and I wanted my daughter to learn Greek, too. **Besides** learning the culture of my parents, she was also learning another language. The more languages she learns, the better off she'll be in the future." She added, "Sometimes it was a **struggle** to get her to classes, in terms of convenience and other school activities, but I kept her in the classes." When the daughter was older, she even took a trip to Greece with her classmates at the school.

B **Word Builder** **Find the boldfaced words in the reading. Circle the correct definition.**

1. What can immigrant parents do to help their children learn or **maintain** their native language and culture? *Maintain* means _____.

    a. to repair   **b.** to continue   **c.** to take care of   **d.** to speak

2. The **mission** of most programs is to help children of immigrant parents and / or grandparents to learn the native language and culture. A *mission* is _____.

    a. a goal   **b.** a map   **c.** a lesson   **d.** a fight

3. The school teaches reading and conversation, Korean history, and Korean **fine arts**, including art, music, and calligraphy. Which of the following is not a *fine art*?

    a. drawing   **b.** painting   **c.** chemistry   **d.** photography

4. **Besides** learning the culture of my parents, she was also learning another language. *Besides* means _____.

    a. but   **b.** in addition to   **c.** next to   **d.** if

5. Sometimes it was a **struggle** to get her to classes. *It was a struggle* means _____.

    a. it was easy   **b.** it was confusing   **c.** it was challenging   **d.** it was exciting

C **Discuss.**

1. Are you more similar to Family 1 or Family 2? Explain your answer.

2. Is it important to you that your children or future children learn to speak, read, and write your native language? Why or why not?

3. What do you think about weekend language and culture schools for children?

A **Read the composition.**

My Regrets

Manny Arias
March 2010
English IV

It's difficult to move to a new city, especially in a new country. Looking back, there are many things that I should have done to prepare.

First of all, there's the language. I studied English in high school, but I didn't take it seriously. I should have studied harder. Also, I could have taken another English class before I came here. Of course, now I'm taking English classes.

Second, good jobs are hard to find. I finished my degree back in my country, but I didn't bring my transcripts. Now, it's difficult to get the transcripts; I should have brought them with me. I've ordered my transcripts from the university, but it's taking a long time for them to arrive. When they arrive, I may be able to find a job in my field.

Finally, I didn't know how to drive when I arrived. In my country, public transportation was very convenient and cheap. But in this state, many jobs are outside of the city and there isn't any public transportation to those locations. One of my friends is teaching me how to drive, but I should have learned earlier. Those are a few of the things that I should have done before I came here.

B **You are going to write a composition about your regrets when you moved to this country.** Answer the following questions to give you some ideas.

1. What did you forget to bring with you to this country that you needed?

2. What did you bring with you that you didn't need?

3. What should you have done before you came here?

4. Could you have studied English before you came to this country?

5. Did you contact relatives in this country when you were planning your move to this country?

6. Where did you live when you first came to this country?

7. Did you have information about job opportunities before you came to this country? Were you happy with your first job?

WRITING NOTE

Quotation Marks

Use *quotation marks* to write someone's exact words. Report exact words with a verb such as *said, shouted, yelled, cried, asked,* or *complained.* Put punctuation <u>inside</u> the quotation marks.

> She said, "I studied Greek in an after-school program when I was a child, and I wanted my daughter to learn Greek, too."

C **Complete the sentences.** Use a verb from the box. Add punctuation.

> asked   shouted   explained   said   complained

1. Sylvia _____ shouted, _____ "Stop slamming the door!"

2. Ivan _____ When can I take the test

3. Marlene _____ We should've called the police

4. Juliette _____ Do you have any job openings

5. Karen _____ I must have overslept. I'm sorry I'm late

6. Al _____ I've lived here a long time and you've never visited me

7. José _____ You should have invited her to the party

D **Write your composition.** Use quotation marks at least once.

E **Sharing Our Stories** **Read your partner's composition.** <u>Underline</u> the punctuation. What does your partner regret?

F **Find and correct the mistakes.**

1. I could have ~~study~~ studied to be a doctor, but I chose computers instead.

2. We should have not eaten so much. I think I've gained five pounds.

3. You must had enjoyed the party.

4. Peter might has called after 10:00.

5. Edward should enjoyed his surprise party, but he didn't.

6. That TV must have be expensive. It's the newest model.

7. The performance must have be exciting.

8. You might been upset when I called.

A **Complete the conversations.** Use the verb in parentheses and a modal from the box. Use the present or past modal form.

have to	doesn't / don't have to	should (not)	may (not)
had to	didn't have to	had better (not)	might (not)
must (not)			could (not)

1. **A:** Are you free this weekend?

   B: No, I'm not. I (work) _____ overtime.

2. **Driver:** What's the problem, Officer?

   Officer: You (not make) _____ a left turn at that corner. Now, (give) I _____ you a ticket.

3. **A:** How's the weather?

   B: It's very cloudy. It (rain) _____ . You (take) _____ your umbrella.

4. **A:** Why are you so late?

   B: It's a nice day, so I decided to walk. I (take) _____ the bus instead.

5. **A:** Did you hear? Connie's husband was laid off last week.

   B: She (be) _____ very upset.

6. **A:** Why does Steven wear blue shirts every day?

   B: I don't know. He (like) _____ the color blue.

7. **Teacher:** This is your last chance. You (not / miss) _____ another class.

   Student: I promise I won't be absent again.

8. **A:** Why didn't Peter take his driving test last Friday?

   B: I'm not sure. He (be) _____ ready.

Subject	*Be*	Past Participle	
Tuna	is	caught	by fishermen in Oregon.
Apples	are	grown	in Washington State.

Active sentences emphasize the subject that does the action.

Subject	Verb	Object

Fishermen **catch** *tuna and salmon* in Oregon.

Passive sentences emphasize the object that receives the action.

Object	Verb	Subject

Tuna and salmon **are caught** by fishermen in Oregon.

Note: When the subject is obvious, unknown, or not important, "by" and the subject are **not** necessary.

Tuna and salmon **are caught** in Oregon. (The subject is obvious: We know that fishermen catch the fish, so "by fishermen" isn't necessary.)

A **Write each product from the chart next to the correct verb.**

A count noun requires either a singular or plural verb.

This apple **is** delicious.
Apples **are** grown in Washington State.

A non-count noun requires a singular verb.

Lettuce **is** grown in Arizona.

Count Nouns		Non-count Nouns	
apples	potatoes	coal	lettuce
cattle (plural)	sheep (plural)	copper	milk
chili peppers	shrimp (plural)	cotton	natural gas
computers	tomatoes	gold	petroleum
grapes	tuna (plural)	hay	
lumber products	Christmas trees		

1. mine   coal, _____

2. catch   shrimp, _____

3. grow   apples, _____

4. manufacture   computers, _____

5. produce   lumber products, _____

6. raise   cattle, _____

B **In your notebook, write ten sentences about the map on page 162, five with count nouns and five with non-count nouns.** Use the passive.

Apples are grown in Washington State. _____

C Circle the correct form of the verb.

1. Farmers **grow** / **are grown** corn in Iowa.

2. Sheep **raise** / **are raised** in Ohio.

3. Milk **produces** / **is produced** in Wisconsin.

4. Auto companies **manufacture** / **are manufactured** cars in Michigan.

5. Steel **produces** / **is produced** in Illinois.

6. Coal **mines** / **is mined** in Illinois and Kentucky.

7. Many companies **produce** / **is produced** cereal in Michigan.

8. Owners **raise** / **are raised** horses in Kentucky.

9. Cattle **raise** / **are raised** in Tennessee.

WORD PARTNERSHIPS	
grow	vegetables
	flowers
	trees
raise	animals
	children

D With a partner, ask and answer questions about the product map.

Is	milk	**produced** in Wisconsin?
Are	tires	**manufactured** in Ohio?

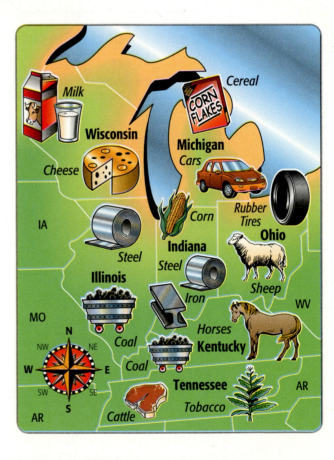

| Where | **is** | rice | **grown**? |
| How | **are** | cars | **manufactured**? |

CD3·TR1

A **Listen and write the questions.** Then, look at the product map and write the answers.

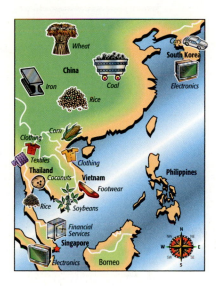

Count Nouns	Non-count Nouns
automobiles	clothing
coconuts	coal
electronics	corn
financial services	footwear
soybeans	iron
textiles	rice
	wheat

1. Where are electronics manufactured?

   They are manufactured in South Korea.

2. _____

   _____

3. _____

   _____

4. _____

   _____

5. _____

   _____

6. _____

   _____

B **In your notebook, write three more questions.** Ask and answer the questions with a partner.

> Use *by* when the **subject** of the action is important and is not obvious.
> This candy **is produced** *by* Royal Sweets.
> This toy **is made** *by* an American company.

A **Rewrite the sentences in the passive.** Use *by* when necessary.

1. Farmers grow rice in Louisiana.

   Rice is grown in Louisiana.

2. Construction workers build skyscrapers in New York City.

   _____

3. Cardiologists perform heart surgery.

   _____

4. A technician usually does my blood test.

   _____

5. In Maine, fishermen trap lobsters.

   _____

6. All over the world, soccer fans watch the World Cup.

   _____

7. Someone cuts and fertilizes his lawn.

   _____

8. Specially trained bakers design wedding cakes.

   _____

9. Flight attendants serve beverages during flights.

   _____

10. Cranberry farmers grow cranberries in New Jersey and Massachusetts.

    _____

Student 1: Choose a product from the pictures below. Name a company that makes the product. Use the passive and *by* with a verb from the box.

Other students: Try to guess the product.

Student 1: If the students are wrong, make a new statement and give the name of another company that makes the product.

This product is made by _____.

name of company

It's a copy machine!

deliver	refine
design	manufacture
make	produce

1.

2.

3.

4.

5.

6.

7.

8.

9.

10.

11.

12.

C **Write four products that you and your family use at home.** Complete the sentences. Write one of your sentences on the board.

1. **I / We** use _____.

product

It / They _____ by _____.

passive verb   name of company

2. **I / We** use _____.

product

It / They _____ by _____.

passive verb   name of company

3. **I / We** use _____.

product

It / They _____ by _____.

passive verb   name of company

4. **I / We** use _____.

product

It / They _____ by _____.

passive verb   name of company

Describing a Process

CD3·TR2

A **Pronunciation: Syllable Stress** Listen and repeat.

Verb	Noun	Adjective
1. pasteurize	pasteurization	pasteurized
2. sterilize	sterilization	sterilized
3. immunize	immunization	immunized
4. separate	separation	separated
5. refrigerate	refrigeration	refrigerated
6. evaporate	evaporation	evaporated
7. ferment	fermentation	fermented

CD3·TR3

B **Listen again.** Underline the stressed syllable of the words in the chart.

pas<u>teur</u>ize   pasteuri<u>za</u>tion   pas<u>teur</u>ized

C **Write a sentence under each picture on page 169 to describe the process of gathering chocolate beans.** Use the cues below. Two sentences require active verbs, and the others require passive verbs.

1. the ripe pods / gather / every few weeks during the season

2. the workers / cut down / the pods / from the cacao trees

3. the pods / split open / and / the seeds / remove

4. the seeds / put in large wooden boxes for fermentation

5. the seed pulp / drain / for six to eight days

6. the seeds / dry / by machine or the sun

7. the workers / put / the seeds / into large sacks

8. the beans / export / to chocolate makers all over the world

1. The ripe pods are gathered every few weeks during the season.

2. _____

3. _____

4. _____

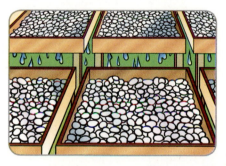

5. _____

6. _____

7. _____

8. _____

T-shirts—From the Field to Your Closet

   A **Talk about the pictures.** Then, listen and take notes.

CD3·TR4

1.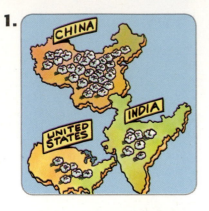

2.

3.

4.

5.

6.

7.

8.

9.

CD3•TR4

B Listen again and answer the questions.

1. Which countries are the three top cotton producers in the world?
2. How is cotton picked in China—by hand or by machine?
3. What happens at the ginner?
4. Where are the bales of cotton sent?
5. What percent of the cotton fabric is dyed different colors?
6. Does one person complete an entire T-shirt? Explain.
7. What is the original cost for a T-shirt?
8. Why is the T-shirt price increased in the warehouse?
9. How much is the price increased at the department store?
10. How long does it take before a T-shirt is sent to a discount store?

C Complete the sentences. Use an active or passive verb.

clean	knit	send
dye	~~pick~~	sew
embroider	sell	ship

1. The cotton _____is picked_____ by the workers.
2. The cotton _____ at the ginner.
3. The bales of cotton _____ to spinners.
4. Knitting machines _____ the cotton yarn into fabric.
5. The dye houses _____ the fabric different colors.
6. The fabric _____ to a sewing plant.
7. The T-shirts _____ together piece by piece.
8. The printers _____ designs on the T-shirts.
9. The T-shirts _____ to warehouses.

D Complete the sentences.

1. After the patterns are cut, the workers _____.
2. When the T-shirts are sold to the department stores, the price _____ by over 200 percent.
3. Before a T-shirt is discounted, the store _____ it for the full price.
4. The T-shirts are discounted after they _____.
5. The unsold T-shirts _____ for $14 or less when _____.

A **Discuss.** Then, read.

1. Can you list two sources of alternative energy?

2. How can today's cars save energy?

> **READING NOTE**
>
> **Listing Pros and Cons**
>
> Some readings discuss the pros and cons of an issue. As you read, make a list of the pros and cons. This will help you discuss the reading more easily.

"**Hybrid**" cars—cars that use two sources of power—are becoming more and more popular. These cars use gasoline, but they also have batteries to supply power to an electric motor. Hybrid cars send fewer pollutants into the air. Consumers need clean sources of electricity to run their hybrid cars. They also need clean energy to run other appliances, such as microwaves, TVs, and computers. What new power sources are being used to help protect our environment?

A significant source of **green**, environmentally safe energy is wind. For hundreds of years, windmills have been used by farmers to pump water. Today, millions of windmills and wind turbines are found throughout the world. Cities such as Houston, Texas, and Chicago, Illinois, are using wind energy to generate some of their power. A number of U.S. universities are using wind energy as one of their power sources. About 2.3 percent

of California's power is generated by wind turbines. In West Texas, wind turbine engines have become a source of income for people who own groups of wind turbines, or **wind farms**.

Wind has an advantage over other energy sources, such as coal and gas, which cause pollution. It does not generate harmful emissions like coal and gas do. The average household **consumes** approximately 10,000 kilowatt-hours (kWh) of electricity. With green energy, a household can use less energy. A 10-kWh wind turbine generates enough power to serve a typical household for a year. Wind energy is included as one of the options in "green power" plans in some of today's electric companies. The top three energy users of wind energy in 2009 were Germany, Denmark, and the United States.

Although wind is a clean source of energy, not everyone is in favor of wind turbine engines. First of all, **opponents** of wind energy say that large birds may fly into the moving blades and be killed. **Advocates**, or supporters, of wind energy say that more birds are killed by cars than by wind turbines. Second, opponents say that wind turbine generators are noisy and disturb neighborhoods. Advocates say that wind turbines are no louder than refrigerators. Third, residents complain that wind turbines are ugly and reduce the value of their property. However, one wind advocacy group says that one wind farm attracted over 350,000 visitors, and there has been no evidence that housing prices have been affected. There are both positives and negatives of wind energy, but it looks as though it is here to stay.

B **Answer the questions.**

1. What were windmills originally used for?

2. Which cities are using wind as a source of power?

3. What percent of California's power is wind energy?

4. Why have wind turbine farms become popular in West Texas?

5. What type of wind turbine can save energy for a household?

6. Which countries were the top three users of wind energy in 2009?

C **Word Builder** **Complete the definitions.**

1. A **hybrid** car _____uses two sources_____ of power.

2. **Green** energy is _____ energy.

3. A **wind farm** is _____ wind turbines.

4. Households **consume**, or _____, a lot of energy.

5. **Opponents** of wind energy are people who _____ wind energy.

6. **Advocates** of wind energy are _____ of the energy choice.

D **Read the sentences.** Write *pro* or *con*.

1. Windmills send no pollutants into the air. _____

2. Wind energy does not generate harmful emissions. _____

3. Wind energy may harm birds. _____

4. Wind turbine generators are noisy. _____

5. A wind turbine is no louder than a refrigerator. _____

6. Wind turbine engines may lower housing prices in a neighborhood. _____

A Read.

Business and Industry in Japan

Hideo Tokuda

April 2010

English IV

I am from Tokyo, Japan. Tokyo is located in the eastern part of Japan on Honshu, the largest of the four islands in Japan. Tokyo is also the capital city. Japan is an island. It is bordered by the Pacific Ocean to the east, the Sea of Japan to the west, and the China Sea to the southwest. Because much of Japan is mountainous, the Japanese people live in a small area of the country. Japan has a very large

population of 127,078,679 (2009), and we need to import many products, such as wood and natural gas, because many natural resources are not found in my country.

Rice is an important product for Japanese people. Rice is grown in many parts of Japan. Many vegetables, including sugar beets and radishes, and fruit, such as apples, are grown on Japanese farms. Fishing is also a large industry. In fact, Japan supplies about 15 percent of the world's fish.

Japan is best known for its automobiles and electronics. Three of the largest automobile companies in the world are Japanese. Japan is also known for its consumer electronics. For example, televisions, game consoles, and DVD players are manufactured by Japanese companies. Look in your home. How many Japanese-made electronics can you find?

WRITING NOTE

For example, such as, including

For example, such as, and **including** introduce examples, but they are used in different ways. Note the punctuation and placement of the transitions in the examples.

Many minerals, **such as** copper and iron ore, can be found in my country.
Many industries are in trouble right now. **For example,** two steel plants have laid off workers.
Tourists can visit a number of famous places in Japan, **including** Kyoto and Mt. Fuji.

B Complete the sentences with examples.

1. Dye houses dye the T-shirts a variety of colors, such as _____ and _____.

2. T-shirts are sold at discounted prices at many stores, including _____, _____, and _____.

3. There are many countries represented in my class. For example, there are students from _____, _____, and _____.

4. My country has natural resources, including _____ and _____.

5. Agricultural products, such as _____ and _____, are grown in my country.

C In your notebook, draw a map of your native country. Show the bordering countries. Then, add products and natural resources.

D Write a composition about your native country's industry and products. Use the questions to guide you.

1. What city and country are you from? Where is it located?

2. What are three major products that are produced in your country?

3. What are the major industries or businesses in your country?

4. What natural resources are found in your country?

E Sharing Our Stories Exchange papers with a partner. Answer the questions.

1. What city and country is your partner from?

2. What are three products that are produced in your partner's country?

3. What natural resources does your partner's country have?

F Find and correct the mistakes.

1. Coffee is grow in South and Central America.

2. Italy is bordering by Switzerland, France, Austria, and Slovenia.

3. After the cotton picked, it is sent to the ginner.

4. France and Italy is known for their fashions.

5. Dairy cows raise by farmers.

6. My country locates near an ocean.

A **Look at the map.** Complete the sentences using verbs in the box.

build
design
make
manufacture
produce
raise

1. Watches _____ in Switzerland.

2. Automobiles _____ in _____.

3. Glass and crystal _____.

4. Ships _____.

5. Footwear _____.

6. Sheep _____.

B **In your notebook, write three more sentences about the map.**

C **Write questions and answers about the product map.**

1. (watches) <u>Where are watches designed and manufactured?</u>

   <u>They're designed and manufactured in Switzerland.</u>

2. (software) _____

   _____

3. (textiles) _____

   _____

 A **Working Together** **Work in a group of three or four students.** Choose a state to research.

B **Go online.** Find information about the state you chose. Draw a map of the state in the space below. Mark the places and location of products on your map.

1. Put a star next to the state capital.

2. Label the bordering states.

3. Label three major cities.

4. Label the largest airport in the state.

5. Write three agricultural products that are grown in the state.

6. Write three major industries that are operated in the state.

 **C** **Working Together** **Present your research to your classmates.**

Technology: Yesterday and Today

 A **Listen.** Write the year that each item was invented.

CD3·TR5

1. an insulin pump
Dean Kamen, *1960s*

2. an anti-shoplifting device
Arthur Minasy, _____

3. video games
Ralph Baer, _____

4. a compact fluorescent bulb
Ed Hammer, _____

5. an artificial heart
Robert Jarvik, _____

6. the hepatitis B vaccine
Baruch Blumberg, _____

7. a space shuttle
NASA, _____

8. a laptop computer
Sir Clive Sinclair, _____

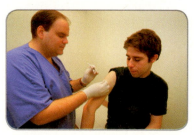

9. a personal human transpor
Dean Kamen, _____

Subject	Be	Past Participle	
The space shuttle	was	completed	in 1981.
		invented	by NASA.
747 jumbo jets	were	developed	in 1970.
		designed	by Boeing.

A **Complete the information.** Use the present or past form of the passive. Use the past or the present tense.

1. The first anti-shoplifting device (invent) _____was invented_____ by a consultant for the New York City Police Department, Arthur Minasy. These tags (attach) _____ to store merchandise. When a customer bought the item, the tag (remove) _____. The tag set off an alarm if a customer walked through the door without paying. The tags (use) _____ in many department stores today.

2. The first compact fluorescent bulb (invent) _____ by a General Electric engineer named Ed Hammer. Hammer (assign) _____ to develop more energy-efficient bulbs in the mid-70s, when there was an energy crisis in the U.S. Hammer worked for years. Finally in 1976, the compact fluorescent bulb shape (create) _____. General Electric didn't sell the bulb at first because of production costs. Then, the design (discover) _____ by other designers and it (copy) _____ by other companies. Today, the bulbs (sell) _____ in all stores.

B **Answer the questions.** Use the past form of the passive.

1. When was the first artificial heart invented?

2. Why was it invented?

3. By whom was the artificial heart invented?

4. When was the hepatitis B vaccine developed?

5. Why was the fluorescent bulb created?

6. When was the first space shuttle launched?

7. Which organization was the shuttle developed by?

A **Read the paragraph.** Underline the passive verbs. Circle the active verbs.

The automobile <u>was developed</u> before 1900, and cars were already used in Europe on a limited basis. In the United States, Henry Ford (developed) a more affordable car in 1908 called the Model T. The first moving assembly line was installed in his factory in 1913. This reduced the cost and time of producing a car. A Model T was assembled in 93 minutes and cost $850. By 1927, more than fifteen million cars were on the roads in the United States.

B Circle *A* for active or *P* for passive.

1.	The first cars didn't have windshield wipers.	A	P
2.	People got out of their cars to clean their windshields.	A	P
3.	The first windshield wipers were invented by Mary Anderson.	A	P
4.	They were operated from the inside of the car.	A	P
5.	The electronic ignition system was invented by Kettering and Coleman.	A	P
6.	Before this, people turned a crank to start their engines.	A	P
7.	Before 1929, people could not listen to the radio in their cars.	A	P
8.	The first car radio was designed by Paul Galvin.	A	P
9.	The radio was not installed at the automobile factory.	A	P
10.	Car owners took their cars to a separate company for radio installation.	A	P
11.	Turn signals were invented by Buick in 1938.	A	P
12.	Before this, people used their hands to signal a turn.	A	P

C **Talk about each advance in car and traffic technology.** Use the chart below. What did people do before each item was invented?

> The electronic ignition system was invented by Charles Kettering and Clyde Coleman in 1911. Before that, people turned a crank by hand in order to start their cars.

WORD PARTNERSHIPS

parking	lot
	meter
	place
	spot

Invention	Inventor	Year
1. windshield wipers	Mary Anderson	1903
2. automatic traffic signal	Garrett Morgan	1923
3. car radio	Paul Galvin	1929
4. parking meter	Carlton Cole Magee	1932
5. turn signals	Buick	1938
6. air-conditioning	Packard	1939
7. air bags	General Motors	1973

D **Complete the sentences.** Use the passive voice.

1. One of the first automatic traffic signals (develop) ___*was developed*___ by Garrett Morgan.

2. Before this, many people (kill) _____ in traffic accidents.

3. Three positions (feature) _____ on this device: Go, Stop, and All-Direction Stop. The All-Direction Stop allowed pedestrians to cross safely.

4. Morgan's device (use) _____ until today's system of red, yellow, and green lights was invented.

5. The first parking meters (install) _____ in Oklahoma City.

6. They (meet) _____ with resistance by drivers.

7. Several of the first parking meters (destroy) _____ by angry citizens.

8. The air bag (invent) _____ by General Motors.

9. Air bags (offer) _____ as an option in the 1973 Chevys.

10. For more than ten years, air bags (consider – *negative*) _____ important by drivers. Now they are standard equipment.

In early times, the medicine man cured people.

In early times, people were cured **by the medicine man**.

Many years ago, hospitals did not sterilize equipment.

Many years ago, equipment was not sterilized.

Use *by* when the subject of the action is important or is not obvious.

A **Rewrite the sentences.** Use the passive voice. Use *by* when necessary.

1. The Romans began the first hospitals.

   The first hospitals were begun by the Romans.

2. Today, doctors and hospitals sterilize all equipment.

   Today, all equipment is sterilized.

3. Sir Alexander Fleming discovered penicillin in 1928.

   _____

4. Bernard Fantus established the first blood bank in the United States in 1937.

   _____

5. Ian McDonald invented ultrasound in 1958.

   _____

6. Sound waves create pictures of internal organs.

   _____

7. The Federal Drug Administration (FDA) approved the hepatitis B vaccine in 1981.

   _____

8. Most colleges require students to have the hepatitis B vaccine.

   _____

9. Doctors performed the first laser surgery to correct vision in 1987.

   _____

10. Doctors perform many operations on an outpatient basis.

   _____

B **Pronunciation: Compound Nouns** **Listen and repeat.**

1. **saf**ety razor
2. **air** conditioner
3. **lie** detector
4. **mi**crowave oven
5. **ball**point pen

6. **park**ing meter
7. **con**tact lenses
8. **seat** belt
9. **la**ser printer
10. **cell** phone

> The first word receives more stress than the second word.

 C **Working Together** **List nine inventions you can see or find in your classroom or in your bag.** Then, answer the questions about each invention.

1. _____
2. _____
3. _____

4. _____
5. _____
6. _____

7. _____
8. _____
9. _____

1. What is the name of the invention?

2. How many years ago do you think it was invented?

3. What is it made of?

4. What is it used for?

5. What did people use before we had this invention?

> This is called "liquid paper." I think it was invented about 20 years ago. I don't know what it's made of. It is used for covering up mistakes on paper. Before this was invented, people used special erasers and special paper.

D **Listen and answer the questions.**

1. Where was Hui-Fen educated?

2. What were some of the rules in her school?

3. How were students punished if they did not do their homework?

4. When were students allowed to date?

5. What language is spoken at home in Taiwan? In what language are students educated?

6. When is school closed?

7. What other information do you remember about Hui-Fen's education?

 E **Interview a partner from another country (if possible).**

1. When were you born? Where were you born?

2. Where were you raised?

3. Were you educated in private school or in public school?

4. Were you involved in any after-school sports or activities?

5. Were you required to wear a uniform?

6. Were you allowed to date?

7. When was school closed for vacations?

8. What languages were taught?

9. Were students expected to stand when they answered a question?

10. How many hours of homework were you assigned?

11. How often were exams given?

F **Write two things about your education and your partner's education that were similar.** Then, write two things that were different.

Similarities	Differences
1.	1.
2.	2.

  G **In a group of three or more students, talk about your partner's education.** Your original partner must be in a different group.

The Passive: Other Tenses

Tense	Passive Form
Simple present	Air bags **are installed** in all cars.
Present continuous	Those cars **are being repaired**.
Simple past	Air bags **were** first **installed** in 1973.
Past continuous	My car **was being repaired** while I was waiting.
Future with *will*	A new model **will be delivered** tomorrow.
Future with *be going to*	That car **is going to be inspected** tomorrow.
Present perfect	Many improvements **have been made** to today's cars.

> All passives have a form of the verb *to be*.

A **Complete the sentences.** Use the passive with the correct tense.

1. The tallest building in the world (build) _____ **was built** _____ in Dubai.

2. A memorial (install) _____ in downtown Manhattan in the future.

3. I believe that future cars (manufacture) _____ with solar panels.

4. Many diabetics' lives (change) _____ since the invention of the insulin pump.

5. When (the book / write) _____?

6. An AIDS vaccine (research) _____ now.

7. 3D movies (already / produce) _____ for theaters.

8. When _____ TVs with 3D technology (sell) _____ at the price of other TVs?

9. Some inventions (discover) _____ by mistake.

10. The traffic signal (repair) _____, so a police officer was directing traffic.

CD3·TR8

A **Listen as you look at the pictures of shopping technology.**

CD3·TR8

B **Listen again.** Then, complete the chart.

Invention	Date	How did the invention help people?
1. catalogs		
2. a cash register		
3. a shopping cart		
4. a credit card		
5. a bar code (U.P.C.)		
6. online shopping		

C Match each statement with an invention from the chart on page 186.

1. Before this invention, all receipts were handwritten. __2__

2. This invention was invented in 1973. _____

3. With this advance in technology, it's easy to compare prices. _____

4. This idea was developed by a traveling salesman. _____

5. This invention was designed by a grocery store owner. _____

6. This advance was first used by business travelers. _____

D Read the questions. Then, listen again and answer the questions.

CD3·TR8

1. Why was a traveling salesman necessary?

2. How did Ward travel?

3. How did his idea help his customers?

4. Where did store owners keep their money before 1884?

5. How did the cash register make shopping simpler?

6. Why did customers need shopping carts?

7. Who were the first credit card users?

8. What invention do supermarket clerks use?

9. How does the bar code make supermarket clerks' jobs easier?

10. How does online shopping save customers money?

E Complete the sentences. Use the active or passive.

1. The first mail-order catalog (print) _____ in 1872. Customers (look) _____ through the catalog and (order) _____ the items they wanted.

2. Before 1950, customers (pay) _____ for their purchases with cash or by check. The first credit cards (issue) _____ to business travelers. With a credit card, people (*negative* - need) _____ to carry a lot of cash.

3. The first U.P.C. scanner (install) _____ in a supermarket in Ohio. Today, supermarket clerks simply (scan) _____ each item. The price (appear) _____ on their cash register's screen.

A **Discuss.**

1. Do you own a cell phone? Is it hand-held or hands-free?

2. Does your state have any laws about the use of cell phones when driving?

B **Word Builder** **Match.**

<u> c </u> **1.** controversy   **a.** not permitted by law

<u>   </u> **2.** relationship   **b.** the time it takes to react

<u>   </u> **3.** banned   **c.** disagreement or argument

<u>   </u> **4.** evidence   **d.** to limit; to control

<u>   </u> **5.** distraction   **e.** a connection or association

<u>   </u> **6.** response time   **f.** facts that prove something is true

<u>   </u> **7.** to restrict   **g.** something that causes a person to lose concentration

> ### READING NOTE
>
> **Reading Long Passages**
>
> As you read a long passage, it is a good idea to summarize each paragraph. This will help you remember what you have read.
>
> **Example**
>
> Summary of Paragraph 1: More people are using cell phones than ever before, and this has created controversy.

C **Read.**

Cell phone technology was developed during the 1970s and 1980s. It was not until the 1990s, however, that cell phones came into everyday use. In 1995, 24 percent of adults in the United States reported that they owned a cell phone. By 2009, that number was 89 percent. This little invention has produced a major **controversy**. What is the **relationship** between hand-held phones and car accidents? Some people think that hand-held phones are responsible for car accidents. Do you know the law for cell phone usage in your area?

In June 2001, the governor of the state of New York signed the first law in the United States that **banned** the use of hand-held phones by drivers. Violators are now fined $180 for a violation. New York followed the example set by other countries. The use of cell phones by drivers is banned in Portugal and India. In several other countries, including Germany and Spain, drivers are required to use hands-free sets. Many countries are beginning to add text messaging to this law.

Some people in the cell phone industry are trying to fight these laws. They say that there is not enough **evidence** to prove that only cell phone usage causes accidents. A study by the American Automobile Association (AAA) said that other distractions, such as eating or applying makeup, are more serious.

Other studies show that cell phone use contributes to accidents. According to the National Highway Traffic Safety Administration (NHTSA), in 2008, almost 6,000 people were killed and half a million were injured due to drivers who were **distracted** by cell phones. Men and women under the age of 20 were the most frequent offenders.

A study at the University of Utah showed that all cell phone use in cars is a distraction. Sixty-four drivers were asked to perform simple tasks, such as changing a radio station, listening to music, talking on a hands-free cell phone, and talking on a hand-held cell phone. Then, researchers measured their **response time** when they were braking or stopping a car. When people were using a cell phone, their responses were much slower. This was true of both hands-free phones and hand-held phones.

What can drivers expect in the future? More laws will be passed to **restrict** the use of hand-held cell phones, especially text messaging. Manufacturers will continue to encourage cell phone safety in their instructions. Some auto companies have already installed voice-activated dialing services in their new models. You can be sure that companies are busy inventing technology for safer ways to use cell phones.

D (Circle) *True* or *False.*

1. The U.S. was the first country to enact cell phone restrictions.   True   False

2. The American Automobile Association said that using a hand-held phone is more distracting than eating in a car.   True   False

3. The NHTSA reported that young people were most often caught using cell phones while driving.   True   False

4. A study at the University of Utah showed that hands-free cell phones are safer than hand-held cell phones.   True   False

5. Response time slowed down when drivers used cell phones.   True   False

6. According to the reading, auto companies have begun installing voice-activated dialing services.   True   False

E **Complete the sentences.** Use words from Exercise B.

1. Television is a _____ for children when they are doing homework.

2. The museum _____ the use of cell phones. Visitors must go outside to make phone calls.

3. What is the _____ between drinking and driving?

4. After the accident, the parents decided to _____ their daughter's driving privileges. She can only drive during the day with an adult in the car.

5. The _____ shows that the car's brakes failed.

6. There is an ongoing _____ about how to spend taxes.

A **Read the letter from a customer to a restaurant owner.**

25 Glen Street
Tampa, Florida 33661
March 17

Dear Mr. Lombardi:

Please consider a ban on cell phones at your restaurant. This past Friday evening, my husband and I were enjoying dinner at your restaurant when a woman at the next table received a call. Her loud conversation continued for ten minutes. My husband and I were looking forward to a relaxing evening, a good dinner, and quiet conversation. We didn't pay $47.00 to listen to another customer's personal problems.

Please follow the example of several other restaurants in the city that have posted signs, "Cell phone usage limited to emergencies only."

Sincerely,

Teresa Santiago

Teresa Santiago

WRITING NOTE

A Letter Expressing Your Opinion

1. Put your address at the top on the left side.
2. Begin with *Dear* [name of official / *Sir* or *Madam*]
3. State your problem. Be clear. State your reasons for your complaint.
4. End with *Sincerely*.
5. Sign your name.
6. Print your name clearly underneath your signature.

B **Work with a partner.** Write the reasons under the correct heading. Add one more reason under each heading.

> **a.** Drivers need two hands on the wheel.
>
> **b.** Drivers spend hours in traffic. Talking to friends passes the time.
>
> **c.** There are not enough studies to prove that drivers using hand-held cell phones cause more accidents.
>
> **d.** A person who is talking on the phone is not concentrating on the road.

Drivers should be allowed to use hand-held cell phones:

1. b, _____

2. c, _____

3. _____

Drivers should not be allowed to use hand-held cell phones:

1. a, _____

2. d, _____

3. _____

C **Write a letter to your mayor.** Express *your* opinion.

Your city is considering a ban on using cell phones in cars and in restaurants.

1. Give your opinion in the first sentence, and then give two or three reasons.

2. End your letter according to the Writing Note.

D **Sharing Our Stories** **Exchange papers with a partner.** Answer the questions.

1. What is your partner's opinion?

2. What are your partner's reasons for his / her opinion?

E **Find and correct the mistakes.**

1. The accident was ~~causing~~ *caused* by a driver talking on a cell phone.

2. The driver distracted when her cell phone rang.

3. Yesterday I was seen an accident.

4. Olivia's parents were bought her a headset for her cell phone.

5. The man at the next table talking on his cell phone.

6. She was gave a ticket for driving while using a cell phone.

A **Complete the article.** Use the active or passive and the correct verb tense.

Heart disease is the number one cause of death in the United States. For years, doctors have been developing tests, medications, and procedures to help patients with heart disease. In the most serious cases, a heart transplant (require) _____.
₁

On December 3, 1967, Dr. Christiaan Barnard (perform) _____ ₂ the first heart transplant in Cape Town, South Africa. The heart of an auto accident victim (transplant) _____ into the body of Louis ₃ Washkansky, a 55-year-old man. He (live) _____ for 18 days ₄ following the operation.

Since that day, over fifteen thousand heart transplants have been performed. The major difficulty in these procedures (be) _____ the ₅ rejection of the new heart by the recipient's immune system. In 1969, an anti-rejection drug, cyclosporine, (discover) _____ by Jean- ₆ Francois Borel. Today, heart transplants (perform) _____ ₇ throughout the world.

The first artificial heart (implant) _____ in Dr. Barney ₈ Clark in 1982. This mechanical heart (attach) _____ by ₉ tubes and wires to a large machine. The heart (name) _____ ₁₀ the Jarvik-7 after its inventor, Dr. Robert Jarvik. Dr. Clark (live) _____ for 112 days. The next patient survived for 620 days, ₁₁ but research with the new heart (discontinue) _____. ₁₂

Since then, there (be) _____ many medical advances. ₁₃ A French professor and leading heart transplant specialist, Alain F. Carpentier, (test) _____ a new type of artificial heart in the near future. ₁₄ It (develop) _____ by Dr. Carpentier and (manufacture) ₁₅ _____ by him along with two other companies. ₁₆

B **In your notebook, write seven questions about the article.**

A **Working Together** **Work in a group of three or four students.** Match the problem in each picture with a solution below.

1. _____

2. _____

3. _____

She's been in the shower for half an hour.

4. _____

5. _____

6. _____

a. Take short showers of four to five minutes.

b. Install a programmable thermostat.

c. Use compact fluorescent light bulbs.

d. Plug TVs, DVD players, and other electronics into power strips.

e. Buy energy-efficient appliances. Look for the Energy Star label.

f. Wash full loads of clothes.

Compact fluorescent light bulb

 B **Interview a partner about saving energy at home.** Check (✓) *Yes* or *No*.

Questions	Yes	No
1. Do you have a programmable thermostat?		
2. Do you only wash full loads of laundry?		
3. Do you unplug your TV and other electronics when you are not using them?		
4. Do you take short showers?		
5. If you have a computer, is it plugged into a power strip?		
6. Do you have energy-efficient windows?		

Music

A **Match the musicians with the kind of music.**

classical	hip-hop	pop	R&B (rhythm and blues)
country	jazz	rap	rock
heavy metal	opera	~~reggae~~	salsa

1. Bob Marley
reggae

2. Taylor Swift

3. Celia Cruz

4. Beyoncé

5. The Black Eyed Peas

6. Green Day

 B **Discuss.**

1. What's your favorite kind of music?

2. Who is your favorite singer or band?

> An adjective clause describes or gives information about a noun. Adjective clauses begin with relative pronouns, such as **who, whom, which,** and **whose.**
>
> **who** – replaces a subject (person)
> The student **who is sitting next to me** plays in a rock band.
> **which** – replaces a subject or object (thing)
> I just saw the movie *Crazy Heart*, **which has good music**.
> **whom** – replaces an object
> He's writing a song for his son, **whom he named after his father**.
> **whose** – replaces a possessive form
> This is the singer **whose song you just heard**.

A **Underline** the adjective clauses. (Circle) the relative pronoun and draw an arrow to the noun it modifies.

1. Celine Dion, (who) was born in Quebec, Canada, grew up in a musical family.

2. Dion performed with her family, who toured Canada, when she was a child.

3. When Dion was twelve, she and her mother sent a demo tape, which was later heard by a producer.

4. Her first English-language album was *Unison*, which she recorded in 1990.

5. In 1992, Dion, whose career was steadily building, recorded the theme to the movie *Beauty and the Beast*.

6. In 1994, Dion married her manager, whose second marriage ended in divorce.

7. In 2001, Dion and her husband had a son, whom they named Rene-Charles.

8. In 2003, Dion began a series of performances at Las Vegas's Caesar's Palace, which negotiated a 36-month contract.

B **Look at the picture.** Complete the adjective clauses.

1. The girl who _____ is sitting in the front _____ is saying, "How many shows have you seen?"

2. The couple who _____ is saying, "This is our tenth show."

3. The woman who _____ is saying, "I'm your biggest fan."

4. The woman who _____ is signing autographs.

5. The woman who _____ is taking a picture of her friend.

6. The woman who _____ is saying, "I only bought a few souvenirs."

C **In your notebook, write five sentences about your classmates.**

The student _____ who is sitting next to the window _____ is from
_____.
    name of country

D **Answer the questions about you and your classmates.**

1. Who do you sit next to in class? _____

2. How long have you been in this country? _____

3. Who has a difficult work schedule? _____

4. Who has long hair? _____

5. Who often listens to music before class begins? _____

E **Working Together** **Work with a group of three or four students.** Complete the sentences. Use the information from Exercise D.

> Sung Kul, **who is in a band**, is from Korea.
> Beata, **whom I sit next to**, is from Poland.

1. _____, who ___sits next to me___,
   _{name of student}

   is from _____.
   _{native country}

2. _____, whom _____,
   _{name of student}

   is from _____.
   _{native country}

3. _____, who _____,
   _{name of student}

   is from _____.
   _{native country}

4. _____, whose _____,
   _{name of student}

   is from _____.
   _{native country}

5. _____, who _____,
   _{name of student}

   is from _____.
   _{native country}

F **In your notebook, write five more sentences about your classmates.** Use adjective clauses that begin with *who*, *whom*, *which*, or *whose*.

To introduce an adjective clause, the relative pronoun *that* can be used instead of *who, which,* or *whom*.

Use *that* only with **restrictive adjective clauses**. A **restrictive clause** identifies the noun it describes.

Restrictive clause:	We paid the man **whom we hired to sing at our wedding**. *or* We paid the man **that we hired to sing at our wedding**.
Meaning:	The adjective clause is necessary to understand who "the man" is.
Note:	No commas are necessary with restrictive clauses.

Don't use *that* with **non-restrictive adjective clauses**. A **non-restrictive clause** gives extra information about the noun it describes.

Non-restrictive clause:	We paid Dave Jones, **whom we hired to sing at our wedding**.
Incorrect:	We paid Dave Jones, **that we hired to sing at our wedding**.
Meaning:	We know who Dave Jones is. The adjective clause gives extra information about Dave Jones.
Note:	Use a comma to separate a non-restrictive adjective clause.

A **Rewrite the sentences.** Use *that* where possible. Write *X* if no change is possible.

1. The Black Eyed Peas is a group which sings hip-hop.

   The Black Eyed Peas is a group that sings hip-hop.

2. *Elephunk* is the 2003 album which sold more than any other hip-hop album.

   _____.

3. Green Day, whose band sold 15 million copies worldwide, started in Berkeley, California.

   _____.

4. Taylor Swift, who has already won multiple awards, has a long career ahead of her.

   _____.

5. Beyoncé used to sing with a group which was named Destiny's Child.

   _____.

6. Jay-Z performed in two videos with a singer whom he married in 2008.

   _____.

CD3·TR9

B **Listen.** Then, answer the questions with a partner.

1. What is the grandson listening to?

2. What are the grandmother and grandson talking about?

3. What did the grandmother listen to when she was younger?

4. What was inconvenient about 45s and LPs?

5. What is the grandson glad about?

6. What did some people think about LPs?

7. What does the grandmother have in the basement?

8. What are they going to do next?

9. Have you ever listened to 45s or LPs?

C **Write each adjective clause in the correct sentence.**

that holds digital audio files
~~that holds computer data~~
that plays 45s and LPs
that you insert into your ears
that has a small hole in the middle and plays multiple songs on both sides
that has a large hole in the middle and plays one song on each side

1. A CD is a small disk _that holds computer data_____.

2. An MP3 player is a device _____.

3. Earphones are devices _____.

4. An LP is a record _____.

5. A 45 is a record _____.

6. A turntable or record player is a machine _____.

Adjective clauses can also begin with *when* and *where*.

Tim McGraw has appeared in a movie each year since **2004**, **when** *he appeared in his first movie.*

Faith Hill was born in **Mississippi**, **where** *she grew up singing in church.*

A Complete the sentences about country singer Tim McGraw.

a. Tim McGraw was born in Delhi, Louisiana.

b. He went to Nashville, Tennessee, in the early '90s to start a recording career.

c. In 1995, McGraw had a hit album.

d. He went on tour in 1996 and performed with Faith Hill.

e. McGraw and Hill married in October 1996.

f. McGraw and Hill's first child was born in 1997.

g. The couple recorded a duet in 1998.

1. ____Delhi, Louisiana____ is the town where _____.

2. He went to _____, where he _____.

3. _____ was the year when McGraw _____.

4. In _____, when _____, he met his future wife,
   country performer Faith Hill.

5. _____ is the month when McGraw and Hill _____.

6. _____ is the year when their _____.

7. 1998 is the year when _____.

B Complete the sentences.

1. _____ is the place where I grew up.

2. I attend _____, where I study _____.

3. _____ is the year when I _____.

Your musical preferences

A **Complete the sentences about your musical preferences.**

1. _____ is my favorite musician.

2. _____ is my favorite type of music.

3. _____ is my favorite musical group.

4. _____ is my favorite American singer.

5. _____ is my favorite radio station.

6. _____ is my favorite place to go dancing.

B **Rewrite your preferences from Exercise A.** Then, discuss your preferences with a partner.

1. _____, who is my favorite musician, is from _____.

name of musician   name of country

2. _____, which is popular in _____, is my

type of music   name of country

favorite type of music.

3. _____, which is my favorite musical group, plays

name of group

_____.

type of music

4. _____, whose music is _____, is my favorite

        adjective

American singer.

5. _____, which is at _____ FM/AM, is my

letters of radio station   numbers

favorite radio station.

6. _____, which is located in _____, is my

name of club   name of city

favorite place to go dancing.

C **Complete the questions.** Then, ask a partner the questions.

> Do you know a music store where I can buy some country music?

> Yes, I do. You should try the CD Den. It's on Broad Street.

1. Do you know a music store where _____?

2. Do you know a movie theater where _____?

3. Do you know a dance club where _____?

4. Do you know a restaurant where _____?

5. Do you know a supermarket where _____?

6. Do you know an auto repair shop where _____?

A **Discuss.**

1. Look at the picture. Have you ever heard these instruments?

2. What state is labeled on the map? What do you know about this state?

3. What countries make up the British Isles?

CD3·TR10

B **Listen to the history of country music.** Then, circle *True* or *False*.

1. Today's country music was originated by immigrants from the British Isles.   True   False

2. The people from Appalachia sang all the time.   True   False

3. People sang to make their work go more slowly.   True   False

4. Country music, which the Appalachians sang, was very complicated.   True   False

5. The banjo, which became popular among country musicians, came from South America.   True   False

6. The fiddle was the main instrument of country music.   True   False

7. The first superstars of country music recorded in 1947.   True   False

8. Jimmy Rodgers and the Carter Family, who sang country music, became the first superstars of country music.   True   False

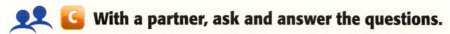

C With a partner, ask and answer the questions.

1. How long ago did the country sound appear in the Appalachian Mountains?

2. What countries did the music come from?

3. Why did the immigrants choose the United States?

4. What kind of banjo did country musicians use?

5. When did the fiddle stop being the main instrument in country music?

6. Which musician played the melody of the songs?

7. Besides the banjo and the fiddle, what other instruments are used in country music?

8. What year did Jimmy Rodgers and the Carter Family first record?

D Complete the sentences. Use a relative pronoun from the box.

that	who	which	whom	whose

1. The music, ____which____ is called country music, came from the British Isles.

2. The people _____ immigrated to this country moved to a land similar to their native land.

3. Today's country music began in the Appalachian Mountains, _____ extend from the northeast to the south.

4. The music, _____ was very simple, was sung all the time.

5. The immigrants, _____ came from the British Isles, brought their music with them.

6. The fiddler, _____ instrument was country music's main instrument until the 1930s, made people dance.

7. The fiddler, _____ the community considered a very important part of the music, was necessary in every band.

8. The banjo, _____ came from Africa, had five strings and was used to play a different kind of music.

9. Jimmy Rodgers and the Carter Family, _____ a Virginia record company first recorded, were the earliest superstars of country music.

A **Discuss.** Then, read.

1. Find New Orleans on the map.

2. What kind of music is New Orleans famous for?

3. Look at the photo. What kind of music do you think they are playing?

READING NOTE

Understanding Word Forms

When you study vocabulary, it is important to learn different word forms so that you can use the words correctly.

Noun	Adjective
culture	cultural
music	musical
popularity	popular

The history of New Orleans is different from many other U.S. cities. The city was founded in 1718 by the French. Then, the city was governed by the Spanish. In 1803, Louisiana territories were again controlled by France, and then France sold the territories to the United States. This transaction was called the Louisiana Purchase.

New Orleans began as a French-speaking **culture** with a love of good food, wine, music, and dancing. Later, Africans, some free and some slaves, came to the city. Many of them came through the Caribbean and brought West Indian culture with them. After that, African Americans and Creoles, who were a mix of French and African cultures, brought another cultural and **musical** mix to the city.

The beginnings of jazz were in the African American communities, but jazz was also influenced by the ethnic variety of New Orleans. Bands led by brass instruments, such as trumpets and trombones, participated in many community events like parades and even funerals. People in the neighborhoods joined the parades and funeral processions and danced along. **Music** was a part of every event.

During the end of the 19th century, some **musicians** began to do something called improvising. As they played, they began to change the music and play what they liked along with the other musicians. This was also a time when the Creoles and black musicians began to combine their styles. Jelly Roll Morton (1890–1941) was one of the musicians that became a well-known composer and piano player. His compositions spread the **popularity** of jazz.

Jazz began to spread to other cities when job opportunities opened in the north. Jazz was especially **popular** in clubs in Chicago and New York City. This also meant that jazz began to change from the original sounds that were in New Orleans.

During the 1920s, Louis Armstrong (1901–1971) developed his style as a solo artist. His recordings with his bands made him an international star.

In 1961, Preservation Hall opened in the French Quarter. It was a place for experienced and new musicians to perform and try to **preserve** traditional jazz, which had to compete with rock and modern jazz.

After Hurricane Katrina hit New Orleans in 2005, many musicians were displaced. Homes were destroyed, and much of the population had to leave the city. Since that time, charitable organizations have donated money, instruments, furniture, homes, and more to aid musicians in rebuilding the musical culture in New Orleans.

B Complete the sentences.

1. _____ was the first country to govern New Orleans.

2. Examples of brass instruments are trumpets and _____.

3. Music was played at _____ processions and parades.

4. Creole is a mix of _____ and African cultures.

5. _____ means that a musician makes original changes to the music while he is playing.

6. Chicago and _____ were popular places for jazz musicians.

7. _____ became an international star.

8. At Preservation Hall, the musicians want to _____ traditional jazz.

9. Musicians have received _____ from charitable organizations since Hurricane Katrina.

C Word Builder (Circle) the correct answers.

1. The **culture / cultural** of New Orleans is different from other U.S. cities.

2. New Orleans has a rich **music / musical** culture.

3. Traditional jazz had to compete with **popularity / popular** rock and modern jazz.

4. One **culture / cultural** tradition in New Orleans is the funeral procession.

5. Jelly Roll Morton helped spread the **popularity / popular** of jazz.

6. The different ethnic groups helped build a different **music / musical** form.

A **Read Armin's time line of his life in the United States.**

Time Line

July 1993	came to the United States
Aug. 1993	began to promote soccer games in local parks
Jan. 1995	enrolled in English class
Aug. 1995	bought 10,000 phone cards to sell
Sept. 1995	started selling phone cards
Oct. 1995	quit the promotion business
Nov. 1995	became a successful phone-card salesman
July 1996	opened a business as a distributor
July 1998	entered a partnership with phone-card makers
Now	has a very successful business

B **Read Armin's autobiography.**

In July 1993, I immigrated to the United States with my wife and children. I didn't have any business contacts here, but in my country I used to be a promoter. I tried to continue the same business here.

Soccer was popular among the immigrants here, so I began to promote soccer games in the local parks. I arranged for closed-circuit TV broadcasts of the games because people were very interested in soccer games, especially professional games between South American teams.

In 1995, a friend of mine told me about phone cards. I offered to sell them for him even though I didn't know anything about phone cards. I was a good salesman and sold more and more cards because I had confidence in myself. In October, the promotion business, which was not very stable, was finished. Sometimes I had no work for two months, so I decided to quit the promotion business in August. I concentrated on selling phone cards. I bought 10,000 cards, which I sold in a short time. In November 1995, my sales were excellent and business was strong, so I decided to become a phone-card distributor.

In July 1996, I opened an office as a phone-card distributor. Many people wanted to sell phone cards, so business grew quickly. Two years later, I was able to form a partnership with phone-card makers. Today, I have two offices and a very successful distribution business, which sells cards in over 5,000 stores.

C **Make a time line.** Choose six to ten significant events in your life. Write the year and a phrase about the event on a time line.

D **In your notebook, write your autobiography.** Use the information in your time line. Try to use a few adjective clauses in your story. Before you turn in your paper, check for run-on sentences.

 E **Sharing Our Stories** **Exchange papers with a partner.** Answer the questions about your partner's paper.

1. When did your partner come to this country?

2. What significant events did your partner describe?

3. What events interested you the most?

F **Find and correct the mistakes.**

1. The singer ~~who his~~ *whose* music I like has written many hit songs.

2. Placido Domingo was a famous tenor whose know worldwide.

3. Faith Hill, whom is married to another country singer, is one of the most popular female country singers.

4. The Beatles toured all over the United States and they went to New York City, and they were very popular.

5. Jeff Bridges performed many of the songs in his movie, who was named *Crazy Heart*.

6. Celine Dion spent three years performing in Las Vegas, her performances regularly sold out.

7. The person who performing there has always been my favorite singer.

A Circle the correct relative pronouns.

1. Nashville, **who /** (**which**) **/ where** is located in Tennessee, is known as Music City.

2. For many years, the headquarters of country music has been Nashville, **when / where / which** many of the singers live.

3. Two music producers, Owen Bradley and Chet Atkins, created the Nashville Sound, **whom / which / where** was a more popular and sophisticated sound.

4. Chet Atkins, **whom / who / which** is the most recorded solo artist, built a billion-dollar business and recording center.

5. Hip-hop, **who / that / which** originated in New York City, is a combination of music, fashion, and culture.

6. Hip-hop culture became a way of expression for teenagers **where / that / whom** were looking for a way out of violence and drugs.

7. Celia Cruz, **whom / which / who** was known as the "Queen of Salsa," won three Grammy awards and four Latin Grammys.

B In your notebook, combine each pair of sentences into one longer sentence with an adjective clause. Use *that, who, whose, which, whom, where,* or *when.*

1. Johnny Cash was one of the most famous country singers. Johnny Cash almost always wore black. *Johnny Cash, who almost always wore black, was one of the most famous country singers.*

2. John Lennon was successful after leaving the Beatles. His wife, Yoko Ono, sang with him.

3. Disco music was popularized in the late 1970s. In the late 1970s, the movie *Saturday Night Fever* was a big hit.

4. Placido Domingo was a famous tenor. Many other artists performed with him.

5. On September 11, 2009, Jay-Z had a concert in New York City. The concert benefited the New York Police and Fire Widows and Children Charity Fund.

6. On June 4, 2004, the city of Union City, New Jersey, dedicated a park to the salsa singer Celia Cruz. Many Cuban refugees live in Union City.

A **Working Together** **Go online.** Work with a partner. Search for a U.S. musical performer. Put the name in quotation marks (" ") and type "bio" in the search area. Find out the following information:

1. What is the performer's original or given name?

2. Where was the performer born?

3. Did this person grow up in a musical family? Describe the family.

4. What kind of music is the performer known for?

5. How did the person get started in a music career?

6. When did the person get a recording contract?

7. What is the name of the performer's first hit song?

8. Find three more interesting facts about the performer.

WORD PARTNERSHIPS	
a hit	song
a popular	

B **Read the suggestions for making a presentation.**

1. Show a picture of your performer.

2. Go online and find a song or excerpt (piece) of a song that you can play for the class.

3. Before your presentation, check the pronunciation of any new words with your teacher.

4. Practice your presentation. Time yourself.

 C **Working Together** **Prepare a five- to seven-minute presentation about the performer.** Present your information to the class.

Student 1: Present the information in 1–4 of Exercise A.

Student 2: Present the information in 5–8 of Exercise A.

Unit 14 Let's Get Organized

A **Look at the picture.** Answer the questions.

1. Does an organized desk indicate an organized person?

2. What can you infer about the person who works at this desk?

3. Is your desk (or room) organized or disorganized?

B **Do you know exactly where these items are in your home?** Circle *Yes* or *No*. Then, compare your answers with a partner.

1.	postage stamps	Yes	No	7. checkbook	Yes	No
2.	scissors	Yes	No	8. car title	Yes	No
3.	pencil sharpener	Yes	No	9. address book	Yes	No
4.	aspirin	Yes	No	10. Social Security card	Yes	No
5.	passport	Yes	No	11. birth certificate	Yes	No
6.	rental agreement or deed	Yes	No	12. last test paper	Yes	No

There are many verbs that require the infinitive form (*to* + base verb). Gradually, you'll learn the list.

I **plan** *to attend* college in the fall.
He **promised** *to babysit* for his cousin tonight.

Use an infinitive after the following verbs:

(be) able	forget	manage	remember
afford	hate	need	seem
agree	hope	offer	try
ask	intend	plan	volunteer
choose	know how	prefer	wait
decide	learn (how)	prepare	want
expect	like	promise	wish
fail	love	refuse	would like

A **Complete the sentences about yourself.**

1. I would like to _____ next year.

2. I plan to _____.

3. I need to _____.

4. I want to _____.

5. I have decided to _____.

6. I will try to _____ next year.

7. I know how to _____.

8. I expect to _____.

B **Ask your teacher these questions.**

1. Why did you decide to become a teacher?

2. Do you know how to speak another language?

3. Would you like to learn my first language?

4. Do you want to teach English in another country?

5. Where would you like to travel?

6. In addition to teaching, what else do you like to do?

7. Do you know how to cook any ethnic foods?

8. Would you agree to end class early today?

CD3·TR11

A **Listen and read.** Then, discuss.

Are You a Procrastinator?

Everyone has plans and goals. Some plans are short-term and can be accomplished in a few hours or on a weekend: I'm going to wash the car. I plan to organize my closet. I want to gather all my photos from the past five years and put them in a photo album. I need to study for the test next week. I plan to start an exercise program. Some goals are far in the future and will take years to accomplish: I expect to get my nursing degree. I want to start my own business. Do you find yourself making plans but not accomplishing them? Is it difficult to take the first step? Is it impossible to find the time? Could you be a procrastinator? A procrastinator waits for the last minute. A procrastinator believes, "There is always tomorrow."

CD3·TR12

B **Listen.** Answer the questions about Scott's plans.

1. When did Scott plan to paint the kitchen?

2. Why didn't he paint the kitchen?

3. When does he plan to paint the kitchen?

4. Who did he intend to call?

5. Why didn't he make the call?

6. When is he going to make the call?

7. What did he promise to do with his daughter?

8. Why didn't he help his daughter?

9. When is he going to help his daughter?

10. How much was he supposed to read?

11. When does he need to finish the assignment?

12. Why does he need to finish the assignment?

🔊 CD3•TR13

C **Listen and read.** Then, discuss.

It's hard to get started on your plans. It's easy to make excuses! Once you start on a goal, there are always distractions. You sit down to work at the computer, but first you check your e-mail, and then you start to chat with friends. Or, you are supposed to write a paper for class, but a friend calls and wants to go to the mall with you. Or, you sit down to type your paper, and you realize that it's time for your favorite TV show.

D **Write your top three distractions.**

Example: _____the telephone_____

1. _____ 2. _____ 3. _____

E **Work with a partner.** Write excuses for not doing your homework. Use the verbs in the box.

| had to | forgot to | didn't know how to | needed to | promised to |

1. I didn't do my homework because I had to . . . _____

2. _____

3. _____

4. _____

5. _____

F **Working Together** Student to Student.

Student 1: Turn to page 266. Read **Set A** sentences to Student 2.

Student 2: Listen to Student 1 and write the sentences you hear.

Then change roles. Student 2, turn to page 266. Read **Set B** sentences. Student 1, write the sentences you hear.

1. _____

2. _____

3. _____

4. _____

5. _____

Many verbs require an object or an object pronoun.

Use an **object + the infinitive form** after the following verbs:

advise	encourage	hire	remind	urge
allow	expect	invite	require	want
ask	forbid	permit	teach	warn
convince	help	persuade	tell	

My mother **asked _me_ to clean** my room.

The teacher **expected _us_ not to arrive late**.

A **Advice for Paul.** Restate each comment using an infinitive.

1. His teacher said, "Turn in your report on time." (expect)

2. His teacher said, "Don't hand in your report late." (tell)

3. His teacher said, "Buy a notebook and organize your papers." (advise)

4. His mother said, "Get up earlier." (urge)

5. His sister said, "Buy a wall calendar for your bedroom." (tell)

6. His boss said, "Don't be late for work again." (warn)

7. His father said, "Don't talk on your cell phone when you study." (remind)

8. His grandmother said, "Let's clean up your room." (help)

His teacher expected him to turn in his report on time.

His teacher told him not to hand in his report late.

 B **Working Together Complete the sentences about Manika and her family.** She is starting college, and her parents are about to leave. Use your imagination.

1. Manika's family helped her to _____.

2. Manika's father is telling her to _____.

3. Manika's mother advised her to _____.

4. Her mother is reminding her to _____.

5. Her parents allowed her to _____.

6. Manika's sister asked her to _____.

7. Manika's sister doesn't want Manika to _____.

8. Manika's parents expect her to _____.

C Write your to-do list for today or tomorrow. Number the items in order of importance. Look at a partner's list. Do you think your partner will complete everything?

D Work with a partner. Complete the sentences.

1. Gloria got a speeding ticket in another state. She doesn't want to pay the fine. She believes that she only needs to pay a ticket for the state she lives in.

   a. Her friend _told her not to pay the ticket_ .

   b. Her brother convinced _her to sign the ticket and send in the fine_ .

2. Your brother lost his credit card.

   a. You advised _____ .

   b. The bank expects _____ .

3. John has begun to hang around with a group of troublemakers. Two of them have dropped out of school and two have been in trouble with the law.

   a. His parents have forbidden _____ .

   b. The baseball coach has invited _____ .

4. Ella was accepted to college, but she doesn't have enough money for tuition.

   a. Her parents have persuaded _____ .

   b. Her high school counselor advised _____ .

Use the infinitive form *after* these adjectives:				
dangerous	good	important	polite	selfish
difficult	hard	impossible	possible	stressful
easy	healthy	interesting	reasonable	terrible
expensive	helpful	necessary	romantic	wonderful

A **Listen and read.** Then, discuss. Underline the adjectives. Circle the infinitives.

CD3·TR14

It's <u>important</u> (to make) a schedule of your day, and it's <u>necessary</u> (to schedule) your study time. It's <u>easy</u> (to say,) "I'll get it done sometime today." It's more <u>helpful</u> (to make) an appointment with yourself. If <u>possible</u>, find a time that is the most productive for you. What is your most productive time (to do) your schoolwork? Maybe it is immediately after class or as soon as you get home.

B **Pronunciation: Stressed Syllables** **Listen and mark the stressed syllables.**

CD3·TR15

1. dán · ger · ous
2. i · de · a · lis · tic
3. im · pos · si · ble
4. in · ter · est · ing
5. po · lite

6. rea · son · a · ble
7. re · a · lis · tic
8. ro · man · tic
9. stress · ful
10. thought · ful

C **Work with a partner.** Make sentences about your daily lives. Then, say the sentences to each other.

> It's difficult to find time to exercise.

It's difficult It's impossible It's stressful	to	work and go to school. find time to exercise. stick to a schedule. get to class on time. keep my school papers in order. get enough sleep. find time for myself.

D **In your notebook, write your sentences from Exercise C.**

E **Give suggestions for staying organized.** Use the adjectives in the box.

> easy   helpful   important   necessary

1. file your important papers
2. check your appointment calendar daily
3. make a to-do list
4. hang a calendar in your kitchen or bedroom
5. plan your day
6. schedule your study time
7. organize your desk
8. post notes on your desk to help you remember things

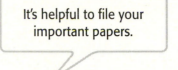
It's helpful to file your important papers.

 F **Give two more suggestions to a partner for organizing your day.**

 G **Working Together** **Look at Ali's list of weekend homework assignments.** Ali likes to study in the morning. With a group of classmates, plan his study time. Write the assignments in the chart. Does Ali have enough time to complete all his work?

Grammar workbook – pages 153–156

Read article about Elvis (two pages)

Go to library and research a musician

Write a composition about a popular musician

Study infinitives for quiz on Monday

Saturday	Sunday
9:00	9:00
10:00	10:00
11:00	11:00

A **Look at the picture.** Then, discuss.

1. Diana is supposed to be studying. Is her bedroom a good place to study?

2. What do you think her father is going to say?

CD3·TR16
B **Listen to Diana's telephone conversations.** In your notebook, take notes about her phone calls. Who called? What did each person want?

CD3·TR16
C **Listen again.** (Circle) *True* or *False*.

1. Susan was able to stop and talk with Diana.	True	False
2. Susan has to study for the math test.	True	False
3. Diana's father expects her to do well in school.	True	False
4. Diana called Jake at his job.	True	False
5. Jake needs to write his lab report.	True	False
6. He plans to see Diana later tonight.	True	False
7. Alex is at school now.	True	False
8. Alex asked her to join his study group.	True	False
9. Katie invited Diana to go to the mall.	True	False
10. Diana decided to stay home and study.	True	False

D **Listen again.** Then, complete the sentences. Use the infinitive form.

Susan

1. Susan isn't able _to talk on the phone now_____.

2. She needs _____.

3. She promised _____.

Dad

4. He expects _____.

5. He reminded _____.

Jake

6. He plans _____.

7. He encouraged _____.

Alex

8. He asked _____.

9. He volunteered _____.

10. They agreed _____.

Katie

11. She invited _____.

12. Diana decided _____.

  E **Diana failed the math test.** Her mother asked her some questions. With a partner, ask the questions and give Diana's answers.

1. Why / agree / go to the mall?

2. When / plan / talk to your teacher?

3. How many hours / plan / study every night?

4. When / expect / organize your room?

5. need / quit your job?

6. expect / pass this course?

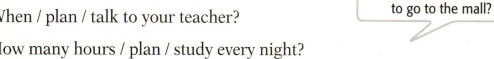

Why did you agree to go to the mall?

  F **Work with a partner.** In your notebook, write a conversation between Diana and her mother. Diana is upset about the test, and her mother is giving her advice.

A Circle the techniques you use when you study English. Add one more.

1. I make lists and charts.

2. I look at the book.

3. I use an English study site on the Internet.

4. I study with a partner.

5. I try to read the newspaper.

6. I listen to a CD.

7. I repeat the sentences in the book aloud.

8. _____

_____

READING NOTE

Active Reading

When you read, try to be active. Take notes in the margins. Use a highlighter to mark new vocabulary. Write questions that you can ask the teacher about the reading.

B **Read.**

It is helpful to become an active student outside of class. These students are all "active learners." How do they approach learning?

. . . .

Because I**'m pressed for time**, I have to plan carefully to find study time. One of the only places I have **downtime** is in my car. After we study a unit, I record ten or fifteen sentences from the book on a CD. I listen to the CD and memorize the sentences as I sit in traffic. I'm sure that other drivers think I'm crazy!

Richard

. . . .

For me, it's important to have a study partner. When I'm taking a new class, I look for a person who is serious about studying. After class, we meet in the library and review the material we studied in class. For example, I ask my partner the questions we practiced in class, and she answers them. Then, we switch roles. When we learned the past participles, we gave each other quizzes. I think this is the best way to study because my grammar has already **improved**.

Marjorie

. . . .

I take work with me wherever I go. I don't have a lot of time, so I study when I can. Reading is my most difficult subject, so I use index cards to make flash cards of new vocabulary. I also use index cards to take notes on the book I'm reading. Then, when I have a break at work, I review the cards. It's a very **convenient** way to study.

Mary Ann

Country music is my ticket to English. Country music is easy to understand because the songs tell a story. I listen to Carrie Underwood and other popular country singers. I often find the **lyrics** online so I can understand the words and sing along. Sometimes I ask an American student to help me **figure out** the words.

Alex

C (Circle) *True* or *False*.

1. Richard has sufficient time to study.		True	False
2. Richard memorizes songs in his car.		True	False
3. Marjorie studies with a classmate.		True	False
4. Marjorie likes to work with a serious student.		True	False
5. Mary Ann has trouble with reading and vocabulary.		True	False
6. Mary Ann thinks index cards are a difficult way to study.		True	False
7. Alex thinks country music is challenging to understand.		True	False
8. Alex gets help from American students.		True	False

D **Word Builder** **Match the boldfaced words with their definitions.**

___d___ **1.** I'm **pressed for time**.　　　　**a.** understand

_____ **2.** I have **downtime** in my car.　　**b.** words

_____ **3.** My grammar has already **improved**.　　**c.** gotten better

_____ **4.** It's a very **convenient** way to study.　　**d.** very busy

_____ **5.** I sing along with the **lyrics**.　　**e.** free time

_____ **6.** She can help me to **figure out** the words.　　**f.** easy

E **Complete the sentences.** Use words from the box.

pressed for time	downtime	lyrics	convenient	improved	figure out

1. I like to read the _____ of songs. It helps me to learn vocabulary.

2. It's _____ to listen to English CDs in my car.

3. I haven't been able to _____ how to do this math problem.

4. When I'm _____, I do at least one homework assignment.

5. During my _____, I take out my cards and study.

6. My English has _____ since I began studying with a partner.

Let's Get Organized · **221**

Read.

I think I have good study habits. My study area is a large table in the corner of my bedroom. There's a large desk lamp in the corner. On the left side of my desk is my laptop. The printer is in back of the computer. Above the desk, attached to the wall, is a long, narrow shelf, about six inches wide. It holds envelopes, a pencil sharpener, a small clock, a jar with pens and pencils — everything I need — all in easy reach. To the right of my desk is a small bookcase for my books, notebooks, and papers. I keep a large calendar over my desk for my work schedule and appointments. I'm glad I have such a good place to study!

I like to study in the evening from 7:00 to 9:30. I always do my writing first because it's my least favorite assignment. When I'm finished with my writing, I relax a little and start my reading assignments. I leave my grammar and vocabulary for last because that is the easiest homework for me.

It's difficult to study after 9:30 because I share my bedroom with my older sister. When she gets home from work, she likes to watch TV in the bedroom or talk on the phone with her boyfriend. That's the time that I go online and chat with my friends. Study time is over.

B **Underline the prepositional phrases of location in the paragraphs above.**
Then, describe the locations in the picture below.

1. The MP3 player is _____.

2. The cell phone is _____.

3. There's a cup of coffee _____.

4. _____ is a photo of his girlfriend.

5. The laptop computer is _____.

6. There is a bottle of water _____.

7. The wastebasket _____ is overflowing.

C Write a composition about your study area and study time.

1. Draw a picture of your study area. It could be your kitchen table, a desk in your bedroom, or the school library.

2. Look at the picture. Does it include everything you use? Where are your books, your pencils, your dictionary, your backpack or bag? What other items are in the picture?

3. Carefully write a description of your study area. Details add interest. Describe the locations.

4. Write about how you organize your study time.

D Sharing Our Stories Exchange papers with a partner. Answer the questions.

1. Where does your partner study? _____

2. What subject does your partner like to study first? _____

3. What time does your partner study? _____

E Find and correct the mistakes.

1. I like *to* study at the kitchen table.

2. It's difficult find time to study.

3. My mother told he to be home by 12:00.

4. Is impossible to complete all this homework.

5. She promised to helped me.

6. My father encouraged my sister did her best.

7. The teacher urged to us to use the computer lab.

8. My grandfather offered to paid my tuition.

WORD PARTNERSHIPS	
a place to	eat
	relax
	study

A **Write questions.** Give answers about your weekend plans.

1. How many hours / need to study?

A: <u>How many hours do you need to study this weekend?</u>

B: _____

2. Where / plan / go?

A: _____

B: _____

3. Who / expect / visit?

A: _____

B: _____

4. What movie / would like / see?

A: _____

B: _____

5. What / hope / do?

A: _____

B: _____

B **Rewrite each sentence.** Use the verb in parentheses. You will need to change the wording in some of the sentences.

1. Luis's parents said, "We know you will do well in college." (expect)
   <u>Luis's parents expect him to do well in college.</u>

2. Laura's father said, "Take art lessons." (encourage)

   _____

3. My brother said, "Become an engineer." (tell)

   _____

4. My high school counselor said, "Apply for a scholarship." (advise)

   _____

5. My friend said, "Don't turn in your paper late." (warn)

   _____

 **A Working Together Work in a group of three or four students.** Complete the chart about your study areas.

Name	Where do you study?	Is it quiet?	Is it comfortable?	Is it free of distractions?	Is there good lighting?

B Read.

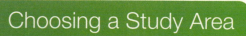

"What is a good place to study?"

1. A good place to study is quiet.

2. A good place to study is comfortable. You should have a comfortable chair. Beds and sofas are not good places to sit while studying.

3. A good place to study has space for your books and computer and a place for you to write.

4. A good place to study is free of distractions. Turn off your cell phone. Do not sit in front of a window. Do not study in front of your computer, where you might want to chat with friends.

5. A good place to study has good lighting. Use a desk lamp or a ceiling light. It is a good idea to study in a room with a window for natural light, but don't study in front of the window.

6. A good place to study has easy access to study materials, such as highlighter markers, pens, pencils, a pencil sharpener, an eraser, and a dictionary.

7. A good place to study is free of unnecessary materials, such as magazines, MP3 players, or bills.

 C Working Together Look at the chart in Exercise A. How can you improve each person's study area?

Unit 15  Becoming a Citizen

A **Discuss.**

1. Are you a United States citizen? Is anyone in your family a citizen?

2. What are the benefits of becoming a citizen?

3. What are the responsibilities of being a citizen?

B **Listen to Marco and Luciana's story about becoming United States citizens.**

CD3·TR17

1.

2.

3.

4.

5.

6.

The Naturalization Process

1. Fill out the application.

2. Send the application, three photographs, and copies of requested documents and check(s) to your regional United States Citizenship and Immigration Service (USCIS) office. Send your letter via certified mail.

3. Send copies of your fingerprints.

4. Go for your interview and English test.

5. Take the Oath of Allegiance to the United States at your swearing-in ceremony.

WORD PARTNERSHIPS	
file	an application an extension a tax return
fill out	an application a check a form

Use a *gerund* form (base verb form + *ing*) after the following verbs:

admit	consider	enjoy	miss	regret
anticipate	continue	finish	postpone	resent
appreciate	delay	hate	practice	start
avoid	discuss	imagine	quit	stop
begin	dislike	like	recall	suggest
can't help	doesn't / don't mind	love	recommend	understand
can't stand				

They **missed** *seeing* their family during the holiday season.
She **regretted not** *working* with people who spoke English.

CD3·TR18

A **Listen.** Complete each sentence with the gerund you hear.

1. Marco and Luciana discussed _____ citizens.

2. They delayed _____ the process because Luciana's English was not strong.

3. Luciana regretted _____ English classes earlier.

4. She began _____ English at a local adult school.

5. A friend recommended _____ in a citizenship class.

6. They didn't mind _____ class one night a week.

7. Marco and Luciana enjoyed _____ about U.S. history.

8. They practiced _____ one another questions.

9. Luciana couldn't help _____ nervous before the test.

10. They enjoyed _____ with their friends after the ceremony.

B **Say the sentences aloud.** Use the gerund form.

> People usually discuss *leaving* their countries for many years before making a final decision.

1. People usually discuss (leave) their countries for many years before making a final decision.

2. They all anticipate (have) a better life for their children.

3. New immigrants can't help (worry) about money and work.

4. Some immigrants begin (study) English soon after they arrive.

5. Other students postpone (enroll) in English classes.

6. Many new immigrants start (work) in low-paying jobs.

7. Older immigrants recommend (find) friends and activities in the United States.

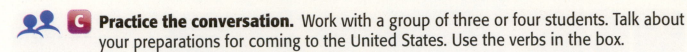 **C** **Practice the conversation.** Work with a group of three or four students. Talk about your preparations for coming to the United States. Use the verbs in the box.

A: I began learning English before I came here. How about you?

B: No, I didn't study English. I regret not taking classes before I left.

A: I continued working until a few days before I left.

B: Me, too. I couldn't stop working.

anticipate	discuss	recall	start
begin	finish	regret	stop
continue	quit	remember	

 **D** **What do you like about the United States?** What don't you like? Write two or three items in each column.

like / enjoy	don't mind	dislike / don't like	can't stand

 E **Working Together** **Work in a group of three or four students.** Compare your information from Exercise D.

A: I **can't stand** *wearing* a heavy winter coat, hat, and gloves.

B: Why?

A: I come from a tropical country. I **don't like** *wearing* heavy clothing.

Preposition + Gerund

Use a gerund (base verb + *ing*) after the following prepositions:

after   before   besides   by   in addition to   instead of   while   without

After *studying* for the naturalization test, she easily passed the test.

A **Restate the sentences.** Use a gerund.

> Before applying for citizenship, I lived here for ten years.

1. Before I **applied** for citizenship, I lived here for ten years.
2. After I **obtained** the application for naturalization, I had my fingerprints taken.
3. After I **filled out** the application, I wrote the check.
4. Before I **sent** in the paperwork, I needed to include three photographs.
5. After I **sent** in the papers, I waited a long time.
6. While I **waited**, I studied for the naturalization test.
7. Before I **took** the Oath of Allegiance, I had an interview.
8. After I **took** the Oath of Allegiance, I became a citizen.

B **Look at Paul's activities from 1998 to 2010.** Complete the sentences.

1998 – applied for a visa
2001 – received his visa
2002 – arrived in the United States
2003 – began to study English; worked as a taxi driver
2005 – found a job at an auto body repair garage
2007 – applied for citizenship
2008 – became a citizen
2010 – married girlfriend; opened his own garage

1. After ____waiting____ for three years, Paul ____received____ a visa.
2. After _____ his visa, Paul _____ to the United States.
3. Instead of _____ English in Poland, Paul waited until he _____ to the United States.
4. While _____ as a taxi driver, Paul _____ English.
5. After _____ a taxi for two years, Paul _____ a new job.
6. After _____ his girlfriend, Paul _____ his own garage.

Use a gerund (base verb + *ing*) after the following verb and preposition phrases:

adjust to	complain about	give up	succeed in
approve of	count on	insist on	talk about
argue about	depend on	keep on	think about
believe in	dream about	look forward to	warn about
care about	forget about	plan on	worry about

Use a gerund (base verb + *ing*) after the following *be* + adjective and preposition phrases:

be afraid of	be good at	be interested in	be tired of
be capable of	be guilty of	be opposed to	be upset about
be famous for	be in favor of	be proud of	

 A **Complete the sentences.** Then, read your sentences to a partner.

Before coming to the United States, ...

1. I dreamed about _____.

2. I planned on _____.

3. I looked forward to _____.

4. I worried about _____.

5. I was interested in _____.

After coming to the United States, ...

6. I am proud of _____.

7. I have adjusted to _____.

8. I often complain about _____.

9. I think about _____.

10. I'm tired of _____.

B **Pronunciation: Linking** **Listen to the conversation.** Then, practice the conversation with a partner.

> When a word begins with a vowel, link it with the word before.
>
> I **plan‿on** working full time.　　　He's **good‿at** fixing things.

A: I thought life here was going to be easy. I just can't‿adjust to living here. I miss seeing my family.

B: You'll‿always miss them. I plan‿on visiting my family once‿a year.

A: And, I'm afraid‿of losing my job if‿I leave.

B: Yesterday you were complaining‿about working so much‿overtime!

A: I gave‿up working‿at my family's business to come here.

B: You didn't like working there anyway. And you plan‿on‿opening your own business some day, don't you?

A: You're right, but I'm tired‿of listening to English‿all day! I'm thinking‿of going back to Korea.

B: You've‿only been here for nine months. Everybody feels like‿you at first. Concentrate‿on learning‿English and making‿a few friends.

C **Work with a partner and give your opinion and reasons for your opinion.** Use the phrases in the box.

I agree with	I approve of	I'm not in favor of
I'm in favor of	I disagree with / I don't agree with	I'm against

1. Limit new immigration

2. Require English only in government offices

3. Issue national identity cards

4. Prohibit the sale of automatic weapons

5. Increase the tax on cigarettes

6. Build fences on the Mexican and Canadian borders

7. Raise the retirement age

D **With a partner, name two more controversial issues in your city, state, or nation.** Give your opinion about the issues.

Active Grammar

Contrast: Infinitives and Gerunds

> It was **impossible** *to find* a job in my country.
>
> My friends **didn't encourage** me *to speak* English.
>
> He **enjoyed** *working* at the real estate office.
>
> **After** *working* for a few years at the factory, I found another job.

A **Complete the sentences.** Use the gerund or the infinitive form of the verb in parentheses.

1. It was impossible (find) __to find__ a job in my country.

2. I have missed (see) __seeing__ my family and friends.

3. I intend (visit) _____ my native country next year.

4. I expect my cousin (arrive) _____ soon.

5. Have you ever considered (become) _____ a citizen?

6. How long do you plan on (stay) _____ in this country?

7. He is capable of (learn) _____ another language.

8. My parents appreciated (receive) _____ a check from me each month.

9. She's proud of (start) _____ her own business.

10. My sister promised (e-mail) _____ me often.

11. Besides (have) _____ difficulty finding a job when I first arrived, I didn't like (live) _____ with my uncle.

12. Carlos enjoys (read) _____ books about U.S. history.

13. My uncle refused (change) _____ his long name when he came here.

14. Sometimes I regret (come) _____ to this country.

15. My cousin complains about (wear) _____ heavy winter clothes.

16. In addition to (sponsor) _____ his sister, Andre is supporting his parents.

B **Ask and answer the questions with a partner or in a small group.**

1. When do you anticipate finishing your English studies?

2. Why did you decide to come to the United States?

3. Have you ever considered becoming a citizen?

4. What have you missed doing since you came here?

5. What do you enjoy doing in this country?

6. What do you advise new immigrants to bring with them?

CD3·TR20

C **Listen.** An immigrant is talking about citizenship. Write the questions. Then, ask and answer the questions with a partner.

1. why / they / decide / come / to the United States?

   Why did they decide to come to the United States?

   Because of the job opportunities.

2. what / be / their families / worried about?

   _____

   _____

3. who / help / them / find an apartment?

   _____

   _____

4. what / be / Martin / good at?

   _____

   _____

5. what / he / design?

   _____

   _____

6. what / they / can afford / do?

   _____

   _____

7. what / they / appreciate / have?

   _____

   _____

8. what / he / would like / do?

   _____

   _____

A Discuss.

1. Look at the pictures. Who is running for political office?

2. What are the people doing?

 B **Listen.** Then, retell the story about the local political campaign.

CD3·TR21

CD3·TR21

C **Listen again and** (circle) *True* **or** *False***.**

1. Manuel is a U.S. citizen.		True	False
2. Manuel has always been involved in politics.		True	False
3. Manuel votes in every election.		True	False
4. Manuel and John are good friends.		True	False
5. Manuel's and John's families enjoy spending time together.		True	False
6. John owns a bookstore and community computer center.		True	False
7. John hires senior citizens for his bookstore.		True	False
8. John is running for mayor.		True	False

D **Complete the sentences.**

donate	have	set	spend
give	organize	~~shake~~	work

1. John complained about ____shaking____ hands.

2. John is looking forward to _____ interviews.

3. Andrea is good at _____ people.

4. Their friends have been talking about _____ a voter-registration drive.

5. They're thinking about _____ up tables at the supermarkets.

6. They are not worried about _____ too much money.

7. John's friends have insisted on _____ services.

8. Kathy quit _____ to help with her husband's campaign.

E **Ask and answer the questions about the story with a partner.**
Use the names in the box. Use different verb tenses.

1. who / enjoy / spend time together

2. who / interested in / work on the campaign

3. who / quit / work

4. who / interested in / make signs

5. who / insist on / donate services

6. who / like / help John practice for the debate

7. who / enjoy / stuff envelopes

> Who enjoys spending time together?

> The families do.

Manuel
Kathy
everyone
friends
the children
the families

A **Discuss.**

1. Do you know anyone who has taken the Naturalization Test?

2. What is the best way to prepare for the test?

CULTURE NOTE

The Naturalization Test is required for anyone who wants to become a U.S. citizen. An USCIS examiner asks a citizenship applicant a group of questions from a list of 100 questions. The questions are about U.S. history and government.

READING NOTE

Multiple-Choice Test Strategies

Before taking a multiple-choice test, remember to:

1. Read the directions first. Ask the teacher or test examiner questions if you do not understand something.

2. Read the question carefully.

3. Read all of the answers. Try to eliminate wrong answers.

4. Select your answer. Fill in the circle next to your answer.

5. Watch the time. If you have limited time, make sure you know how much time is left. You may have to work more quickly.

B **Read the Naturalization Test sample questions.** Fill in the circle next to the correct answer.

1. What do the stars on the flag mean?
   - ○ **a.** There is one star for each one hundred citizens.
   - ○ **b.** There is one star for each citizen.
   - ● **c.** There is one star for each state of the union.
   - ○ **d.** There is one star for each president.

2. How many states are there in the United States?
   - ○ **a.** 48
   - ○ **b.** 49
   - ○ **c.** 50
   - ○ **d.** 51

3. When is Independence Day?
   - ○ **a.** January 1st
   - ○ **b.** July 4th
   - ○ **c.** September 1st
   - ○ **d.** November 25th

4. What do the thirteen stripes on the flag represent?
   - ○ **a.** The first thirteen presidents
   - ○ **b.** The original thirteen colonies
   - ○ **c.** The first thirteen days of the country
   - ○ **d.** Thirteen laws

5. From which country did the United States fight to win independence?

    ○ **a.** Ireland   ○ **c.** France

    ○ **b.** Germany   ○ **d.** Great Britain

6. Who was the first president of the United States?

    ○ **a.** Abraham Lincoln   ○ **c.** George Washington

    ○ **b.** John Adams   ○ **d.** Benjamin Franklin

7. Who becomes the president of the United States if the president dies?

    ○ **a.** the Secretary of State   ○ **c.** the First Lady

    ○ **b.** the Secretary of Defense   ○ **d.** the Vice President

8. Who makes the laws in the United States?

    ○ **a.** judges   ○ **c.** the president

    ○ **b.** congress   ○ **d.** the governors

9. Who was president during the Civil War?

    ○ **a.** Abraham Lincoln   ○ **c.** Richard Nixon

    ○ **b.** George Washington   ○ **d.** Franklin D. Roosevelt

10. What is the 50th state of the union?

    ○ **a.** Alaska   ○ **c.** Puerto Rico

    ○ **b.** Hawaii   ○ **d.** Florida

11. Who was the president during the Great Depression and World War II?

    ○ **a.** Franklin D. Roosevelt   ○ **c.** John F. Kennedy

    ○ **b.** Thomas Jefferson   ○ **d.** Dwight Eisenhower

12. In what month do we vote for the president?

    ○ **a.** January   ○ **c.** July

    ○ **b.** April   ○ **d.** November

13. Which state borders Canada?

    ○ **a.** Montana   ○ **c.** Tennessee

    ○ **b.** Arizona   ○ **d.** North Carolina

14. What movement tried to end racial discrimination?

    ○ **a.** the Boston Tea Party

    ○ **b.** the Vietnam War protests

    ○ **c.** the Civil Rights Movement

    ○ **d.** the Women's Suffrage Movement

Check your answers below.

1. c 2. c 3. b 4. b 5. d 6. c 7. d 8. b 9. a 10. b 11. a
12. d 13. a 14. c

A Read the two political platforms. Which person would you vote for? Why?

> I believe in improving our community by attracting development to our town. I'm in favor of lowering taxes in order to attract much-needed new businesses, including the new paint factory, to our town. Our town must begin building the factory right away. We need new jobs for our citizens. I'm opposed to building a new library. We already have a library. The new library can wait, but jobs can't. In addition to creating jobs, I'm in favor of increasing parking meter fees to fifty cents per half hour. I manage a successful business, and the downtown areas need income to improve parking and the sidewalks. I have fifteen years of experience on the town council. You can count on me to serve you.
>
> Douglas McMurphy

> It's time for a change. The citizens of this town are used to hearing the same promises. They're tired of seeing heavy traffic and breathing factory pollution. They miss having peace and quiet in their community. We don't need more development. Instead of building a paint factory, we should start building a new library. As a former high school teacher and member of the Board of Education, I'm proud of the improvements we've made in educating our children. More students are applying to college than ever before. Imagine having a place where adults and children can enjoy reading, using free computer facilities, and listening to authors read from their books. A vote for me is a vote for education in a livable community.
>
> Angela Luisa Velez

B Imagine you're a candidate for the town council. In your notebook, write your opinion of (1) the new factory, (2) the new library, and (3) the increase of parking meter fees to fifty cents per half hour. Choose one other issue to discuss. Use the phrases in the box.

> be opposed to   be in favor of   believe in

C (Circle) **Fragment** or **Correct.**

1. After the airplane landed.   Fragment   Correct

2. He regrets not studying English before.   Fragment   Correct

3. When I considered leaving my country.   Fragment   Correct

4. Because I needed to learn English.   Fragment   Correct

5. I dislike taking the bus instead of driving myself.   Fragment   Correct

6. Is easy to learn English.   Fragment   Correct

D **Before you turn in your paper, check for sentence fragments.**

 E **Sharing Our Stories** **Exchange your papers from Exercise B with a partner.** (Circle) **the answers.**

1. My partner is **opposed to / in favor of** the new factory.

2. My partner is **opposed to / in favor of** the new library.

3. My partner is **opposed to / in favor of** the parking increases.

F **Find and correct the mistakes.**

1. The mayor isn't interested in ~~run~~ *running* for another term.

2. The students have finished to read two novels.

3. Because I haven't registered to vote yet.

4. I'm tired of walk in the snow.

5. I've missed see my family.

6. The council is opposed building a new parking garage.

7. When I arrived in this country.

8. My daughter can't stand wears heavy winter clothes.

A **Complete each sentence.** Use the gerund form of the verb.

1. Before (register) _____registering_____ for classes, she has to complete an application.

2. She can't stand (wait) _____ in long lines to register.

3. She has postponed (look) _____ for a job until she knows her class schedule.

4. She is going to buy her textbooks after (attend) _____ her first class.

5. After she begins (study) _____, she will have more confidence.

6. She liked (go) _____ to class and (meet) _____ new people.

7. She has missed (see) _____ her family, so she started (send) _____ them e-mails every other day.

8. In class, she practices (speak) _____, (read) _____, and (write) _____.

9. She believes in (work) _____ as hard as possible to achieve her goals.

10. After (study) _____ for a year, she will be ready to enroll in an accounting degree program.

B **Complete the sentences with the gerund or infinitive form.**

1. After (arrive) _____ in this country, Pierre lived with his brother.

2. He didn't mind (take) _____ care of his nieces and nephews.

3. He didn't know how (speak) _____ much English, but he could read.

4. His brother persuaded him (enroll) _____ in English classes.

5. Instead of (work) _____ full time, he decided (take) _____ a part-time job at his brother's company.

6. He has enjoyed (study) _____ and he is a good student.

7. He has been trying (speak) _____ as much English as possible.

8. He hopes (finish) _____ his English classes in a year.

CULTURE NOTE

To become a U.S. citizen, you must show that you understand basic English. During your Naturalization Test:

1. You must read one or more sentences and show that you understand the meaning.

2. You must write one of three sentences, and the testing officer must be able to understand your writing.

3. You must answer questions about your application.

4. You must answer six out of ten questions about the U.S. government correctly. The testing officer will ask the questions.

CD3·TR22

A **Listen and write the questions.** Then, match each question with the correct answer.

_____ f ____ 1. What is the Bill of Rights _____ ?   **a.** The president

_____ 2. _____ ?   **b.** George Washington

_____ 3. _____ ?   **c.** Congress

_____ 4. _____ ?   **d.** Four years

_____ 5. _____ ?   **e.** Eighteen years of age

_____ 6. _____ ?   **f.** The first ten amendments of the Constitution

_____ 7. _____ ?

_____ 8. _____ ?   **g.** Freedom of speech

h. 100

B **Working Together** **Work with a small group of students.** Answer the questions.

1. Who is the president of the United States? _____

2. Who is the vice president of the United States? _____

3. Who is your state's governor? _____

4. What is the capital of your state? _____

5. Who is one of your state senators? _____

C **Go online.** Find information on the naturalization process. Try to find a practice test. Enter "naturalization test" or "how to become a citizen" in the search box. Do the practice activities.

Grammar Summary

Unit 1

Simple Present Tense

STATEMENTS

Subject	Verb	
I	**study**	
You	**do not study**	
They	**don't study**	English.
He	**studies**	
She	**does not study**	
	doesn't study	

> **Note:**
> Use the present tense to describe everyday activities, habits, and repeated actions.

YES / NO QUESTIONS

Do/Does	Subject	Verb
Do	I	
	you	**work**?
	they	**study** in the library?
Does	she	**walk** to school?
	he	

SHORT ANSWERS

Yes, you **do**.	No, you **don't**.
Yes, I **do**.	No, I **don't**.
Yes, they **do**.	No, they **don't**.
Yes, she **does**.	No, she **doesn't**.
Yes, he **does**.	No, he **doesn't**.

> **Note:**
> Use the auxiliaries *do* and *does* to form present tense questions. Do not change the main verb.

WH- QUESTIONS

Question Word	Do/Does	Subject	Verb
What		I	
Where	**do**	you	
Why		they	**study**?
How	**does**	she	
How often		he	

WHO QUESTIONS

Who	Verb with -s	
	studies	English?
Who	**goes**	to work?
	lives	close to school?

> **Notes:**
> 1. *Who* asks about the subject.
>
> 2. *Who* takes a singular verb. The answer may be singular or plural.
> **Who** studies English?   Joe **does**.
> **Who** goes to work?   Joe and Sara **do**.

242 · Grammar Summary

Present Continuous Tense

STATEMENTS

Subject	Be	(not)	Verb + -ing
I	**am**		
He She	**is**	(not)	us**ing** a computer. study**ing** for a test. sitt**ing** at a desk.
We You They	**are**		

Notes:
1. Use the present continuous to talk about an action that is happening now.
   I **am using** a computer.
2. Use the present continuous to talk about an action that is temporary.
   He **is not studying** right now.

YES / NO QUESTIONS

Be	Subject	Verb + -ing
Am	I	
Is	he she	speak**ing** English?
Are	we you	

SHORT ANSWERS

Affirmative	Negative
Yes, you **are**.	No, you **aren't**.
Yes, he **is**.	No, he **isn't**.
Yes, she **is**.	No, she **isn't**.
Yes, we **are**.	No, we **aren't**.
Yes, I **am**.	No, I'm **not**.

WHO QUESTIONS

Who	**is**	speak**ing** English?

ANSWERS

You **are**.
Joe **is**.
Marta **is**.
Marta and I **are**.
Marta and Joe **are**.
I **am**.

WH- QUESTIONS

Wh- Word	Be	Subject	Verb + -ing
What Where Why	**am**	I	study**ing**? read**ing**? writ**ing**?
	is	he she	
	are	they	

Non-action Verbs

appear	have	miss	smell
believe	hear	need	sound
belong	know	own	taste
feel	like	prefer	understand
hate	look	see	want

Notes:
1. Some verbs in English do not usually take the present continuous tense. They are called non-action verbs. These verbs often show feelings, senses, beliefs, and possession.
   He **knows** my name.
   I **miss** my grandparents.
2. Some verbs can show both action and non-action.

   I **have** a computer.   They are **having** a party.
   I **think** he is a good   She is **having** a baby.
   teacher.   I'm **thinking** about my
                                   vacation.

Simple Past Tense

STATEMENTS		
I You He They	**moved** **didn't move**	to the United States.

WH- QUESTIONS			
Wh- Word	*Did*	Subject	Verb
Where	**did**	you	**go** to school?
What	**did**	they	**study** at school?
When	**did**	she	**come** here?
Why	**did**	he	**leave** his countr
How	**did**	it	**happen**?

YES / NO QUESTIONS		
Did	Subject	Verb
Did	you they he she	**have** any pets? **live** in the country? **play** sports?

SHORT ANSWERS	
Yes, I **did**.	No, I **didn't**.
Yes, they **did**.	No, they **didn't**.
Yes, he **did**.	No, he **didn't**.
Yes, she **did**.	No, she **didn't**.

Past Tense of *Be*

STATEMENTS		
I He She It	**was** **was not** **wasn't**	fast.
You We They	**were** **were not** **weren't**	young.

Note:
Use the past tense to describe past actions or events.
> I **was** young.
> It **wasn't** difficult.
> They **were** young.

PAST STATEMENTS WITH *THERE + BE*		
There	**was**	a garden.
	was not **wasn't**	a refrigerator.
	were	few schools.
	were not **weren't**	large schools.

YES / NO QUESTIONS		
Be	Subject	Place / Adjective
Was	he it	in the city?
Were	you they	busy?

SHORT ANSWERS	
Yes, he **was**.	No, he **wasn't**.
Yes, it **was**.	No, it **wasn't**.
Yes, I **was**.	No, I **wasn't**.
Yes, they **were**.	No, they **weren't**.

Used to

Subject	*Used to*	Verb
I You She They	**used to**	**live** in Peru. **use** candles for light. **grow** all of our vegetables.

Notes:
Use *used to* to talk about a habit or a routine that you did in the past, but that you don't do now.

I **used to live** in New York.
Now I live in Sacramento.

Simple Past Tense Questions with *Who* as Object

WHO QUESTIONS			
Who	*Did*	Subject	Verb
Who	**did**	you	**come** here with?
		she	**call**?
		they	**visit**?

ANSWERS

I came here **with my family**.

She called **her sister**.

They visited **their cousins**.

> Note:
> In these questions, *Who* is the object.

Simple Past Tense Questions with *Who* as Subject

WHO QUESTIONS	
Who	Past verb
Who	**came** here alone?
	brought a pet here?
	left family behind?

ANSWERS

Julia did.

Beata did.

Li did.

> Note:
> In these questions, *Who* is the subject.

Unit 3

Future with *Be Going To*

STATEMENTS			
Subject	*Be*	*Going to*	Verb
I	**am (not)** / **'m not**	**going to**	**move**.
You	**are (not)** / **'re not**		**change** jobs.
He / She	**is (not)** / **isn't**		**get** married.
They	**are (not)** / **'re not**		

Notes:
1. Use *be going to* to talk about future plans.
2. Use *be going to* when you already know something will be true.
   *It **is going to rain**.*
   Meaning: I heard the weather report.
   *We **are going to have** a test.*
   Meaning: The teacher announced the test.
3. *Going to* is often pronounced *gonna* in speaking. Do not write *gonna*. Use the long form.
   *It **is going to be** a difficult test.*

YES / NO QUESTIONS			
Be	Subject	*Going to*	Verb
Am	I	**going to**	**move**?
Are	you		**change** jobs?
Is	he / she		**go** to college?
Are	they		

SHORT ANSWERS	
Yes, you **are**.	No, you **aren't**.
Yes, I **am**.	No, I **'m not**.
Yes, he **is**.	No, he **isn't**.
Yes, she **is**.	No, she **isn't**.
Yes, they **are**.	No, they **aren't**.

WH- QUESTIONS

Wh- Word	Be	Subject	Going to	Verb
What	am	I		**do** tomorrow?
Where	are	you		**study** next year?
How	are	they	going to	**get** there?
Who	is	he		**visit**?
Who	is	—		**help** you?
When	is	it		**happen**?

ANSWERS

You**'re going to work**.

I**'m going to study** in California.

They**'re going to drive**.

He**'s going to visit** his cousins.

My teacher **is going to help** me.

It**'s going to happen** tomorrow.

Present Continuous with Future Meaning

If a specific time in the future is stated or clear, the present continuous can express future time.

I**'m working** tomorrow.　　　　He **is leaving** at 4:00.

Future with *Will* for Promises and Offers

STATEMENTS

Subject	Will	Verb
I You He She They	**will** **'ll** **will not** **won't**	do it.

Notes:
1. Use *will* to make a promise or an offer to help.

2. It is common to use the contraction *'ll*.
   I**'ll** help you.

3. The negative contraction of *will not* is *won't*.
   I **won't** forget.

Future with *Will* for Predictions

Use *will* to make a prediction about the future.

The United States **will make** *new immigration laws.*

There **will be** *more electric cars.*

Future Time Clauses: Statements

If I **study** hard, I**'ll graduate** in two years.
(time clause)　　　　**(main clause)**

When I **have** time, I**'m going to finish** my degree.
(time clause)　　　　　**(main clause)**

I**'ll graduate** in two years if I **study** hard.
(main clause)　　　　(time clause)

I**'m going to finish** my degree when I **have** time.
(main clause)　　　　　(time clause)

Notes:
1. *After, before,* and *when* also introduce time clauses.

2. Use a comma when the time clause is at the beginning of a sentence.

3. Do *not* use a comma when the time clause is at the end of a sentence.

4. Use the simple present tense in the time clause. Use the future tense in the main clause.

Modals: *Must / Must not*

STATEMENTS		
Subject	*Must*	Verb
I You	**must**	**stop** at a red light. **drive** at the speed limit.
He Drivers	**must not**	**drive** without a license.

Notes:
1. *Must* shows rules, obligation, or necessity.
   You **must stop** at a stop sign.

2. *Must not* shows that an action is not permitted.
   Drivers **must not drive** through a red light.

3. *Must* in the question form is very formal and is rarely used.
   Must I pay my ticket?

Modals: *Have to*

AFFIRMATIVE STATEMENTS		
Subject	*Have to*	Verb
I You	**have to**	**stop** at a red light. **drive** with a license. **wear** a seat belt.
He She	**has to**	
They	**have to**	

Notes:
1. *Have to* shows necessity or obligation.
   I **have to get** car insurance.
   She **has to babysit** her niece.

2. *Have to* can substitute for *must*.
   You **must stop** at a red light.
   You **have to stop** at a red light.

NEGATIVE STATEMENTS		
Subject	*Don't / Doesn't have to*	Verb
I You	**do not have to** **don't have to**	**buy** a new car. **work** today. **go** to school today.
She	**does not have to** **doesn't have to**	
They	**do not have to** **don't have to**	

Notes:
1. *Doesn't have to / Don't have to* show that something is not necessary.
   You **don't have to own** a car.

2. Do not confuse *don't have to* with *must not*.
   I **must not buy** a new car.
   (Incorrect: It is not against the law.)
   I **don't have to buy** a new car.
   (Correct: It is not necessary.)

YES / NO QUESTIONS WITH *HAVE TO*			
Do / Does	Subject	*Have to*	Verb
Do	I you	**have to**	**do** laundry? **buy** stamps? **see** the dentist?
Does	he she		
Do	they		

Modals: *Can / Can't*

AFFIRMATIVE STATEMENTS		
Subject	*Can*	Verb
I You She He They	**can** **can't**	**drive**. **park** in this area.

YES / NO QUESTIONS		
Can	Subject	Verb
Can	I you she they	**drive** a truck? **swim**? **speak** French?

Notes:
1. *Can* shows ability. *Can't* shows inability.
   I **can** drive a car.
   I **can't** drive a truck.

2. *Can* also shows that an action is permitted. *Can't/Cannot* shows that an action is *not* permitted.
   I **can drive** at night by myself.
   You **can't drive** through red lights.

Modals: *Could – Past Form*

STATEMENTS		
Subject	*Could*	Verb
I You He They	**could** **couldn't**	**speak** English. **find** a job. **register** for classes.

YES / NO QUESTIONS		
Could	Subject	Verb
Could	I he she	**speak** English? **find** a job? **register** for classes?

Note:
Could shows past ability.
I **could** drive when I came to this country.
My uncle **could** find an apartment for us easily.
I **couldn't** speak English when I came here.

Modals: *Should / Should not*

STATEMENTS		
Subject	*Should*	Verb
I You She He They	**should** **should not** **shouldn't**	**drive** carefully. **buy** a new car. **drive** at night. **park** there.

Note:
Should expresses an opinion or advice.
I **should buy** a smaller car. Small cars get good gas mileage.
Should not / Shouldn't show that something is *not* a good idea.
You **shouldn't park** there. There is not enough space.

Modals: *Had better / Had better not*

STATEMENTS		
Subject	*Had better*	Verb
I You She He They	**had better** **'d better** **had better not** **'d better not**	**wear** a seat belt. **use** a car seat. **drive** without a license. **forget** to fill the gas tank.

Note:
Had better expresses a strong warning.
Had better is stronger than **should**.
   You'd better check your tire.
   (Or you'll get a flat tire.)
   I'd **better not miss** another class.
   (Or I'll fail the class.)

Unit 5

Note: Refer to Units 1 to 4 for questions with present tense, present continuous tense, past tense, and future questions with *be going to* + verb.

CAN; FUTURE WITH *WILL*

Can Will	I you they she he	**play** soccer?

QUESTIONS WITH *WHO* AND *WHOSE*

Whose umbrella is that?	It's mine.
Who likes sports?	I do.
Who do you play cards with?	With my cousins.

Notes:
1. *Whose* asks questions about possession.
2. *Who* asks questions about the subject or object.

Who Questions

PRESENT

Subject	**Who** goes	to the gym every day?	Beth <u>does</u>.
Object	**Who** does Beth go	to the gym with?	She goes <u>with her sister</u>.

PAST

Subject	**Who** went	to the gym?	<u>Jim</u> did.
Object	**Who** did Jim go	to the gym with?	He went <u>with his wife</u>.

Questions with *How*

How do you get to work?	By bus.
How far do you live from school?	About three miles.
How long did you wait?	Thirty minutes.
How much money do you have?	$4.39
How many tickets do you have?	Just two.
How often do you come to school?	Three days a week.

Tag Questions

Present with *be*	You **are** from Thailand,	**aren't** you?
	It **isn't** cold today,	**is** it?
Present continuous	They **are having** a nice time,	**aren't** they?
	They **aren't having** a bad time,	**are** they?
Simple present	He **plays** soccer every day,	**doesn't** he?
	He **doesn't play** tennis,	**does** he?
Past *be*	They **were** at the park,	**weren't** they?
	They **weren't** at home,	**were** they?
Past	You **took** some pictures,	**didn't** you?
	You **didn't take** these pictures,	**did** you?
Future with *will*	She **will plant** more roses,	**won't** she?
	She **won't plant** any vegetables,	**will** she?

Unit 6

Modals: *May* and *Might* for Possibility

STATEMENTS		
Subject	*May / Might*	Verb
I	**may**	
You	**may not**	**go** on vacation.
They	**might**	**need** a visa.
He	**might not**	

Note:
Use *may or might* to express possibility.
  I **might go** on vacation. = Maybe I will go on vacation.
  He **may not need** a visa. = Maybe he will not need a visa.

Continuous Modals: *May, Might, Could*

STATEMENTS			
Subject	*May / Might*	*Be*	Verb + *-ing*
I			
You	**might**		**going** away.
They	**may**	**be**	**driving**.
She			

Note:
Use the continuous modal form to discuss possibilities about something that is happening now.
  A: *Where are they going?*
  B: *They **might be going** to Europe.*

Modals: *Must* for Deduction

STATEMENTS		
Subject	*Must*	Verb
I		
You	**must**	**have** the flu.
They		**speak** French.
He		

Notes:
1. Use *must* to make a deduction.
   Situation: Ann is in Paris. She is talking to a store clerk in Paris, and she is having no trouble communicating.
   *Ann **must speak** French.*
   *The clerk **might be speaking** English to her.*

2. Use *must* to express empathy (show that you understand another person's feelings).
   *You **must be** tired.*

Modals: *Could* for Suggestions

> Note:
> Use *could* to make a suggestion.
>   **A:** *How should I go to the airport?*
>   **B:** *You **could take** the shuttle.*

Modals: *Would rather* and *Would prefer to*

YES / NO QUESTIONS			
Would	Subject	*Rather*	Verb
Would	you he she they	**prefer to** **rather**	drive or fly?

ANSWERS			
Subject	*Would*	*Prefer to / Rather*	Verb
I You They He	**would** **'d**	**prefer to** **rather**	fly. drive.

> Notes:
> 1. Use *would rather* and *would prefer to* to express a preference.
>   *I **would rather go** to New York than Miami.*
>   *I **would prefer to go** to Chicago than Dallas.*
>
> 2. The contraction is *'d rather* or *'d prefer to*.
>   *He**'d rather fly**.*
>   *They**'d prefer to drive**.*

Unit 7

Present Perfect Continuous

STATEMENTS			
Subject	*Have*	*Been*	Verb + *-ing*
I You	**have**	**been**	play**ing** tennis for an hour.
He	**has**		
They	**have**		

> Notes:
> 1. The contractions for the present perfect:
>   I have – *I've*   you have – *you've*
>   he has – *he's*   they have – *they've*
>
> 2. The *present continuous* describes an action that is happening now.
>   *I **am playing** tennis.*
>
> 3. The *present perfect continuous* describes an action that began in the past and is continuing now.
>   *I **have been playing** tennis for an hour.*

For and *Since*

> Notes:
> 1. *For* shows an amount of time.
>   **for** *a few minutes*
>   **for** *three days*
>
> 2. *Since* shows when an action started.
>   **since** *2009*
>   **since** *Monday*
>   **since** *she moved to the city*

YES / NO QUESTIONS

Have / Has	Subject	Been	Verb + -ing
Have	you		watch**ing** a game?
Has	she	**been**	play**ing** with a team?
Have	they		work**ing** hard?

ANSWERS

Yes, I **have**.	No, I **haven't**.
Yes, she **has**.	No, she **hasn't**.
Yes, they **have**.	No, they **haven't**.

How long Questions

How long	Have	Subject	Been	Verb + -ing
How long	**have**	I you	**been**	study**ing** English? liv**ing** here?
	has	he		
	have	they		

Note:
How long asks about a length of time.
He**'s been studying** English <u>for two months</u>.
I**'ve been living** here <u>for three years</u>.

Unit 8

Present Perfect Tense

STATEMENTS WITH *FOR / SINCE*

I You	**have** **haven't**		
He	**has** **hasn't**	**worked** there	**for** two years. **since** January. **since** the company opened.
They	**have** **haven't**		

Notes:
1. To form the present perfect tense, use *have/has* and the past participle.

2. Use the present perfect tense to describe an action that began in the past and is still <u>true in the present.</u>
   They **have been** in the city **for** many years.   She **hasn't seen** him **since** they broke up.

3. Use the present perfect tense to describe changes.
   He **has lost** over fifty pounds **since** he started exercising.   In the past year, Lily **has grown** three inches.

PAST PARTICIPLES

See page 116 for irregular verb chart.

Present Perfect Tense for the Recent Past

Notes:
1. Use the *present perfect tense* with words such as *just, lately,* and *recently* to describe an action in the recent past.

2. Put *just* between *have / has* and the main verb.
   I **have just quit** my job.

3. Put *lately* at the end of a sentence.
   He **hasn't been** in class **lately**.

4. Put *recently* between *have / has* and the main verb or at the end of the sentence.
   They **have recently become** grandparents.
   They **have become** grandparents **recently**.

Present Perfect with *Already* and *Yet*

> **Notes:**
> 1. *Already* shows that an action is completed. Use *already* in affirmative sentences. You can use the present perfect tense or the past tense with *already*.
>   She has **already bought** the invitations.   She **already bought** the invitations.
>
> 2. Put *already* between *have / has* and the main verb or at the end of the sentence.
>   She **has already bought** the invitations.   She **has bought** the invitations **already**.
>
> 3. *Yet* shows the action has not been completed. Use *yet* in questions and negative sentences. Use the present perfect tense or the past tense with *yet*. Put *yet* at the end of the sentence.
>   **Has** she **sent** the invitations **yet**?   Did she **send** the invitations **yet**?   She **hasn't sent** the invitations **yet**.

Contrast: Present Perfect, Present Perfect Continuous, and Simple Past

> **Notes:**
> 1. Use the *present perfect tense* to describe actions that began in the past and are true in the present. The present perfect also describes events in the recent past.
>   I **have been** in this country for three years.   They **have just won** the lottery.
>
> 2. Use the *present perfect continuous tense* to describe actions that began in the past and are continuing now.
>   We **have been living** in this country for three years.
>
> 3. Use the *past tense* to show an action <u>completed</u> in the past.
>   She **graduated** from college <u>in 2009</u>.   They **moved** to New Mexico <u>two years ago</u>.

Unit 9

Present Perfect with *How long* and *How many*

> **Notes:**
> 1. *How long* asks about an amount of time. Use *how long* with the present perfect continuous.
>   **How long has** she **been repairing** TVs?
>   She **has been repairing** TVs <u>for two hours</u>.
>
> 2. *How many* asks about a specific number. Use *how many* with the present perfect .
>   **How many TVs has** she **repaired**?
>   She **has repaired** <u>three TVs</u>.

Present Perfect for Repeated Actions

> **Notes:**
> 1. Use the *present perfect tense* for repeated past actions.
>
> 2. The following time expressions often signal a repeated action.
>   from time to time   I have been late **from time to time**.
>   a few times   She has worked overtime **a few times**.
>
> 3. *Ever* and *never* are often used with the *present perfect*. *Ever* means "in your lifetime" or "in your experience."
>   **Have** you **ever been** to China? Yes, I have. / No, I've never been to China.

Present Perfect: Word Order

1. Place definite and indefinite time expressions **at the end of the sentence**.
   I began to work here **in 2005**.
   I have been working here **for two years**.
   I have changed jobs **twice**.
   She's taken four breaks today **so far**! (Meaning: up until now)

2. Place adverbs of frequency **before the main verb**.
   Laura has **never** received a warning at work.
   She has **always** been an excellent employee.

3. Place *just* and *finally* **before the main verb**.
   Henry has **just** gotten a raise.
   Andrea has **finally** finished her project.

4. Place *already* before the main verb or at the end of the sentence.
   They have **already** repaired three computers.
   They have repaired three computers **already**.

5. Place *yet* and *recently* at the end of the sentence.
   I've spoken to him **recently**.
   Bill hasn't finished the project **yet**.

Contrast: Present Perfect and Present Perfect Continuous

Notes:
1. Some verbs can be used in either the simple present perfect tense or the present perfect continuous tense.
   I **have lived** in this town for six years.
   I **have been living** in this town for six years.

   They **have worked** on this project since last month.
   They **have been working** on this project since last month.

2. Other verbs, especially non-action verbs, use the simple present perfect tense.

| **Non-action:** | hear | see | need | think (to express an opinion) |
| **Action:** | listen | watch | deliver | think |

Contrast: Simple Past and Present Perfect

Notes:
1. Use the past tense to describe an action at a <u>specific time</u> in the past.
   I **finished** my deliveries <u>an hour ago</u>.
   We **had to work** overtime <u>from 5:00 to 8:00</u>.

2. Use the present perfect to describe an action that happened at an <u>unspecified time</u> in the past.
   They**'ve never used** this equipment.
   I**'ve applied** to that company twice.

Past Modals: *Should have* for Regret and Expectation

STATEMENTS		
I You We They He She It	**should have** **shouldn't have**	**left** earlier. **studied** harder.

Notes:
1. Use *should have* to discuss regret about a past action.
   *I **should have studied** more.*
   Meaning: I didn't study enough.
   *We **should have brought** warm clothes.*
   Meaning: We didn't bring warm clothes. Now we're cold.
   *They **shouldn't have left** their umbrellas at home.*
   Meaning: It rained; they weren't prepared.
2. Use *should have* to show an expectation.
   *The bus **should have arrived** by now.*
   Meaning: The bus is late.
   *I **should have done** better on this exam.*
   Meaning: My grade is lower than expected.

May have, Might have, and *Could have* for Past Possibility

STATEMENTS		
Subject	*May / Might / Could + Have*	Past Participle
I You She They	**may (not) have** **might (not) have** **could (not) have**	**gone** to the movies. **forgotten** to bring it. **bought** a new car.

Notes:
1. Use *may have, might have,* or *could have* to express past possibility.
   *I **may not have taken** it.* (Meaning: Maybe I didn't take it.)
   *She **might have remembered** it.* (Meaning: Maybe she remembered it.)

2. *Could not have / Couldn't have* express past impossibility.
   *He **couldn't have been** at work that day. He was in the emergency room with his daughter.*

Past Modals: *Must have*

STATEMENTS		
Subject	***Must + Have***	**Past Participle**
I You She They	**must have** **must not have**	**left** his keys at home. **had** a doctor's appointment.

Notes:
1. Use *must have* to express a deduction about a past action.
   He **must have left** his keys at home.

2. Use *must have* to express empathy.
   A: *I didn't pass my driver's test.*
   B: *You **must have been** disappointed.*

Unit 11

The Passive: Present Tense

Active sentences emphasize the subject that does the action.
> **Subject   Verb   Object**
> Fishermen **catch** *tuna and salmon* in Oregon.

Passive sentences emphasize the object that receives the action.
> **Object   Verb   Subject**
> *Tuna and salmon* **are caught** by fishermen in Oregon.

Note:
When the subject is obvious, unknown, or not important, "by" and the subject are **not** necessary.
> *Tuna and salmon* **are caught** in Oregon. (The subject is obvious: We know that fishermen catch the fish, so "fishermen" isn't necessary.)

YES / NO QUESTIONS		
Is	milk	**produced** in Wisconsin?
Are	tires	**manufactured** in Ohio?

SHORT ANSWERS	
Yes, it **is**.	No, it **isn't**.
Yes, they **are**.	No, they **aren't**.

WH- QUESTIONS			
Where	**is**	rice	**grown?**
How	**are**	cars	**manufactured?**

ANSWERS
Rice **is grown** in many Asian countries.
Cars **are manufactured** in factories on assembly lines.

Passive with *By*

Notes:
1. Use *by* when the **subject** of the action is important and is not obvious.

This candy **is produced** by Royal Sweets. *This toy* **is made** by an American company.	(This is the name of a particular company.)

2. Don't use *by* if the doer of the action is obvious.

This chocolate **is made** in Switzerland.	(*By* is not necessary. We know that a candy company makes the candy.)
Cows **are raised** on farms.	(The meaning is clear. It is obvious that farmers raise the cows.)

Unit 12

The Passive: Past Tense

Subject	*Be*	Past Participle	
The space shuttle	**was**	**built**	in 1976.
		invented	by NASA.
747 jumbo jets	**were**	**developed**	in 1970.
		designed	by Boeing.

Passive with *By*

In early times, the medicine man **cured** people.
In early times, people were cured **by the medicine man.**

Many years ago, hospitals **did not sterilize** equipment.
Many years ago, equipment **was not sterilized.**

Note:
Use **by** when the subject of the action is important or is not obvious.

The first hospitals were begun **by the Romans**.

The Passive: Other Tenses

Tense	Passive Form
Simple present	Airbags **are installed** in all cars.
Present continuous	Those cars **are being repaired**.
Simple past	Airbags **were** first **installed** in 1973.
Past continuous	My car **was being repaired** while I was waiting.
Future with *will*	A new model **will be delivered** tomorrow.
Future with *be going to*	That car **is going to be inspected** tomorrow.
Present perfect	Many improvements **have been made** to today's cars.

Note:
All passives have a form of the verb *to be*.

Unit 13

Adjective Clauses with *Who, Which, Whom,* and *Whose*

Adjective clauses begin with relative pronouns such as **who, whom, which,** and **whose**.

who – replaces a subject (person)
<u>The student</u> **who is sitting next to me** plays in a rock band.

which – replaces a subject or object (thing)
I just saw <u>the movie</u> Crazy Heart, **which has good music**.

whom – replaces an indirect object
He's writing a song for <u>his son</u>, **whom he named after his father**.

whose – replaces a possessive form
This is <u>the singer</u> **whose song you have just heard**.

Adjective Clauses with *That*

Notes:
To introduce an adjective clause, the relative pronoun *that* can be used instead of *who, which,* or *whom.*

1. Use *that* only with **restrictive adjective clauses**. A **restrictive clause** identifies the noun it describes.
   Restrictive clause: *We paid the man* ***whom we hired to sing at our wedding.***
   or *We paid the man* ***that we hired to sing at our wedding.***
   Meaning: The adjective clause is necessary to understand who "the man" is.

2. No commas are necessary with restrictive clauses.

3. Don't use *that* with **non-restrictive adjective clauses**. A **non-restrictive clause** gives extra information about the noun it describes.
   Non-restrictive clause: *We paid Dave Jones,* ***whom we hired to sing at our wedding.***
   Incorrect: *We paid Dave Jones,* ***that we hired to sing at our wedding.***
   Meaning: We know who Dave Jones is. The adjective clause gives extra information about Dave Jones.

4. Use commas to separate non-restrictive clauses.
   Dave Jones, ***whom we hired for our wedding***, *has a popular wedding band.*

Adjective Clauses with *When* and *Where*

Adjective clauses can also begin with *when* and *where.*

Tim McGraw has appeared in a movie each year since **2004,** **when** <u>he appeared in his first movie</u>.

Faith Hill was born in **Mississippi,** **where** <u>she grew up singing in church</u>.

Unit 14

Verb + Infinitive

Note:
There are many verbs that require the infinitive form (*to* + main verb). Gradually, you'll learn the list.
   I **plan** **to attend** *college in the fall.*   *He* **promised** <u>**to babysit**</u> *for his cousin tonight.*

Use an infinitive after the following verbs:

(be) able	fail	like	prefer	try
afford	forget	love	prepare	volunteer
agree	hate	manage	promise	wait
ask	hope	need	refuse	want
choose	intend	offer	remember	wish
decide	know how	plan	seem	would like
expect	learn (how)			

Verb + Object + Infinitive

Notes:

1. Many verbs require an object or an object pronoun.

advise	encourage	hire	remind	urge
allow	expect	invite	require	want
ask	forbid	permit	teach	warn
convince	help	persuade	tell	

2. Use an **object + the infinitive form** after the following verbs:

   *My mother **asked <u>me to clean</u>** my room.*
   *The teacher **expected <u>us to prepare</u>** for the test.*

Be + Adjective + Infinitive

Use the infinitive form after the following adjectives:

dangerous	good	important	polite	selfish
difficult	hard	impossible	possible	stressful
easy	healthy	interesting	reasonable	terrible
expensive	helpful	necessary	romantic	wonderful

*It**'s important <u>to make</u>** a schedule of my activities.*
*It **was helpful <u>to have</u>** a study partner.*

Unit 15

Verb + Gerund

Use a gerund form (base verb + *ing*) after the following verbs:

admit	dislike	practice
anticipate	doesn't / don't mind	quit
appreciate	enjoy	recall
avoid	finish	recommend
begin	hate	regret
can't help	imagine	resent
can't stand	like	start
consider	love	stop
continue	miss	suggest
delay	postpone	understand
discuss		

*They **missed <u>seeing</u>** their family during the holiday season.*
*She **regretted not <u>working</u>** with people who spoke English.*

Preposition + Gerund

> **Use a gerund (base verb + *ing*) after the following prepositions:**
>
> | | | | |
> |---|---|---|---|
> | after | besides | in addition to | while |
> | before | by | instead of | without |
>
> ***After <u>studying</u>*** *for the naturalization test, she easily passed the test.*
> ***In addition to <u>playing</u> tennis,*** *he also plays soccer.*

Verb + Preposition + Gerund

> **Use a gerund (base verb + *ing*) after the following verb and preposition phrases:**
>
> | | | | |
> |---|---|---|---|
> | adjust to | complain about | give up | succeed in |
> | approve of | count on | insist on | talk about |
> | argue about | depend on | keep on | think about |
> | believe in | dream about | look forward to | warn about |
> | care about | forget about | plan on | worry about |

Be + Adjective Phrase + Gerund

> **Use a gerund (base verb + *ing*) after the following *be* + adjective and preposition phrases:**
>
> | | | | |
> |---|---|---|---|
> | be afraid of | be good at | be interested in | be tired of |
> | be capable of | be guilty of | be opposed to | be upset about |
> | be famous for | be in favor of | be proud of | |
>
> *I **am good at** <u>understanding</u> spoken English.*
> *She **is not interested in** <u>going</u> to that film.*

Contrast: Infinitives and Gerunds

> *It was **impossible <u>to find</u>** a job in my country.*
> *My friends **didn't encourage** me **<u>to speak</u>** English.*
> *He **enjoyed <u>working</u>** at the real estate office.*
> ***After <u>working</u>*** *for a few years at the factory, I found another job.*

Present Continuous Verbs

1. For most verbs, add *-ing*.
   walk-walking   *play-playing*   *eat-eating*

2. If a verb ends in *e*, drop the *e* and add *-ing*.
   write-writing   *come-coming*   *drive-driving*

3. If a verb ends in a consonant + vowel + consonant, double the final consonant and add *-ing*.
   sit-sitting   *run-running*   *put-putting*

Present Tense: Third Person

1. For most verbs, add *-s*.
   make-makes   *call-calls*   *sleep-sleeps*

2. If a verb ends with a consonant and a *y*, change the *y* to *i* and add *-es*.
   try-tries   *cry-cries*   *apply-applies*

3. If a verb ends with *sh, ch, x,* or *z*, add *-es*.
   wash-washes   *watch-watches*   *fix-fixes*

4. These verbs are irregular in the third person.
   have-has   *do-does*

Past Verbs

1. For most verbs, add *-d* or *-ed*.
   rent-rented   *save-saved*

2. If a verb ends in a consonant + *y*, change the *y* to *i* and add *-ed*.
   try-tried   *study-studied*

3. If a verb ends in a consonant + vowel + consonant, double the final consonant and add *-ed*.
   stop-stopped   *rob-robbed*

4. If a verb ends in *w, x,* or *y*, do not double the consonant. Add *-ed*.
   play-played   *relax-relaxed*   *snow-snowed*

Comparative Adjectives: *-er*

1. For most adjectives, add *-r* or *-er*.
   cold-colder   short-shorter   tall-taller

2. If a one-syllable adjective ends in a consonant + vowel + consonant, double the final consonant and add *-er*.
   big-bigger   thin-thinner   sad-sadder

3. If an adjective ends in a consonant + *y*, change the *y* to *i* and add *-er*.
   happy-happier   heavy-heavier   friendly-friendlier

Superlative Adjectives: *-est*

1. For most adjectives, add *-st* or *-est*.
   large-largest   short-shortest   tall-tallest

2. If a one-syllable adjective ends in a consonant + vowel + consonant, double the final consonant and add *-est*.
   big-biggest   thin-thinnest   sad-saddest

3. If an adjective ends in a consonant + *y*, change the *y* to *i* and add *-est*.
   busy-busiest   noisy-noisiest   friendly-friendliest

Dictations

Unit 1

Page 8, Exercise C

1. Are any students eating?
2. Are all the students writing in their notebooks?
3. Does anyone have a pencil sharpener?
4. Do you go to work after class?
5. Who is sitting next to you?
6. How many hours do you study for this class?

Unit 3

Page 39, Exercise C

1. We'll have better jobs after we learn English.
2. She'll help you with the party.
3. He won't need to work next semester.
4. The environment will be cleaner.
5. You'll need to prepare for the final exam.
6. Cars will be more efficient.
7. I'll help you after class.

Student to Student

Unit 5

Page 72, Exercise A

Student 1: Read the questions in Set A to Student 2.

Student 2: Read the questions in Set B to Student 1.

Set A

1. Who cooked when you were growing up?
2. Who taught you how to cook?
3. Do you watch cooking programs on TV?
4. Is your kitchen big enough for you?
5. What kind of cooking classes did you take before now?

Set B

6. Does your husband like to cook?
7. What classes did you take together?
8. What was the first dish that you cooked?
9. How does your husband like the food you cook?
10. Why did you decide to go to cooking school?

Unit 6

Page 89, Exercise C

Student 1: Read Set A sentences to Student 2. Then, turn to page 89. Listen to Student 2 and write each sentence you hear next to the correct picture.

Student 2: Read Set B sentences to Student 1.

Set A

1. They might move to a warmer climate.
2. They may not go to college right away.
3. They could take their honeymoon later.
4. They may get full-time jobs.
5. They would rather rent an apartment first.
6. They would prefer to be closer to their grandchildren.

Set B

1. They may volunteer at the library.
2. They'd prefer to buy a house in a couple of years.
3. They may not work at the same place.
4. They could move in with their children.
5. They would rather study part time.
6. They might wait to have children.

Unit 7

Page 103, Exercise C

Student 1: Read Set A sentences to Student 2. Then, turn to page 103. Listen to Student 2 and write each sentence next to the correct picture.

Student 2: Read Set B sentences to Student 1.

Set A

1. You haven't been coming to work on time.
2. It's been making a strange noise.
3. They've been running for two hours.
4. It's been leaking oil.
5. We've been receiving a lot of complaints.
6. They've been drinking a lot of water.
7. I've been feeling very tired.
8. My stomach has been bothering me.

Set B

1. It's been overheating in traffic.
2. I've been having trouble sleeping.
3. They've been getting lots of support.
4. You've been making mistakes in your work.
5. Roger has been leading for 30 minutes.
6. It hasn't been running smoothly.
7. You've been arguing with your co-workers.
8. I haven't been eating well.

Unit 9

Page 137, Exercise F

Student 1: Read Set A questions to Student 2. Then, turn to page 137 and listen to Student 2. Write the answer under the correct picture. Use complete sentences.

Student 2: Read Set B questions to Student 1.

Set A

1. Has she fired any employees this year?
2. How many doctors did she talk to this morning?
3. How many cars has he repaired today?
4. How long has she been selling homes?
5. What time did he start work this morning?
6. How long has he had his own business?

Set B

1. How many employees did she hire?
2. How many patients has she helped today?
3. How long has he been working at this garage?
4. Did she sell any homes this month?
5. How many streets has he cleared so far?
6. Has he installed more than one system today?

Unit 10

Page 153, Exercise B

Student 1: Listen to Student 2 talk about the weekend. Be a good listener and give an appropriate response. Use *must have been* and an adjective from the box. Then, turn to page 153.

Student 2: Listen to Student 1 talk about the weekend. Be a good listener and give an appropriate response. Use *must have been* and an adjective from the box.

Example: My homework / be / very difficult

My homework was very difficult.

You must have been frustrated.

excited	surprised	proud
scared	thrilled	frustrated
pleased	disappointed	worried
exhausted		

Page 213, Exercise F

Student 1: Read Set A sentences to Student 2. When you are finished, turn to page 213. Write the sentences you hear.

Student 2: Read Set B sentences to Student 1.

Set A

1. Every time I start to study, my kids interrupt me.
2. I wanted to get up early, but I forgot to set the alarm clock.
3. I want to exercise after work, but I'm too tired when I get home.
4. I need to get a cavity filled, but I hate to go to the dentist.
5. I've decided to buy a computer, but I can't decide which one to buy.

Set B

1. I'd like to save some money every month, but I love to shop.
2. I would love to travel, but I can't afford it right now.
3. I need to study more, but I often have to work overtime.
4. I decided to clean the basement, but there was a good movie on TV.
5. We need to write our wills, but we haven't hired a lawyer yet.

Audio Scripts

Unit 1

CD 1, Track 1, Page 5
A. Listen to the story about Sophie and Lizzy, two college roommates. Complete the questions with *Do* or *Does*. Then, answer the questions.

Sophie: Hi, I'm Sophie, and I'm a morning person. When the sun comes up, I feel great. I get a lot of things done in the morning, so I take courses early in the morning. I'm finished with my classes by noon. I like to keep everything neat and in order. If things are out of place, I go crazy! My favorite subjects are science and math, so I think I'm going to major in chemistry or computer science. I really like computers. I do all of my work on my computer, so I prefer to study in my room at my own desk. I almost never write by hand. Oh, and I always hand in my class work on time. But my roommate, Lizzy, is completely different from me. We get along well, though.

Lizzy: Hi, I'm Lizzy. Sophie and I are complete opposites. She's a morning person, but I'm a night owl. I rarely go to bed before 2 A.M., so I don't get up until noon. I take all afternoon classes. I don't care about keeping my things in order. I can always find my things even if I have to look on the floor or under the bed. Sophie hates that. She's really neat. My favorite subjects are literature, writing, and art. I love to write, and I love to draw. I think I'll major in art history or English literature. I have a computer, but I almost never use it. I prefer to write everything by hand. I only use the computer to type my papers, which are sometimes late. I often have to talk to my professors about my late papers. Sophie is completely different from me, but she's a great roommate.

CD 1, Track 2, Page 6
B. Pronunciation: Linking */do you/.* Listen and repeat.
1. What do you do?
2. Where do you work?
3. How do you get home?
4. Where do you live?
5. Why do you study here?
6. What do you do on weekends?

CD 1, Track 3, Page 10
The Big Picture: The University of Texas at San Antonio
The University of Texas is a large university with many campuses all over Texas. This is a description of the University of Texas at San Antonio, which is located in southeastern Texas.

The University of Texas at San Antonio, or U.T.S.A., is a four-year public university with a graduate school. U.T.S.A.'s main campus is located on a suburban campus, 15 miles from downtown San Antonio. The university has a large undergraduate student population of over 24,000. Two percent of the students come from other countries. In addition, over three thousand students are in graduate programs. The university employs 1,224 faculty.

Students who want to attend U.T.S.A. must turn in the following: first, a completed application with a $40 application fee. An online application is available. Second, they must have an official high school transcript and official ACT or SAT scores. There is no minimum score for students in the top 25 percent of their high school classes.

Like most other universities, U.T.S.A. offers many academic majors. Students can major in the liberal arts, sciences, or technical fields. Here are just a few of the possible majors: accounting, criminal justice, engineering, and international business.

U.T.S.A. offers many facilities and student services to help the students be successful in their college studies. For students who need extra help for their college courses, there is academic help. There is also a health clinic and personal counseling for students. When the students aren't studying, they can take advantage of the many extracurricular activities. There are many athletic teams for both men and women. There are also student organizations that cover many different interests including sports teams and drama.

To help prepare new and transfer students for life at U.T.S.A., the university offers an orientation program. Students learn about life on a college campus, get help registering for courses, and find out about the student services available. Family members are welcome, too.

CD 1, Track 4, Page 11
C. Listen and write short answers to the questions about the university.
1. Is the university a two-year university?
2. Does the university have only one campus?
3. Is there a graduate school at the university?

4. Does the university require students to pay an application fee?
5. Is it a private university?
6. Are there opportunities for women to participate in sports?
7. Is there an orientation for new students?
8. Are families welcome to come to the orientation?

Unit 2

CD 1, Track 5, Page 19
B. Look at the pictures and listen to the comparison between life in colonial times and life today. Number the pictures.
The colonial period in the United States lasted from 1607 to 1776. Most early colonists were men and women from England who decided to start a new life in North America. They settled along the eastern coast of what is now the United States. Life at that time was very different from life today.
1. Most people lived on small farms. People grew their own food.
2. They didn't cook on stoves. They cooked their food over open fires.
3. When they needed milk, they milked their own cows. They didn't buy milk at the supermarket.
4. Houses functioned without electricity or modern conveniences. People read and worked by candlelight.
5. They didn't sleep on mattresses with box springs. They used to sleep on feather beds.
6. In the evening, instead of watching TV, they read to each other and played games.
7. When people wanted to communicate with friends or relatives far away, they didn't have phones or e-mail. They used to write letters.
8. For transportation, there were no cars. People used horses and wagons.

CD 1, Track 6, Page 22
A. Pronunciation: *Used to*. Listen and repeat.
1. In colonial times, people used to drive horses and wagons.
2. People used to cook over open fires.
3. People used to grow their own food.
4. They used to write letters.
5. They used to attend very small schools.

CD 1, Track 7, Page 24
A. Complete the questions. Then, listen to Eric talk about his childhood. Take notes in your notebook. Answer the questions.
Oscar: Eric, where were you born?
Eric: I was born in a small town in Peru. On the coast.
Oscar: How many brothers and sisters do you have?

Eric: There are four boys—and I'm the youngest.
Oscar: Did your grandparents live in the same town?
Eric: Yes, my grandparents, my two aunts, my five uncles. We all lived in the same town. And, I had a lot of cousins.
Oscar: Did you live in the city or the country?
Eric: In the country. My family owned a small farm. In the winter, I had to get up early and milk our cow.
Oscar: How about school? Did you walk to school or take the bus?
Eric: In our town, there were no school buses. I used to ride my bike to school.
Oscar: What did you do after school?
Eric: After school, I played soccer with my brothers and cousins.
Oscar: How about the summer? What did you do in the summer?
Eric: In the summer, we used to work in the fields with my father.
Oscar: Did you go on vacation?
Eric: We never went on vacation. My mother said that we didn't need a vacation because we lived in the country. A few times each summer, my mom packed a big lunch, and we drove to the ocean.
Oscar: Did you see your relatives a lot?
Eric: All the time. There was always something to celebrate: a birthday, a wedding, or a holiday. We all used to go to grandmother's house. My mother and aunts used to cook inside, and the men barbecued a pig outside. My grandmother always made the desserts. They were wonderful—cakes and rice pudding and *mazamorra morada*.

CD 1, Track 8, Page 26
The Big Picture: Benjamin Franklin
Benjamin Franklin was born in Boston, Massachusetts, on January 17, 1706. At that time, school was not required, and Franklin only attended school for two years. For the rest of his life, he continued to read and study on his own, and he even learned five foreign languages. When he was 12, he began to work at his brother's printing office and learned quickly. By the age of 17, he was an excellent printer. Franklin then moved

to Philadelphia in 1728, and at the young age of 22, he opened his own printing shop in that city. He published a newspaper, the *Pennsylvania Gazette*. He knew that many people could not read well, so his publications had many cartoons and pictures.

Benjamin Franklin was respected in Philadelphia. He helped to improve everyday life for the people in the city. In 1732, he started the first public library in America so that people could borrow and read books. In 1736, he helped to organize the first fire department in Philadelphia because most of the houses were wood, and there were many fires. He was also postmaster in Philadelphia and helped to set up the routes for mail delivery. He also spoke to the officials of the city and encouraged them to pave the city streets.

Franklin was also an inventor. He was always asking questions and trying to improve everyday life. At the time, colonial fireplaces sent black smoke throughout the house. Franklin invented a stove that used less wood and gave off more heat. As postmaster, he invented the odometer. The odometer measured distance, and Franklin used it to set up mail routes in the city. Franklin wore glasses and became tired of taking his glasses off to see far away, so he invented bifocals. Franklin also experimented with electricity and realized that lightning is a form of electricity. He invented the lightning rod to protect homes from lightning.

As the years passed, Franklin became a leader in the city and in the country. He signed the Declaration of Independence, which stated that the 13 colonies were a free and independent nation. He served as a minister to France during the war with England. When he returned, he signed the Constitution, which established the new government.

Benjamin Franklin died on April 17, 1790, and was buried in Philadelphia.

Unit 3

CD 1, Track 9, Page 34
A. Listen. Write the number of each statement under the correct picture.
1. I'm going to pay attention and take careful notes.
2. I'm going to apply for unemployment.
3. I'm going to vote in the next election.
4. The children are going to live with you on the weekends.
5. My mother will help me after the baby comes.
6. I will send e-mails to my family every night.
7. We're going to live in my apartment because it's bigger.
8. I'm going to register for only two courses this semester.
9. I will start working in a law office in two weeks.

CD 1, Track 10, Page 35
A. Listen. Complete the sentences. Some of the sentences are negative.
Ellie: Congratulations, Julie! We're high school graduates!
Julie: Finally! I'm so excited. How do you feel, Ellie?
Ellie: I'm great. So, what are you going to do? Are you going away to college?
Julie: No, I'm not. Things are tough right now, so I'm going to live at home and go to the community college.
Ellie: So am I. Your mother's a teacher. Are you going to study education, too?
Julie: Me? No. I'm going to study engineering and architecture. What about you?
Ellie: I'm not sure. I'm going to talk to a counselor on Monday. Are you going to study full time?

Julie: No. I'm going to keep my job at the department store. I'm going to take classes at night.
Ellie: Too bad. We're not going to have the same schedule. I'm going to take classes during the day and work in my father's restaurant at night.
Julie: OK. Well, good luck. Maybe I'll see you on the weekend.
Ellie: OK. See you around.

CD 1, Track 11, Page 37
B. Listen and circle the meaning.
1. They're watching TV.
2. I'm doing laundry tonight.
3. She's taking her daughter to the doctor on Tuesday.
4. The students are writing essays.
5. I'm taking two classes next semester.
6. I'm listening to the radio.
7. He's not going to class next week.
8. We're not taking a vacation this year.
9. I'm texting a friend.

CD 1, Track 12, Page 38
A. Pronunciation: 'll. Listen and repeat.
1. I'll do it.
2. I'll get it.
3. I'll call you.
4. I'll help him.
5. I'll be there.
6. They'll paint it.
7. She'll do it.
8. He'll answer it.
9. We'll help you.

The Big Picture: After the Baby Comes

Laura: Thanks for arranging the baby shower, Melissa. I had a great time.

Melissa: So did I. It was a lot of fun. So, are you still looking for a house?

Laura: No, we looked at a few houses, but some of them were too expensive, and others needed a lot of work.

Melissa: So, what are you going to do? You need a bigger place.

Laura: I know, but I think we have a solution. We really like our building and our neighborhood, so we're going to look at a few bigger apartments in our building. Besides, it's close to work.

Melissa: Speaking of work, what about your job? Are you still working?

Laura: This is my last week.

Melissa: Then, what are you going to do?

Laura: Well, I have two months maternity leave, but first Brady and I have to finish shopping for the baby.

Melissa: Where are you going to put everything? Your apartment is small!

Laura: We're going to look at apartments tonight. We might get lucky and find one we like. If we do, we're going to move as soon as possible.

Melissa: You're an only child, Laura. Do you even know how to change diapers?

Laura: I used to babysit when I was a teenager, so yes, I know how to change diapers. And Brady and I are taking a parenting class. We're learning a lot.

Melissa: Good. You know, you're going to have to make some big changes. No more late nights out on the town.

Laura: You're right. We used to go out three or four times a week, but we'll be spending a lot of time at home. Besides, I'm too tired to go out, and the baby's not even here yet.

Melissa: What about the cats? Are you going to give them away?

Laura: No! Are you crazy? But we're not going to leave them alone with the baby. That's another reason why we need more space.

Melissa: Is your mother going to help?

Laura: Yes. She's going to be a big help. Brady can only take two weeks off.

Melissa: Are you going to go back to work full time?

Laura: Mm-hmm, but I'm going to work a three-day schedule. My mother will take care of the baby while I'm at work.

Melissa: You're lucky. Call me if you need help.

Laura: Thanks! I will.

Unit 4

CD 1, Track 14, Page 53
D. Listen. Rebecca is talking about her schedule. Check the tasks that she has completed.

Uh, let's see, what do I have to do today? Do I need stamps? Hmm. I don't think so. I bought a few yesterday. Here they are. OK, so I have to mail my gas bill and my phone bill. I can mail them in the mailbox near the Laundromat. I have to do some laundry, or I won't have any clean clothes to wear. While my clothes are in the wash, I can go to the supermarket. I have to get some eggs, milk, and something for dinner. Oh, did I deposit my check? Yes, I did, and here's the deposit slip from last Saturday. And, . . . I have to call to confirm my dentist's appointment. I don't remember if my appointment's at 9:00 or at 10:00. All right. I'm ready to go, but I have to remember to put gas in the car. The tank's almost empty.

CD 1, Track 15, Page 54
A. Pronunciation: *Can* and *can't*. **Listen.** Marcus is talking about his driving experience. Complete the sentences with *can* or *can't*.

I'm a new driver, and I'm a terrible driver. I finally got my driving permit three months ago. It took me three tries to pass the written test. Now, I can only drive with a licensed driver in my car, so my mom or dad has to be in the car with me. I can back up, but I can't parallel park. I'm a terrible parker, so I sometimes drive around the block a few times to find an easy space to park in. I can drive on a busy highway, but I feel nervous. I can't drive at night alone because I'm only 17. I can't drive with the radio playing because I can't concentrate. Maybe I need to take the bus.

CD 1, Track 16, Page 57
A. Pronunciation: *'d better / 'd better not.* **Listen and complete the sentences.** Then, listen again and repeat.
1. **I'd better stay** home. I don't feel well.
2. **You'd better put** the baby in the car seat.
3. **She'd better call** the police and report the accident.
4. **We'd better take** the party inside. It's beginning to rain.
5. **He'd better not have** another piece of cake. He'll get sick.
6. **You'd better not get** a dog. Your landlord won't allow it.
7. **She'd better slow** down. The roads are icy.
8. **I'd better not buy** that. I can't afford it.

CD 1, Track 17, Page 58
The Big Picture: Getting a Driver's License

I'm so excited. Tomorrow, my mother's taking me to the Department of Motor Vehicles to get my learner's permit. I have to have my parent's signature on my application because I'm only 16. I have to show proof of my age, too. I grew up in Peru, but I was born here in the U.S., so I can show my U.S. passport. People can also use original birth certificates, a permanent resident card, or citizenship papers. I've already taken the D.A.T.A. course, and I'm going to take the written test today. There are 40 questions and signs on the test. I have to get 75 percent correct to pass the test. I speak English well, but my reading is still a little weak. I don't have to take the test in English because the DMV gives the test in 30 languages, including mine—Spanish. I also have to take a hearing test and a vision test to check my eyesight. Then, they're going to take my picture.

After I pay 48 dollars, I can get my learner's permit. My permit is good for two years, but I have to practice for 50 hours and have my permit for a year before I can get an intermediate license. I was hoping that my sister could teach me to drive, but in my state, I must have an adult 21 years or older in the car with me. That's the law for people under 18. My sister's only 19, so my mother's going to teach me.

I'm going to practice as much as I can before the road test. My mother will drive me to the road test because I must have a licensed driver 21 years or older in the car with me. My parents will get the auto insurance card, and we need to show the car's registration. Of course, I also have to show my learner's permit. Then, I can take the road test. Wish me luck!

CD 1, Track 18, Page 65
A. Listen and repeat.
1. accelerator
2. brake
3. bumper
4. clutch
5. hood
6. horn
7. signal
8. steering wheel
9. gear shift
10. tires
11. trunk
12. windshield
13. windshield wipers

Unit 5

CD 1, Track 19, Page 68
A. People are talking about activities they enjoy. Circle the question word. Then, listen and answer the questions.

Gina: How do I spend my free time? I like to go dancing. My friends and I go dancing almost every weekend. Every Friday and Saturday night, we go dancing at clubs in our area. We get together with other friends, and we make new friends. We like all kinds of music, but we usually go to clubs that play Latin music. A couple times a month, I take a dance class. Dancing is a really good way to keep in shape. I don't need to work out at a gym. Dancing keeps me fit.

Roberto: I spend my time taking care of my tropical fish. I have a large aquarium in my living room, and I take good care of my fish. I have many books about tropical fish. I also have a few friends who like keeping fish, too. We get together once a week at a coffee shop nearby and talk about what's new with our fish and what new fish we've bought. I also participate in an online discussion with other people who keep fish. Watching my fish is very relaxing after a hard day at work.

Yelena: After I retired, I was bored and I needed something to do. One day, I saw two men playing chess in the lounge in my building.

It brought back memories for me. My father taught me how to play chess, and I even joined the chess team in high school. When I was in college, I didn't have time for chess. And then, I began to work, and I stopped playing chess. Now, I'm playing again. Chess is a game for people who like to think. I'm getting older, and I want to keep my mind sharp. I play every evening. Tomorrow, I'm going to start teaching my grandson how to play.

CD 1, Track 20, Page 71
A. Pronunciation: Tag Questions. Listen and repeat. Pay attention to the arrows.
1. They like to fish, don't they?
2. Fishing isn't expensive, is it?
3. They will cook their fish, won't they?
4. They don't fish every day, do they?
5. They're fishing in a lake, aren't they?
6. It isn't a hot day, is it?
7. Fishing isn't tiring, is it?
8. They hope to catch a lot, don't they?

CD 1, Track 21, Pages 74 and 75
The Big Picture: A Trip to Vancouver, British Columbia

The Yang family is now in Vancouver staying with Victor, William's younger brother. Victor and his family moved to Vancouver three years ago.

Victor decided to move to Vancouver after he visited the city on a business trip. He liked the clean streets, the natural setting, and the economic opportunities. At first, his wife, Lin, didn't want to move there, but after a couple of months, she met a few other immigrants from Hong Kong. They introduced her to more people in the neighborhood. Now, Lin likes Vancouver very much, and she has a job. She works three mornings a week at her daughter's elementary school. There are many other children there who speak Cantonese or Mandarin, so the school needs experienced teachers like Lin, who can speak both languages.

Right now, Victor and Lin are taking William and his family around Vancouver. This morning, they visited Granville Island. They walked around in the Public Market and enjoyed looking at the local and imported fruits, vegetables, and other foods and flowers. They decided to have some tea at an outdoor café and watch the boats come into the harbor.

It's 12:00 now, and they're on their way to Gastown, the oldest part of Vancouver. Later, they're going to take a trolley tour around the city. They're going to stop at Queen Elizabeth Park and visit the Rose Garden. They're also going to visit the zoo. After that, they're going to have dinner in Chinatown with some friends.

William and his family are having a wonderful time. They can't wait until Victor and his family come to San Francisco next year.

Unit 6

CD 1, Track 22, Page 86
A. Listen. Write the number next to the correct response.
1. My husband had a car accident yesterday, but his injuries were minor.
2. We moved last month, and my son has never been away from his friends and grandparents before.
3. I have to get up at 5:00 every day this week.
4. Anna has an important job interview.
5. It doesn't snow in Lilia's native country. She doesn't have any winter clothes yet.
6. My friends are studying for exams, so they can't go out with me this weekend.
7. There was a hurricane in my cousin's area. We're waiting for him to call.
8. My son and his wife are going to have their first child.

CD 1, Track 23, Page 86
C. Listen and complete each suggestion.
1. **A:** My car broke down. I need to get to work.
   B: You could **take the bus**.
2. **A:** We want to take a vacation, but we can't afford to spend a lot of money.
   B: You could **go to the beach**.
3. **A:** My sister's going to Rome, but the hotels are expensive.
   B: She could **exchange apartments**.
4. **A:** My family wants to stay at my house, but I don't have enough beds.
   B: They could **bring sleeping bags**.
5. **A:** My children are coming home from college, but flights are too expensive.
   B: They could **take an overnight train**.
6. **A:** My brother wants to study Spanish in another country.
   B: He could **go to Mexico**.

CD 1, Track 24, Pages 90 and 91
The Big Picture: Planning a Vacation
Gina: Hi, Drew, how are you today?
Drew: I'm doing well, Gina, and you?
Gina: OK, thanks. I guess it's that time of year. I thought you would be coming into the office soon.
Drew: Well, you've been helping to plan our vacations for a long time. This year, I want to do something different.
Gina: Is this going to be a family vacation?
Drew: Yes, our kids are getting older. They like to travel.
Gina: How old is Gabby? She must be ten.
Drew: No, she's 12, and Leo is eight.
Gina: I can't believe it! I remember when Gabby was born.
Drew: Time flies. So, let's talk about our vacation. We're going to be away during Maryann's 40th birthday, so I want to do something special. It's going to be a surprise from me and the kids.
Gina: That's a great idea. So, where do you want to go?
Drew: I want to go somewhere where we haven't been before. A friend told me something about Flathead Lake in Montana.
Gina: Flathead Lake? Good idea. It's a great place for a family. There's a great lodge there, and it's in a beautiful location. The lake is spectacular, and the view of the mountains is beautiful.
Drew: You know, Leo is 8. He'll do anything, and he's very enthusiastic about this trip. He loves the outdoors. Gabby is almost a teenager. She's becoming a little harder to please.
Gina: Don't worry. Lots of families go there with kids of all ages. There are lots of activities that might interest her. The staff at the lodge organizes events for the kids.

Drew: This is near a lake, so there must be a lot of water sports, right?

Gina: Definitely. You can go sailing, swimming, and waterskiing. And, there's a heated pool, too.

Drew: Maryann might like that. I know she would rather spend time by the pool than in a cool lake.

Gina: I think you're right. And, there are plenty of other sports, too. You and your family are pretty active, aren't you?

Drew: Yes, we are.

Gina: So, you'll enjoy the sports that the lodge offers: basketball, soccer, baseball, and tennis. They give lessons, too.

Drew: What happens when the weather's bad?

Gina: No problem. The lodge offers arts and crafts, games, and movies.

Drew: This place sounds perfect. How far is it from a major town?

Gina: Only ten minutes. There are shuttles from the lodge every hour.

Drew: Is there anything else to see in the area?

Gina: Yes, there's a national park nearby. You can tour the park. And, you can see the wild animals in the area.

Drew: Leo will really like that. Do you have any brochures?

Gina: Let's see. Here you are. Take them home and talk to your kids. Then, give me a call.

Drew: OK, because we need to talk about how much this is going to cost me.

Gina: Don't worry. It's very reasonable.

Drew: We'll have to talk about flights, too. I want to make sure I get an aisle seat.

Gina: I'll start checking flights right away. Call me when you've made a decision.

Drew: Thanks, Gina.

CD 1, Track 25, Page 91
E. Pronunciation: *'d rather*. Listen. Complete the sentences with *I'd, He'd, She'd, We'd,* or *They'd*.
1. **We'd** rather go camping.
2. **They'd** rather stay in a cabin.
3. **He'd** rather go fishing.
4. **She'd** rather go swimming.
5. **She'd** rather not stay in a tent.
6. **He'd** rather not go to malls.
7. **They'd** rather not eat at home.
8. **I'd** rather not stay at a hotel.

CD 1, Track 26, Page 97
A. Listen and answer the questions.
A: Good morning. I'm going to ask you some questions.
B: OK.
A: May I see your passport, please?
B: Yes, here it is.
A: Where did you visit?
B: I went to Barcelona and Madrid.
A: Where did you stay?
B: I stayed in a hotel in Barcelona. And I stayed at my sister's apartment in Madrid.
A: Was your luggage always with you?
B: Yes, it was in the hotel in Barcelona, and in my sister's apartment in Madrid.
A: Did you pack your luggage?
B: Yes, I did.
A: Did anyone ask you to carry anything in your bag?
B: No, just presents from my sister for Christmas.
A: Please put your bag here. Open your bag, please.
B: Oh, they're just presents for my family.
A: I'm sorry. You cannot put wrapped presents in your carry-on bag. You'll have to unwrap them or put them in your checked bag.
B: Right now?
A: Yes, right now.
B: OK.
A: Thank you. Here's your passport.

Unit 7

CD 2, Track 1, Page 100
B. Pronunciation: *'ve been / 's been*. Listen and repeat.
1. **a.** She's taking dancing lessons.
   b. She's been taking dancing lessons.
2. **a.** She's learning how to drive.
   b. She's been learning how to drive.
3. **a.** He's playing baseball.
   b. He's been playing baseball.
4. **a.** I'm looking for a new apartment.
   b. I've been looking for a new apartment.
5. **a.** She's recovering from her accident.
   b. She's been recovering from her accident.
6. **a.** He's studying Chinese.
   b. He's been studying Chinese.
7. **a.** He's working hard.
   b. He's been working hard.
8. **a.** I'm training for a new job.
   b. I've been training for a new job.

CD 2, Track 2, Page 100
C. Listen again. Circle the sentence you hear. Then, practice the sentences with a partner.
1. She's been taking dancing lessons.
2. She's been learning how to drive.
3. He's playing baseball.

4. I've been looking for a new apartment.
5. She's recovering from her accident.
6. He's studying Chinese.
7. He's been working hard.
8. I'm training for a new job.

CD 2, Track 3, Page 100
D. Listen to the conversation.
A: Hi, Juan. What've you been up to?
B: I've been painting the house.
A: And how's your family?
B: We're all fine. Maribel is 16 now, so I've been teaching her how to drive.
A: Good luck with that! And your parents? How are they?
B: They've been enjoying their retirement. They've been visiting their grandchildren a lot.
A: Oh, that's nice. Tell them I asked about them.
B: I sure will.

CD 2, Track 4, Page 105
C. Listen. Then, complete the questions.
Reporter: Congratulations! You just won the state championship!
Robert: Thank you.
Reporter: Robert, how old are you?
Robert: Seven.
Reporter: Seven! And how long have you been playing tennis?
Robert: Since I was three.
Reporter: Who taught you how to play?
Robert: My father. And I take private lessons, too.
Reporter: Here at the tennis club?
Robert: Yes. I've been taking lessons for two years.
Reporter: How many days a week do you play?
Robert: About three or four. I want to practice every day, but my parents say three or four days is enough.
Reporter: Are you going to continue with your tennis?
Robert: Uh-huh. I'm going to be a professional tennis player when I'm older.

CD 2, Track 5, Page 106
The Big Picture: A Soccer Game
Today is the championship match between the Kings and the Stars. The game started at 2:00. It's the second half with only ten minutes left to play. An announcer has been calling the action on the field. The Stars have the lead with the score 2 to 1. The Kings have been fighting back, but the Stars' goalkeeper has been stopping every ball.

The stadium is sold out, with more than 35,000 fans in the stadium. The fans have been cheering, waving their banners, and shouting at the officials. Some fans have been banging drums and dancing in the aisles.

It's hot today, and the concession workers have been working hard. They've been walking up and down the steps selling water, soda, and other drinks. The lines at the refreshment stands are long. People have been waiting for 15 minutes or more to get their food.

The players have been drinking a lot of water and energy drinks because of the high temperatures. The officials have been watching everyone carefully to prevent any illegal moves. One official has been issuing yellow cards, but no red cards yet. A few of the players have been pushing each other and pulling shirts, but so far, no players are out of the game.

The Stars' coach has been shouting at his players and substituting players. He's been putting in his best defensive players. The Kings' coach has been putting in his fastest and best players. Everyone has been watching number 7. He has the ball, and it looks like he's about to score again!

CD 2, Track 6, Page 113
A. Listen and repeat.
1. I have a bruise.
2. She has a sprained ankle.
3. She has tendonitis.
4. He has a concussion.
5. He has a pulled hamstring.
6. He has a torn rotator cuff.

CD 2, Track 7, Page 113
B. Listen. Take notes about each injury and its treatment.

Conversation 1
Patient: Dr. Lopez, my shoulder is very weak. If I try to lift something, it really hurts.
Doctor: I've looked at your X-rays. You have a torn rotator cuff.
Patient: A torn rotator cuff? That's serious.
Doctor: Yes, it is. You're going to need surgery. It'll be two to three months before you can throw a football.

Conversation 2
Patient: My ankle really hurts.
Doctor: Well, fortunately you didn't break it. It's only a sprain.
Patient: Oh, good. So what should I do?
Doctor: First, stay off of it as much as possible. When you go home, you should elevate it. Then, put ice on it for 15 to 20 minutes. After that, take the ice off and wait an hour. Then, you can ice it again. Continue doing that all day today and call me tomorrow.

Conversation 3

Doctor: John, who's the president?

John: The president? George Bush?

Doctor: OK, coach. John has a concussion.

Coach: A concussion? Can he play next week?

Doctor: No! He lost consciousness for about 45 seconds, and he's confused. He's dizzy.

Coach: He's the leader of my team. We need him.

Doctor: I'm sorry, but this is a serious injury. His brain needs time to heal. He needs quiet and rest. He might have headaches, too. I want to take an X-ray. Could you take him into the locker room, please?

Conversation 4

Doctor: How do you feel today, Carl?

Carl: Well, my leg still hurts. I tried to run, but after a minute, the pain in my hamstring came back.

Doctor: Carl, you're going to need surgery on that pulled hamstring. I'll schedule the surgery.

Carl: Surgery. Wow. When will I be able to run again?

Doctor: A physical therapist will work with you. Every person is different. You may need a couple months of therapy.

Conversation 5

Doctor: I've looked at your X-rays. It looks like you have tendonitis in your wrist.

Patient: Tendonitis? What's that?

Doctor: You're doing the same motions over and over when you play tennis. Your tendons need rest.

Patient: Oh, I see. What do I have to do?

Doctor: No tennis or heavy lifting for three weeks. Then, come back and see me.

Patient: What can I take for the pain? I'm having trouble sleeping.

Doctor: I'll write down a few over-the-counter medications that you can take. You don't need a special prescription right now.

Conversation 6

Doctor: Ooh. That's a big bruise you've got there.

Patient: I know. It's really killing me.

Doctor: Have you been putting ice on it?

Patient: No, I put heat on it.

Doctor: Oh, you should ice it instead. Put ice on it for about 15 minutes. Then, let your leg warm up. After that, ice it again. The bruise is going to start to change color. Right now, it's a little swollen and red, but soon it'll turn bluish or greenish. That means it's getting better.

Patient: Oh, I see. I've been taking aspirin. Is that OK?

Doctor: No, I'll give you something else to take for the pain.

Unit 8

CD 2, Track 8, Page 114

B. Listen. Kathy and Gloria are talking about plans for a family reunion. Circle *True* or *False*.

Gloria: Hi, Kathy. This is Gloria.

Kathy: Gloria! How are you? We haven't spoken in ages!

Gloria: I know. We get so busy. Have you heard about the reunion?

Kathy: What reunion?

Gloria: We're going to have a family reunion. Angela's planning it.

Kathy: It's about time. We've been talking about that for years. Has she picked a date yet?

Gloria: It'll be in August. I think she mentioned the weekend of August 15th.

Kathy: August 15th. That's in two months. Where's it going to be?

Gloria: At a resort near Angela's. She was able to get a special family package, so the prices will be very reasonable. She's going to send out invitations soon.

Kathy: She can't do this by herself. What can I do to help?

Gloria: Everybody's going to help with the food. Tom and Will are going to plan the activities. I think they're going to design T-shirts for everyone, too.

Kathy: T-shirts? That'll be fun.

Gloria: How many of us are there?

Kathy: About 75. Plus two more. Jenny just had twins.

Gloria: Twins? That's great news. How's she doing?

Kathy: She hasn't been getting much sleep, but she's fine.

Gloria: Good. Did you hear that Michael has changed jobs?

Kathy: Really? What's he doing now?

Gloria: He's just opened a small business. He installs large-screen TVs and sound systems in homes.

Kathy: Hmm. Maybe he could help my husband.

Gloria: Maybe. OK, I've got some more phone calls to make. I've gotta go.

Kathy: Me, too. It'll be great to see everyone. See you in August.

CD 2, Track 9, Page 116
C. Listen and repeat.

Base form	Simple past	Past participle	Base form	Simple past	Past participle
be	was / were	been	leave	left	left
bear	bore	born	lose	lost	lost
become	became	become	make	made	made
begin	began	begun	meet	met	met
break	broke	broken	pay	paid	paid
bring	brought	brought	put	put	put
buy	bought	bought	quit	quit	quit
catch	caught	caught	read	read	read
come	came	come	ride	rode	ridden
do	did	done	say	said	said
drink	drank	drunk	see	saw	seen
drive	drove	driven	sell	sold	sold
eat	ate	eaten	send	sent	sent
fall	fell	fallen	sit	sat	sat
feel	felt	felt	sleep	slept	slept
find	found	found	speak	spoke	spoken
forget	forgot	forgotten	spend	spent	spent
freeze	froze	frozen	steal	stole	stolen
get	got	got / gotten	take	took	taken
give	gave	given	teach	taught	taught
go	went	gone	tell	told	told
grow	grew	grown	think	thought	thought
have	had	had	throw	threw	thrown
hear	heard	heard	win	won	won
know	knew	known	write	wrote	written

CD 2, Track 10, Page 118
A. Pronunciation: Stress. Listen to the stress as each speaker clarifies the information. Underline the stressed word.

1. **A:** I hear that David has bought a sailboat.
   B: Not exactly. He's bought a <u>motorboat</u>.
2. **A:** I hear that Amy has moved to North Carolina.
   B: Close. She's moved to <u>South</u> Carolina.
3. **A:** I hear that Nora has gotten her driver's license.
   B: No, just the opposite. She's <u>lost</u> her driver's license.
4. **A:** I hear that Joe and Tom have just opened an Italian restaurant.
   B: Not Italian. They've just opened a <u>Mexican</u> restaurant.

CD 2, Track 11, Page 119
A. Angela is planning a family reunion. Listen and check the things that have already been completed.

Gloria: How are the reunion plans coming?
Angela: Very well. Everyone wants to help. I asked a few people to help out with the plans, so I have a small committee. It's made things much easier.
Gloria: And the date is the fifteenth, right? August 15th?
Angela: Yes. We've already made the invitations. Tony's son made the invitations on the computer. We're going to send them out next week.
Gloria: Were you able to find everyone's address?
Angela: I think we have them all.
Gloria: Have you done anything else yet?
Angela: Well, we haven't planned the games or the activities, but we've already planned the menu. The resort is going to grill chicken for us, and everyone is going to bring a salad or a side dish. And, we're going to order a big cake for dessert.
Gloria: How about decorations?
Angela: We're not going to get too crazy with the decorations. But, we have bought some colorful tablecloths. The resort is providing the silverware, of course.
Gloria: Angela, you're not going to try to do everything yourself, are you? You need time to talk to people and have fun yourself.
Angela: That won't be a problem. The resort staff is going to help. We've reserved a large room, and the resort will provide staff to help with the setup, serve the food, and clean up.
Gloria: Well, it was a great idea to have the reunion at a resort. Let me know if there's anything I can do. I've already gathered photos to show at the party.
Angela: Thanks, Gloria. It's going to be a lot of fun. If I think of anything else, I'll give you a call.

CD 2, Track 12, Page 122
The Big Picture: Gossip

Conversation 1

A: Have you heard about Diana?
B: No. What happened?
A: Well, remember her engagement party?
B: Sure.
A: She's not engaged anymore.
B: No! I really liked Chris.
A: She's broken off the engagement. She met this new guy who moved into the apartment building, and she's fallen in love with him.
B: And what about Chris?
A: She's given him back his ring.
B: Really?

Conversation 2

A: Have you seen Rosa lately?
B: Hmm-mm. I spoke to her yesterday.
A: She looks great, doesn't she?
B: Yes, she said her vacation was really relaxing.
A: She didn't take a vacation. She went to a clinic.
B: A clinic?
A: Yes, she had a face-lift. That's why she looks so good.
B: Let me know the name of that clinic! I'm going to make an appointment myself.

Conversation 3

A: Have you heard about Amy? She's in big trouble.
B: What happened this time?
A: She took her mom's car without her permission. And she had an accident on the way to the mall.
B: Oh, no! Was she hurt?
A: No, she hit a mailbox. But she's been grounded for a month. I've tried to call her three times, but her parents won't let me talk to her. They've taken away her cell phone.

Conversation 4

A: You've heard about Paul, haven't you?
B: No. What about Paul?
A: He's just been promoted.
B: Promoted?
A: Yup. To assistant sales manager.
B: You've got to be kidding. He's got the worst sales record in the company. He hasn't made a sale this month.
A: I know. But it helps when your cousin is the head of the sales department.
B: That explains it.

Conversation 5

A: You know Mary Johnson, don't you?
B: Yeah. We used to take the bus together.
A: Well, guess what?
B: What?
A: She's going out with a man twice her age!
B: Twice her age? Let's see. I guess Mary's about 35.
A: That's what I guess. And this guy, he must be about 70.
B: What's the attraction?
A: Money. I've heard that he has lots of it!
B: Well, I hope she's happy.

Conversation 6

A: Have you heard about Grandpa Joe?
B: No. Is he OK?
A: OK? Well, first, he's bought a new convertible.
B: A new convertible? He's 70!
A: He's 72. And he's dyed his hair red.
B: Red? No more gray for Grandpa!
A: And he left yesterday.
B: He left?
A: Yes, he's left on a cross-country trip!
B: Good for him!

CD 2, Track 13, Page 123
E. Pronunciation: Surprise Intonation. Listen and repeat.

1. **A:** He bought a new convertible.   **B:** A new convertible?
2. **A:** He left yesterday.   **B:** He left?
3. **A:** He's just been promoted.   **B:** Promoted?
4. **A:** She's run off with a man twice her age.   **B:** Twice her age?

Unit 9

CD 2, Track 14, Page 136
C. Listen. Circle the letter of the sentence with the correct meaning.

1. The doctor saw all his patients for the day.
2. Jamie has been ironing shirts for five hours.
3. The men have planted five trees so far.
4. The teacher has checked 30 papers.
5. Carlos has delivered 40 packages.
6. Mary called 100 people today.
7. Jenna worked at the hospital for 50 years.
8. Tim drives a truck between New York and Florida. He's driven 300 miles today so far.

CD 2, Track 15, Page 136
D. Pronunciation: 've and 's. Listen and repeat.

1. **a.** I sold five cars.
   b. I've sold five cars.
2. **a.** She worked five hours.
   b. She's worked five hours.
3. **a.** They made 500 donuts.
   b. They've made 500 donuts.
4. **a.** She walked five miles.
   b. She's walked five miles.
5. **a.** I helped ten customers.
   b. I've helped ten customers.
6. **a.** He planted five trees.
   b. He's planted five trees.
7. **a.** She read 20 pages.
   b. She's read 20 pages.
8. **a.** I cleaned seven rooms.
   b. I've cleaned seven rooms.

CD 2, Track 16, Page 136
E. Listen again. Circle the sentence you hear in Exercise D.

1. I've sold five cars.
2. She's worked five hours.
3. They made 500 donuts.
4. She's walked five miles.

5. I helped ten customers.
6. He planted five trees.
7. She's read 20 pages.
8. I've cleaned seven rooms.

CD 2, Track 17, Page 138
The Big Picture: Job Performance

My name is George Pappas, and I'm a bus driver for Metro Transit. I started here in 2005. Before that, I drove a school bus. In the morning, the kids were quiet, but on the way home, they were really noisy and excited. It was too noisy for me.

One day, I saw an ad in the newspaper for a city bus driver, so I decided to apply. I was lucky—my interview went well, and I had a clear background check. I got the job offer the next week. The starting salary was $14.80 an hour, a dollar more than my job as a school bus driver.

There are some rules that everyone has to follow. I have to be at work on time and in uniform. I have to drive carefully and obey all of the traffic and safety laws. I have to pick up and drop off my passengers only at designated bus stops, and I can't make any exceptions. Of course, I have to collect the correct bus fares and greet and treat the passengers with courtesy. I always say "Good morning" to my passengers, and I know the names of many of the regular passengers.

There is a very clear salary policy in our contract. We receive a written evaluation every year. If the evaluation is good, we receive a 75-cent an hour pay raise. I've been here for five years, and I've always received my raise. If a driver doesn't have any accidents in five years, the pay increases to $20.00 an hour.

CD 2, Track 18, Page 139
C. Listen. Write the questions to match the answers.
Use the present or present perfect tense.

A: Thanks for telling me about the job opening, George. What other things should I know about this job?
B: Well, there's lots of opportunity for overtime.
A: Really? How much overtime do you work?
B: Oh, I usually work about ten hours a week overtime. Overtime pay is time and a half.
A: That's nice! What about traffic tickets? Have you ever gotten any tickets?
B: Yes, unfortunately. The company is very strict about tickets. If you get a ticket, you have to pay for it. Also, the company fines you $200.
A: $200! How many tickets have you gotten?
B: Only one. I received a ticket for going through a red light. The light had just turned red when I went through it, but I got a ticket anyway. I had to pay the company $200 plus $100 to the city for the ticket.
A: Wow! Do you know any drivers who have gotten a speeding ticket?

B: Yeah, one of my friends got two. He's not working here anymore. You get fired if you get two or more speeding tickets in the same year.
A: Wow, that's tough.
B: It is, but I guess it's necessary. I don't plan on getting any more tickets. I like this job.

CD 2, Track 19, Page 145
B. Listen to Katie's performance evaluation. Check the correct boxes.

Mr. Davis: Katie, let's go over your evaluation.
Katie: OK.
Mr. Davis: Let's go over some of these areas. You're always available to work, and you dress very professionally, but you've arrived late several times. Since I spoke to you about this, you have improved.
Katie: Well, yes, I've been trying. I was only late once last month.
Mr. Davis: Yes, that is an improvement. OK . . . I see that you also require improvement on showing initiative. Katie, when you don't have a customer, you stand and daydream. If I ask you to do something, you're always willing. But when you don't have customers, you should polish the jewelry and the mirrors, put new paper in the cash register, restock the boxes, and do other things without being asked.
Katie: I understand.
Mr. Davis: You're great with customers—friendly, respectful, complimentary. You seem to enjoy sales, and you're a good salesperson. This is your number one strength.
Katie: Thank you. Customer service is my favorite part of the job.
Mr. Davis: Good, good. . . . Unfortunately, you have made several mistakes. You've entered the wrong price on the register and forgotten to enter in the sales price. You've overcharged some customers and undercharged others. I've received complaints, and the store has lost money. You had several problems during our sale last week.
Katie: I know. When we're busy, I sometimes make mistakes.
Mr. Davis: I've decided to have Ms. Miller retrain you on our sales transactions procedures. Are you available next Saturday? She can work with you then.
Katie: Yes, I am.
Mr. Davis: OK, great. So, Katie, do you have any comments?
Katie: No. I like working here, and I'll try to be more careful. I won't make any more mistakes. You'll see.

Unit 10

CD 2, Track 20, Page 147
B. Listen and complete.

1. I bought a used car, and it's already broken down twice. I **should have bought** a new one.
2. I didn't buy a new car. I **shouldn't have bought** a used one.
3. She didn't study very hard for the test, and she got a D. She **should have studied** harder.
4. I registered for six courses, and now I'm too busy. I **shouldn't have taken** so many courses.
5. I left too late for the airport and missed my flight. I **should have left** earlier.
6. I didn't have a photo ID. I **should have remembered** to bring it.
7. Their car ran out of gas. They **should have filled** the tank.
8. He got a ticket for driving without a license. He **shouldn't have driven** without a license.
9. The electric company charged us a late fee. We **should have sent** the check on time.
10. She forgot to bring her homework. She **shouldn't have forgotten** it.

CD 2, Track 21, Page 149
A. Listen and write the number under the correct picture.

1. You should've typed this paper.
2. There should've been three hamburgers in here. There are only two.
3. You should've finished by now. What have you been doing?
4. The flight should've arrived at 4:00, but it's not here yet.
5. You should've gotten an A. What happened?
6. They should've won. They made too many errors.

CD 2, Track 22, Page 151
A. Listen. A man is calling 911 to report a problem in his apartment. Write the letter of the correct deduction under each picture.

1. I came home and found my lock broken and my door open.
2. My stereo is missing.
3. The window's open, but I'm sure I locked it when I left.
4. My cat has been hiding under the bed, and he won't come out.
5. A steak is missing, and there are dirty dishes in the sink.
6. My favorite suit is missing.
7. My large suitcase is missing and so are some of my shirts.
8. I found a pair of gloves on the floor.

CD 2, Track 23, Page 152
B. Pronunciation: Past Modals. Listen and repeat.

1. You must've left your book at home.
2. She might've studied French.
3. I should've made an appointment.
4. We could've gone on a vacation.
5. He must've had to work.
6. She couldn't have walked that far.
7. We shouldn't have spoken to her.
8. They shouldn't have arrived late.
9. He may not have had an opportunity.
10. I must not have heard you.

CD 2, Track 24, Page 152
D. Pronunciation: Word Stress. Listen to the conversation and underline the stressed words.

A: <u>Hi</u>, Julia. <u>Why</u> didn't you <u>come</u> to my <u>party</u>? Everyone <u>missed</u> you.
B: <u>What</u> party?
A: I had a <u>party</u> last <u>Saturday</u>.
B: Really? You should've <u>called</u> me.
A: I <u>did</u>. I left a <u>message</u> on your <u>voice mail</u>.
B: I <u>changed</u> my number. You <u>could've</u> sent me an <u>invitation</u>.
A: I <u>did</u>. I <u>e-mailed</u> it <u>two weeks</u> ago.
B: You must've <u>sent</u> it to the <u>wrong address</u>. I've <u>changed</u> my <u>e-mail</u>.
A: You should've <u>told</u> me.
B: <u>Sorry</u>. Anyway, how was the <u>party</u>?
A: It was <u>fun</u>. You should've <u>been</u> there.

CD 2, Track 25, Pages 154 and 155
The Big Picture: In the Counselor's Office
A. The high school counselor is talking to Amber, a student. Listen and take notes.

Counselor: Come in, Amber. Have a seat. You look upset.
Amber: Well, you know, I'm the editor of the school newspaper.
Counselor: I know. The paper's been very good this year.
Amber: Thank you. I work very hard on it.
Counselor: Why did you come see me today?
Amber: The vice principal took away my job! I'm not the editor anymore! I need that job for my college applications! How am I going to get into college now?
Counselor: Hold on, hold on. Do you know why he did that?
Amber: I don't know. I'm the best writer on the staff!
Counselor: You must have some idea why he did that.
Amber: Well, I guess maybe he's punishing me.
Counselor: Punishing you? Why would he do that?
Amber: I think he's upset because I wrote a story that wasn't true about the football team.
Counselor: Now, Amber, why did you do that?

Amber: I was upset at my boyfriend. He's the captain of the football team. He had just broken up with me.

Counselor: You must have been very upset.

Amber: Yes, I was.

Counselor: So, do you think the vice principal shouldn't have punished you for printing incorrect information? The team must've been very upset, too.

Amber: I know. Yeah, I guess I shouldn't have done that. I shouldn't have used my job to get back at him. I could print an apology in the newspaper. Do you think the vice principal will give me my job back?

Counselor: It sounds like you're sorry. I'll talk to the vice principal. Maybe he'll suspend you for only one issue, especially if you agree to print an apology.

Amber: Thank you.

CD 2, Track 26, Pages 154 and 155
B. The counselor is talking to Miguel, another student.
Listen and take notes about Miguel.

Counselor: The last time we talked, Miguel, your classes were not going well.

Miguel: You can say that again. I was failing everything.

Counselor: We talked about the people you could've asked for help and the things you should've done to improve. Do you want to talk about that today?

Miguel: Yeah. I'm doing a little better. I got a C+ in math last quarter.

Counselor: Your teacher must've been pleased.

Miguel: She was.

Counselor: Did you see a tutor?

Miguel: No, I didn't. I could've, but when I talked to my math teacher, she volunteered to give me some extra help. She also showed me a computer program in the learning center that could help me.

Counselor: Great. Now, how about your English class? Have your grades improved?

Miguel: Well, you know, I can speak English easily, but writing's really hard for me.

Counselor: Do you go to the writing center for tutoring?

Miguel: I've been once.

Counselor: That's not enough, Miguel.

Miguel: I know, but I didn't like the tutor.

Counselor: Now, Miguel, there must've been another tutor who could've helped you.

Miguel: Yeah, I guess I'll go back and try again. By the way, I got the part-time job at the bookstore. Thanks for telling me about it. My parents are really happy about it, too.

Counselor: Oh, congratulations! How's the job?

Miguel: Great! I work two nights a week and all day on Saturday. I get discounts on everything. It's an easy job.

Counselor: That's wonderful, Miguel.

Miguel: Thanks, Mr. D. I couldn't have gotten the job without your recommendation.

Counselor: That's my job, Miguel. Now, go to the writing center during your study period.

Unit 11

CD 3, Track 1, Page 165
A. Listen and write the questions. Then, look at the product map and write the answers.
1. Where are electronics manufactured?
2. Which grains are grown in China?
3. Where are automobiles manufactured?
4. Where is footwear made?
5. What kind of food is grown in Thailand?
6. Where is coal mined?

CD 3, Track 2, Page 168
A. Pronunciation: Syllable Stress. Listen and repeat.
1. pasteurize   pasteurization   pasteurized
2. sterilize   sterilization   sterilized
3. immunize   immunization   immunized
4. separate   separation   separated
5. refrigerate   refrigeration   refrigerated
6. evaporate   evaporation   evaporated
7. ferment   fermentation   fermented

CD 3, Track 3, Page 168
B. Listen again. Underline the stressed syllable of the words in the chart.

CD 3, Track 4, Page 170
The Big Picture: T-shirts—From the Field to Your Closet
1. The top three cotton producers in the world are China, the United States, and India. China is the top cotton producer of the three.
2. In China, the cotton is picked by hand. Then, it is sent to a ginner where it is cleaned. The cleaned cotton is put into bales, and the quality is determined.
3. The bales are sold to large plants or factories called spinners. At the spinners, the cotton is put on spools. The spools are put on knitting machines, and the cotton is made into cotton fabric.
4. The cotton fabric is sent to a dye house. At the dye house, only 20 percent of the fabric is dyed different colors. The remaining 80 percent is processed white.

5. The fabric is sent to a sewing plant. At the plant, patterns are cut. Then, the pieces are sewn by workers on a line. One worker sews the sleeves, another sews the neck, another does the shoulders, and the last one hems the bottom.

6. The T-shirts are folded and packaged. The T-shirts are sent to printers, where a logo is transferred or embroidered onto the T-shirt. At this stage, the T-shirt only costs about $3.00.

7. The finished T-shirts are shipped to warehouses. Because of many costs, including shipping, warehouse space, and inventory, the T-shirt price is increased.

8. The T-shirts are sold to a department store at an over 200-percent increase to $14. The store immediately doubles the price to $28. The store also has many costs, such as paying for sales help, insurance, and advertising. The T-shirt is marked and offered for sale for $28.

9. After two or three weeks, store customers have bought many of the shirts. Now, not all colors and sizes are available. The store advertises a 15- to 25-percent sale. After two more weeks, the price will be decreased again. Finally, after six weeks, any leftover T-shirts will be sent to discount stores. The price may be reduced to $14 or less.

Unit 12

CD 3, Track 5, Page 178
A. Listen. Write the year that each item was invented.

1. The insulin pump was invented by Dean Kamen in the 1960s. It was invented to give diabetics a better way to control their blood sugar. It was not approved for general use by the Federal Drug Administration until 1983.

2. The first anti-shoplifting tag was invented in 1965 by Arthur Minasy. These tags make it difficult for people to steal items from a store.

3. The first video games were invented by Ralph Baer in 1966. These first games were very simple, not like the colorful realistic games of today. Baer is called the "Godfather of Video Games."

4. The compact fluorescent bulb was first invented in the 1970s by an engineer named Ed Hammer. The bulb was created to save energy.

5. The artificial heart was first designed by Robert Jarvik in 1978. It was developed to keep a patient alive while waiting for a heart transplant.

6. In 1980, a hepatitis B vaccine was developed by Baruch Blumberg. Hepatitis B is a disease that attacks the liver and is often fatal. Today, hepatitis B vaccines are required by most public schools and colleges.

7. NASA is the National Aeronautics and Space Administration. The first space shuttle was launched by NASA in 1981. It orbited the world in less than two hours.

8. The laptop computer was invented by Sir Clive Sinclair in 1987. Today, laptop computers are more popular than desktop computers.

9. The personal human transport vehicle was created by Dean Kamen in 2001. It was designed to be a new type of everyday transportation.

CD 3, Track 6, Page 183
B. Pronunciation: Compound Nouns. Listen and repeat.
1. SAFEty razor
2. AIR conditioner
3. LIE detector
4. MIcrowave oven
5. BALLpoint pen
6. PARKing meter
7. CONtact lenses
8. SEAT belt
9. LAser printer
10. CELL phone

CD 3, Track 7, Page 184
D. Listen and answer the questions.
I'm from Taiwan. I was born there in 1963 and raised in Taipei. I went to public school like most students. School in Taiwan is very strict, and there are a lot of rules. First, we were required to wear a uniform. The girls wore blue skirts and white blouses. The boys wore blue plants and white shirts. I couldn't have long hair. All the girls had to keep their hair above their shoulders. The boys could only have hair one inch long! Very short!

We studied very hard. We went to school from 9:00 to 4:30, and we were assigned about three hours of homework. If we didn't do our homework, we were punished. Maybe the teacher hit our hands with a stick, or we had to stand with a book on our heads. We were given exams in the middle of the year and at the end of the year.

Boys and girls studied in separate classes. The only time we were together was for after-school clubs and activities. We couldn't date in high school. We couldn't call each other on the phone, either. But in college, we were allowed to date.

People in Taiwan speak Taiwanese, but it's a spoken language—not a written language. When we begin school, we are expected to use Chinese for everything. This is very hard for students, especially when we first begin school. Also, when we are in middle school, English is taught as a foreign language. By the time we finish high school, we know Taiwanese, Chinese, and English.

Vacations are similar to the United States. School is closed for two months in the summer, and we have one month off in January or February, around the time of the Chinese New Year.

The Big Picture: Shopping Technology

For many years, shopping was a simple process. A person went into a small local store, bought an item, and paid for it with cash. Another popular way of shopping was to buy merchandise from a traveling salesman. Many people lived far from the city, so salesmen traveled around the country by horse and wagon, showing the customers their merchandise.

In 1872, a traveling salesman named Aaron Montgomery Ward had an idea to help his customers see more of his merchandise. Ward decided to print a catalog with pictures of the items that his company sold. The customers could look through the catalog and order the items they wanted. The first mail-order catalog was printed in 1872 and became an immediate success. Catalogs are still a very popular way to shop.

Before 1884, clerks kept money in the store in a drawer or cash box. When a customer bought a product, the clerk wrote a receipt by hand. In 1884, the first cash register was invented by James Ritty. People could receive an immediate printed receipt.

In the 1900s, stores were becoming larger, especially grocery stores. Customers were buying more items at a time. The owner of one of these grocery stores, Sylvan Goldman, had an idea. He put two baskets and wheels on a folding chair and the first shopping cart was invented. Goldman formed a company to design larger and better shopping carts.

Up until this time, people paid by cash or check. In 1950, the first credit cards were issued. At first, credit cards were only used by business travelers for restaurant and hotel bills. In the 1960s, many companies were offering these cards. People did not need to carry so much cash. They could pay later.

Another idea that was developing at this time was the idea of the bar code. At the time, stock clerks had to put a price on every item. The clerk rang up each item on the cash register, punching in the price of each item by hand. Store owners, especially the owners of large supermarkets, needed a way to automatically read information about products during checkout. Several inventors worked on this idea, but there was not a standard way to identify each item. The Uniform Pricing Code, or UPC, was invented in 1973. In 1974, the first UPC scanner was installed in a supermarket in Ohio. It was no longer necessary to put the price on every item. Now supermarket clerks simply scan each item and the price appears on the register.

In the 1990s, another form of shopping became popular—online shopping. The Internet offers an inexpensive way for companies to advertise their products to a worldwide audience. Customers can look at pictures of products, check prices, and place their orders over the Internet. This has made shopping fast and convenient. Customers can also save money by comparing prices from several companies.

Unit 13

B. Listen. Then, answer the questions with a partner.

Grandmother: What's that thing that you're listening to?

Grandson: It's called an MP3 player.

Grandmother: An MP3 player?

Grandson: It's like a computer. It plays music files that you download from a computer.

Grandmother: That sounds difficult. I used to play 45s and LPs.

Grandson: What's a 45?

Grandmother: It's a small disk like a CD that's made of vinyl. They're usually black. There's one song on one side, and one song on the other. An LP is a bigger disk that can hold an entire album of songs. I used to have lots of 45s and LPs, but they take up a lot of space.

Grandson: Did you have to turn a 45 over to hear the other song?

Grandmother: Yes. If I played a 45, I had to turn it over when the song finished.

Grandson: You're kidding! I'm glad that technology has improved.

Grandmother: Maybe, but some people still think the sound quality that LPs had was better.

Grandson: Really? Do you still have any 45s or LPs?

Grandmother: We have some in the den. I think we have a turntable in the basement.

Grandson: A turntable? Do you have the kind that I see in the dance clubs?

Grandmother: I don't think so. My turntable is like a piece of furniture.

Grandson: Let's go get it. I want to see this old technology.

Grandmother: OK. We'll play one of my dance records from the '70s.

Grandson: Can I call my friends? They'd love to see this.

Grandmother: Sure.

The Big Picture: The History of Country Music

The people who first sang the country sound in the United States lived over a hundred years ago in the

Appalachian Mountains. These people sang all the time—while they were working, while they were doing laundry, while they were worshipping at church, or while they were taking care of their babies. People used to sing to make the work go faster. The music that they sang was very simple.

The music, which is now called country music, came from the British Isles: Scotland, Ireland, England, and Wales. The people who immigrated to the United States moved to a land that was similar to their homeland. These people brought their music with them.

Two instruments were common in country music bands. The five-string banjo, which came from Africa, became popular in country music in the 1920s. The fiddle, which had early roots in Nashville, was the main instrument in country music until the 1930s. The fiddler, who carried the melody of the songs, was usually the main performer in country music bands. Banjos and fiddles are still popular in country music today, but other instruments, such as electric guitars and keyboards, are also used. Jimmy Rodgers and The Carter Family, who first recorded in 1927, became the first superstars of country music.

Unit 14

CD 3, Track 11, Page 212
A. Listen and read. Then, discuss.
Are You a Procrastinator?

Everyone has plans and goals. Some plans are short-term and can be accomplished in a few hours or on a weekend: I'm going to wash the car. I plan to organize my closet. I want to gather all my photos from the past five years and put them in a photo album. I need to study for the test next week. I plan to start an exercise program. Some goals are far in the future and will take years to accomplish: I expect to get my nursing degree. I want to start my own business. Do you find yourself making plans but not accomplishing them? Is it difficult to take the first step? Is it impossible to find the time? Could you be a procrastinator? A procrastinator waits for the last minute. A procrastinator believes, "There is always tomorrow."

CD 3, Track 12, Page 212
B. Listen. Answer the questions about Scott's plans.
I always make a list of the things that I'm supposed to do around the house. I planned to paint the kitchen Saturday, but a big game was on TV. I plan to do it next weekend. A classmate called me, and I intended to call him back, but I forgot. I'll do it tonight. I promised to help my daughter with a school project, but I had to work overtime, so I will try to help her tomorrow. I was supposed to read four chapters in my history textbook, but I haven't done it yet. I need to do it before next Tuesday. The exam will be hard. I really need to be better organized.

CD 3, Track 13, Page 213
C. Listen and read. Then, discuss.
It's hard to get started on your plans. It's easy to make excuses! Once you start on a goal, there are always distractions. You sit down to work at the computer, but first you check your e-mail and then start to chat with friends. Or, you are supposed to write a paper for class, but a friend calls and wants to go to the mall with you.

Or, you sit down to type your paper, and you realize that it's time for your favorite TV show.

CD 3, Track 14, Page 216
A. Listen and read. Then, discuss. Underline the adjectives. Circle the infinitives.
It's important to make a schedule of your day, and it's necessary to schedule your study time. It's easy to say, "I'll get it done sometime today." It's more helpful to make an appointment with yourself. If possible, find a time that is the most productive for you. What is your most productive time to do your schoolwork? Maybe it is immediately after class or as soon as you get home.

CD 3, Track 15, Page 216
B. Pronunciation: Stressed Syllables. Listen and mark the stressed syllables.
1. <u>dan</u> · ger · ous
2. i · de · a · <u>lis</u> · tic
3. im · <u>pos</u> · si · ble
4. <u>in</u> · ter · est · ing
5. po · <u>lite</u>
6. <u>rea</u> · son · a · ble
7. re · a · <u>lis</u> · tic
8. ro · <u>man</u> · tic
9. <u>stress</u> · ful
10. <u>thought</u> · ful

CD 3, Track 16, Pages 218 and 219
The Big Picture: The Procrastinator

Conversation 1
Diana: Hi, Susan.
Susan: Hi, Diana. What are you doing?
Diana: I'm supposed to be studying for my math test.
Susan: That's tomorrow, right?
Diana: Right. I'm not really worried. I understood everything in class.
Susan: Well, good luck. I can't talk now. I'm writing this English paper.

Diana: The one about cities and pollution?
Susan: Yeah. I'm in the middle of it. I'll call you tomorrow.
Diana: OK.

Conversation 2
Diana: Hi, Dad.
Dad: Hi, Diana. Studying for that math test?
Diana: I'm going to start in a few minutes.
Dad: You're great at math. You'll do well.
Diana: I hope so.
Dad: Remember to clean this room. How can you find anything in here?
Diana: Don't worry, Dad.

Conversation 3
Diana: Jake? You at work?
Jake: Uh-huh. I'm getting off in an hour. I can't come over tonight.
Diana: I won't see you?
Jake: No, I've got science homework to finish. You know, that lab report. How's it going with your math homework?
Diana: I haven't started yet. I'm going to start in a few minutes.
Jake: Why don't you go over to the math center at school? It's quiet there.
Diana: Maybe.
Jake: Well, I'll see you tomorrow night. How about 8:00? After I get out of work?
Diana: That's good. Ciao.
Jake: Bye.

Conversation 4
Diana: Hi.
Alex: Diana, it's Alex.
Diana: Hi, Alex. Are you still at school?
Alex: Uh-huh. I'm here with Carlos and Mia. We're at the library now, and we're studying for the math test tomorrow. Why don't you come over here and study with us? This math is really difficult, and it's helpful to work together.
Diana: I don't know. I think I'll study alone this time.
Alex: If you want to meet before class, we could go over a few of the problems.
Diana: OK. The test is at 10:00. Can we meet in the cafeteria at 9:00?
Alex: Sure. See you then.

Conversation 5
Diana: Hello.
Katie: Hi, Diana. It's me, Katie. I'm going to the mall. They're having a big sale at Gabby's. Want to come?
Diana: A shoe sale? You know, I do need a pair of black boots.
Katie: I'm getting in my car now. I'll pick you up in ten minutes.
Diana: I really should be studying for my math test tomorrow.
Katie: Don't worry. We won't stay long. I'll see you in a few minutes.
Diana: Well . . . OK.

Unit 15

CD 3, Track 17, Page 226
B. Listen to Marco and Luciana's story about becoming United States citizens.

1. Marco came to the United States from Brazil in 2000 when he was 24. Many years have passed, and Marco has learned to speak, read, and write English very well. He changed jobs four times, met Luciana—another immigrant from Brazil—and they got married. Over the years, they've had a very busy life here in the United States. They have had two children, a boy named Alonzo and a girl named Zandra. Their children were born in the United States, so they are already U.S. citizens.

2. Marco and Luciana decided that they wanted to become citizens. They obtained their application papers from the United States Citizenship and Immigration Service, or the USCIS. They carefully completed all of the paperwork and mailed in their documents. They expected to wait six months to a year for a response.

3. While waiting for their appointments, Marco and Luciana studied for their naturalization tests. Luciana was nervous because her English was not as strong as Marco's. Marco and Alonzo helped her practice the English sample questions and the questions about U.S. history.

4. Finally, after ten months of waiting, they received an appointment for their naturalization interview and test. The immigration officer spoke to each of them separately. Marco had to answer questions in English, write a sentence in English, and read a sentence in English. Luciana was lucky. The interviewer spoke slowly and Luciana could answer all of the questions about U.S. history.

5. Three months later, Marco and Luciana received their letters of approval. They were going to be U.S. citizens!

6. At the swearing-in ceremony, one hundred other people from many countries recited the Oath of Allegiance to the United States. Then, they signed a paper. They each received a letter from the president of the United States, congratulating them.

A. Listen. Complete each sentence with the gerund you hear.

1. Marco and Luciana discussed **becoming** citizens.
2. They delayed **starting** the process because Luciana's English was not strong.
3. Luciana regretted **not taking** English classes earlier.
4. She began **studying** English at a local adult school.
5. A friend recommended **enrolling** in a citizenship class.
6. They didn't mind **attending** class one night a week.
7. Marco and Luciana enjoyed **learning** about U.S. history.
8. They practiced **asking** one another questions.
9. Luciana couldn't help **being** nervous before the test.
10. They enjoyed **celebrating** with their friends after the ceremony.

B. Pronunciation: Linking. Listen to the conversation. Then, practice the conversation with a partner.

A: I thought life here was going to be easy. I just can't adjust to living here. I miss seeing my family.

B: You'll always miss them. I plan on visiting my family once a year.

A: And, I'm afraid of losing my job if I leave.

B: Yesterday you were complaining about working so much overtime!

A: I gave up working at my family's business to come here.

B: You didn't like working there anyway. And you plan on opening your own business someday, don't you?

A: You're right, but I'm tired of listening to English all day! I'm thinking of going back to Korea.

B: You've only been here for nine months. Everybody feels like you at first. Concentrate on learning English and making a few friends.

C. Listen. An immigrant is talking about citizenship. Write the questions. Then, ask and answer the questions with a partner.

My wife and I decided to come to the United States because of the job opportunities. In our country, there were very few job opportunities. Our families were worried about us finding a place to live, but fortunately, we had a cousin who was living in Chicago. He helped us to find an apartment.

I was lucky. I'm good at fixing things and working with wood, and I found a job with a contractor. I built kitchen cabinets and tables. The contractor liked my work and my work habits. I was always on time, I worked hard, and I rarely missed a day of work. One day, one of the customers asked me to design a kitchen for a relative.

The next thing I knew, I had my own business. Now, we can afford to pay for our daughter's dance classes and my son's math tutor. We're able to take a vacation every summer. We really appreciate having a nice apartment, and I'm thinking about becoming a citizen. My family is here, our children were born here, and my business is doing well. As a matter of fact, I'd like to sponsor my brother. I'm encouraging him to take English classes to prepare for life here.

The Big Picture: Running a Campaign

Hi, my name is Manuel. I've been a citizen for a few years now, but I never thought that I would get involved in politics. In fact, I've always avoided getting involved. I vote in the major elections, but sometimes I forget to vote in the city elections. Let me tell you what happened. A few years ago, a new neighbor moved in. His name is John. He's a nice guy and a great neighbor. He's married, and he has three children—a boy and two girls—and so do I. Our families have become very friendly. We barbecue together in the summer. Our children play together, and our wives enjoy spending time together. We've even taken a vacation together.

John is an entrepreneur. He has a very successful bookstore and community computer center. He hires high school and college students for the computer center. He also has senior citizen volunteers read to young children three times a week at the bookstore. He has a good business, and he provides a wonderful service for our community.

Well, there's an empty seat on the city council, and John has decided to run for the seat. At first, he complained about shaking hands, but now he's looking forward to giving interviews and meeting people in town. My wife, Andrea, is good at organizing people, so she has a group of neighbors and other volunteers at our house almost every night. They've been talking about having a voter registration drive. It's important to get the vote of everyone that we can. So, they're thinking about setting up registration tables in front of the library, the high school, the mall, and the supermarkets. We're not worried about spending too much money because John knows many people who have insisted on donating their services. They've donated envelopes, printing services, and vans to get people to the polls on election day.

John's wife, Kathy, is anticipating doing a lot of work for the campaign. She quit working temporarily to support John's campaign. Kathy's in charge of getting volunteers to make phone calls. I'm enjoying helping John practice for this month's debate. I'm pretending to be one of his opponents or one of the reporters who will be asking John the tough questions.

A campaign is a lot of work, but it's worth it.

CD 3, Track 22, Page 241
A. Listen and write the questions. Then, match each question with the correct answer.
1. What is the Bill of Rights?
2. What is one of the rights of the Constitution?
3. What is the voting age?
4. How many senators are there?
5. Who was the first president?
6. Who makes the laws?
7. Who is the Commander in Chief of the military?
8. How long is a president's term of office?

Skills Index

U.S. Map

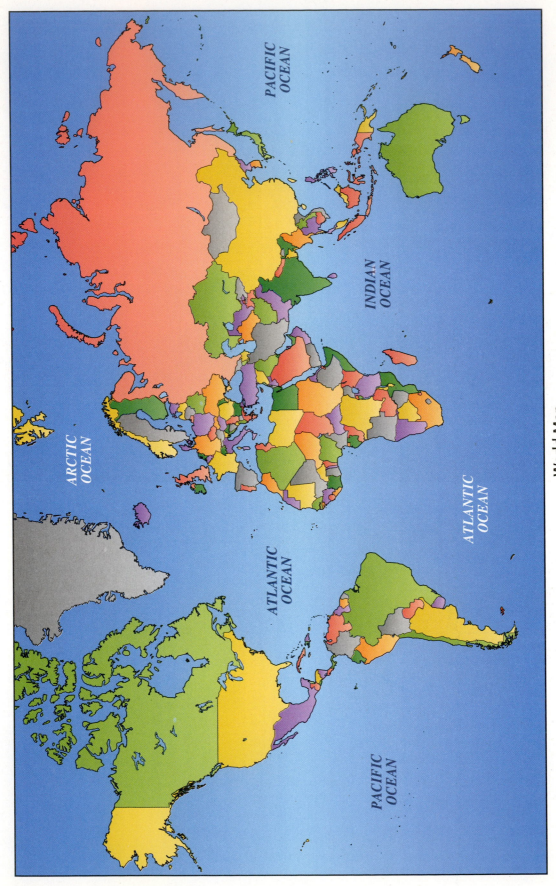

World Map